Contents

KU-075-660

Acknowledgments

I HAVE A LOT OF PEOPLE TO THANK FOR HELP IN THE WRITING of this book. Indeed, I have so many and so kind and such intelligent people to thank that it is a wonder that the book is not so much better. First, and most warmly, I thank members of the Instructional Psychology Research Group at Simon Fraser University. Jack Martin, Phil Winne, Ron Marx, and Roger Gehlbach have given me enormous help, criticism, abuse, and encouragement in writing this book. It is a great pleasure to thank publicly first and foremost people who are likely to disagree with the general argument of the book more strongly than almost any other readers—an empirical claim that may well be disconfirmed in the near future. Suzanne de Castell, Cornel Hamm, and Tasos Kazepides have been most generous in giving their time and philosophic criticisms. Gloria Sampson, Jaap Tuinman, and Dianne Common have kindly and critically read the manuscript or parts of it and offered helpful suggestions. Not content with boring my colleagues at Simon Fraser I have been fortunate in finding a number of people at other institutions who have read parts of the manuscript and made recommendations. They include Charles J. Brainerd (Western Ontario), Francis Schrag (Wisconsin-Madison), N. E. Wetherick (Aberdeen), John Wilson (Oxford), Robin Barrow (Leicester), and Jan Smedslund (Oslo). Without their criticisms, the book would have been worse and certainly longer. Readers, too, will no doubt wish to thank them. Clearly, these kind critics cannot be held responsible for the parts of the book that remain unimproved.

I have been fiddling with this manuscript for some time; parts of it have appeared in various stages of unpreparedness elsewhere. I am grateful for permission to reprint these parts of the manuscript as follows: parts of chapter 2 appeared as "Plato's Theory of Educational Development" in *Curriculum Inquiry*, vol. 11, no. 2 (1981); part of chapter 3 appeared as "What Does Piaget's Theory Describe?" in *Teachers College Record*, vol. 84, no. 2 (1982); bits of chapter 4 appeared in "On the Possibility of Theories of Educational Practice" in *Journal of Curriculum Studies*, vol. 14, no. 2 (1982); and a piece of chapter 5 was used in *The Erosion of Education* (co-authored with David Nyberg, Teachers College Press, 1981). My thanks to the editors for their permission to reprint those pieces here.

During the writing of this book I was the grateful recipient of a Social Sciences and Humanities Research Council of Canada Leave Fellowship. This generous fellowship included money for a research assistant. I am grateful for the efficient and intelligent help provided in this role by Pamela Thomas in Oxford. Finally, and far from least, my grateful thanks to Eileen Mallory, who typed and retyped the manuscript with unfailing cheerfulness and efficiency.

Introduction

IT IS COMMONLY ACCEPTED THAT THERE IS A GULF BETWEEN psychological theories and educational practice and that a bridge of cautious implications is required before we can move from the former to the latter. To the casual observer it may seem a relatively simple matter to move from, say, Jean Piaget's theory of developmental stages to a set of recommendations for teaching, but those psychologists and educators who have worked most intensively on bridging the gulf between psychology and education recognize that the bridge is not at all easy to construct. But, nevertheless, it is accepted as more or less a truism that psychological theories about phenomena such as cognitive development, learning, and motivation can yield implications for educational practice. If one proceeds with due caution, it is commonly assumed, of course one can draw implications from Piaget's developmental theory that will benefit educational practice. This generally accepted truism is exemplified in the current domination of educational research by psychological theories, and in the fact that a significant proportion of all educational writing at present involves drawing implications from psychology to education.

The argument of this book is that no psychological theory has, or can have, legitimate implications for educational practice; or, to continue the metaphor of the previous paragraph, that we lack the materials to build a bridge of implications from psychological theories as they presently exist to educational practice.

In addition, it is argued that proper guidance to educational practice can be provided only by educational theories. Unless articulated within an educational theory, knowledge generated by psychological research must remain educationally silent.

The two preceding paragraphs, intended as statements of complementary parts of the argument of this book, may seem at first glance an ill-matched pair. The former may seem a wild assertion, the latter a commonplace. An attempt to reconcile them might conclude that what is to be argued is that psychological theories do not speak directly to educational concerns and that educational theories, whatever they may be, must guide the drawing of implications from psychological theories to educational practice. Few people would be likely to find such an argument in any way disturbing, concluding that the initial statement of the book's argument was an unnecessarily dramatic way of making a relatively straightforward point, whose only promise of novelty might be merely a technical philosophical argument about the nature of educational theories.

But it is precisely the wild assertion that I hope to substantiate, as I hope to show that the associated argument is far from a commonplace. I hope to show that the notion that one can move, however cautiously, along a line of implication from psychological—or other human or social science—theories to educational practice is mistaken, and is in practice damaging to education; that the dominance psychological theories hold over educational research is responsible for the meager benefits, if not actual losses, to educational practice that have resulted from the massive educational research industry; that the influence of psychological theories on curriculum design tends toward educational vacuousness; that the influence of psychological theories on teaching practice tends to reduce teaching effectiveness; that, in general, the supposition that such theories offer a scientific contribution to the study of education exemplifies misconceptions about the nature of the educational enterprise and fails to perceive the differences between the kind of knowledge educational practice properly requires and the kind of knowledge it can generate.

A frontal attack on a truism presents strategic problems. One such is how to reduce or eradicate a polemical tone. Regret at the uncritical application of psychological theories in education is of course a sentiment widely shared. It is harder to make the more radical case that *any* application of such theories in education is uncritical, without appearing somewhat cranky. The argument, after all, is not just with some more or less casually held opposing position, but rather with what amounts to a presupposition; a presupposition embodied in even the organizational structure of institutions that study to improve education. By implication the argument claims that the very term "educational psychology" involves a fundamental confusion, and that practitioners of educational psychology en masse are not helping but are damaging the practice of education. And that a similar destructive contribution to education is being made by those psychologists who urge educators to seek implications for practice in psychological theories.

Even outlining the argument makes it seem a polemic. But obviously psychology and education are not at war, and I am not a combatant on one side against the other. Nor am I in any way arguing against the propriety of psychological theories as such, nor against the kind of knowledge psychology seeks to secure—though I will discuss some objections to the program of "scientific psychology." Rather my concern is with education, and I hope to show that it is not a sprawling, inchoate field of study in which some things studied by psychologists form one part; some things studied by sociologists form another; and some things studied by anthropologists, philosophers, and so on, form other parts.

The argument against the present role of psychological theories in education is intended to clarify the distinction between what they offer to education and what in fact education needs. Thus I hope to clarify the nature of educationally useful theories. The book pursues this purpose by a simple dialectical movement. It begins, in chapter 1, with a search for the kinds of things educators need to know in order to best do their job, distinguishing these things from what psychological theories tell us. This will produce a sketch of some characteristics of educational theories. With this tentative set of distinctions between educational and psychological theories, the book continues, in chapters 2 and 3, to identify and examine an example of each. In chapter 4, it returns to the distinctions sketched in the first chapter to refine and further clarify them in light of the two examples. For the examples I have chosen theories that have as much in common as possible, in order better to see their differences.

In chapter 1, I will reflect on distinctions between psychological and educational theories. Some of the distinctions have been noted before, but I am not aware of the whole range being noted, nor of their combination into the general argument of this book. I refer occasionally in this chapter to Piaget's theory, assuming that readers will have some knowledge of it.

Plato's developmental theory is described and discussed in chapter 2. The usual accounts of Plato's ideas on education have not isolated his developmental theory, even though he constantly discusses education according to a developmental scheme and provides an explicit general model for organizing the complex process. All of Western philosophy has been described as merely footnotes to Plato. Much the same might be said about all educational thinking. Even people who have never read the *Republic* or the *Laws* carry some of his ideas at second or third or fourth remove in their minds and into their practice.

The discussion of Piaget's theory is, I have tried to ensure, informed by a concept of education which allows a precise sense of why the theory has no implications for educational practice, and which allows a useful critical discussion of the ample literature on Piagetian teaching strategies and curricula. I have chosen to concentrate on Piaget's theory because of its current prominence in education, and the general assumption that it has many implications for education.

Chapter 5 generalizes the argument against Piaget's theory to other psychological theories used in supposedly educational research. In this chapter I try to show why the common analogy—psychology:education::physics:engineering—is false and seriously misleading. This chapter focuses on research on teaching effectiveness; on attempts to articulate a theory of instruction; on behavioral objectives; on social learning theory; and on a few other topics currently prominent in educational psychology. I try to show why none of this research properly has or can have any implications for education.

A book whose argument leads to characterizing the appropriate form of educational theories may seem somewhat distant from the day-to-day business of teaching large groups of children in classrooms. But in a practical enterprise like education the *most* practical thing one can have is an appropriate theory—a common observation, commonly ignored. The general argument of this book is that education, if it is to become a more useful field of study and a more successful field of practice, must generate its own theories about the phenomena of most direct interest to it. If it persists in relying on theories drawn from psychology, or sociology, or anthropology, or whatever, it will fail to come adequately to grips with what we should teach children; how we should teach those things; and when during the process of their development we should teach which things in which ways.

I am neither a philosopher nor a psychologist but—to echo Piaget's claim in reverse—a mere pedagogue. This essay trespasses clumsily in areas where psychologists and philosophers would pass with greater elegance, ease, and confidence. If I go ahead with my trespassing despite my unfamiliarity with the terrain—with its terms, distinctions, methods, and so on—it is because I think I can recognize education when I see it, and its absence when I do not. In this essay I point out why I do not see education in a large range of what passes for educational research.

1/ Education and Psychology
A Sense of Differences

Introduction

EDUCATORS ARE primarily interested in knowing what things
should be taught ("taught" in the sense that implies "learned"), by
what methods, at what stages during a person's educational development, in order to produce a particular kind of educated person.
This suggests four related questions: *What* should we teach? *How*
should we teach those things? *When* should we teach them? What
should our *end-product* be like?[1] Answering these four questions
allows us to construct an educational program or curriculum, and
we might reasonably look to an educational theory to provide such
answers.

In this chapter I want to begin distinguishing between psychologists' and educators' interests in such things as development, learning, and motivation. I will take these four major educational questions
and see what kinds of answers psychology offers to education and
see in what ways these answers are like or unlike what education
requires. For this initial look at the area I will concentrate on theories
of development, because it is this area of psychology that is at present
seen as richest in implications for education. This restricted focus
is for economy's sake; it nevertheless allows dealing with each of
the educational questions. Piaget's developmental theory, after all,
is commonly taken as having implications for the aims, methods,
content, and sequence of educational programs.[2] And while it may
seem odd to use Piaget's atypical theory as a kind of paradigm of

1

psychological theories, I will argue the appropriateness of this procedure in chapter 5.

Introductory to discussing the major educational questions I would like to make three general points. Each concerns differences between psychology and education. They are not contentious, but worth making here because they seem sometimes to be ignored in education.

I. DESCRIBING WHAT IS: PRESCRIBING WHAT OUGHT TO BE

The four major educational questions mentioned above are tightly interrelated. One cannot offer a sensible answer to any one of them without providing some kind of answer to all of them. If our educational theory prescribes learning about, say, the Industrial Revolution in grade nine, we will expect that prescription to be in the context of an outline of normal educational development which makes the set of concepts, facts, and skills to be learned developmentally appropriate, both logically and psychologically; and we will expect it to be in the context of suggestions about the manner in which the topic should be organized and presented to be most engaging and meaningful to typical grade nine students; and also in the context of a description of a desirable end-product which *justifies* such content being taught then and in those ways. Similarly an educational theory will seek to characterize developmental stages partly in terms of the content, concepts, and skills most appropriately mastered during each stage, and in terms of the organization, and forms of presentation, of knowledge that are most meaningful to students at each stage. As the content and forms of presentation will differ if one aims to produce a Spartan warrior rather than a Christian gentleman, so the characterization of the developmental stages leading to such diverse end-products will also differ.

Psychologists, on the other hand, do not seek to answer questions about development in terms of content or programs of cultural initiation. Psychological theories embody the scientific aim of describing what is the case and providing explanations of a particular range of phenomena. Psychology's first task in approaching, say, cognitive development is to isolate the appropriate phenomena and to eradicate all extraneous matters. As the aim is to discover what is necessarily true about cognitive development, psychologists must discount whatever effects on such development are culturally or historically conditioned. Psychologists may perform experiments which involve children at different ages learning certain concepts, or dealing with certain problems. But that content and those problems in themselves are irrelevant, except in so far as they allow the psychologist to see the underlying abstract processes of cognitive development. They are as incidental to the resulting theory as the stain or dye a biologist might use in order to see better the form of a transparent organism. Far from being expressed in terms of something else, especially if that something else is the kind of cultural content which forms a central focus for an educational theory, a psychological theory will if necessary construct its own technical language to refer as precisely as possible to the abstract processes that form its focus of concern.

So first and most generally, a psychological theory is about phenomena that exist in the world; there are psychological processes and patterns of behavior which the researcher may seek to describe and explain. There may be enormous difficulties in the way of providing secure explanations of psychological phenomena, but a presupposition of scientific psychology is that there is a *nature* of things psychological about which increasingly secure theories may be established. So Piaget's claim that "Psychology is a natural science"[3] is a fundamental premise to the program of scientific psychology. There is, however, no such thing as a natural educational process out there that we should be trying to find, describe, and explain. An educational process exists only as we bring it into existence. The main problem for the educator, then, is not to describe the nature of the process but to prescribe what ought to be done to create an ideal or good process.

In considering the differences between psychology and education this rather gross difference should be emphasized. The habit of looking at education through psychology, as it were, tends to suppress or disguise this profound and far-reaching difference. We would expect theories about phenomena that exist to be significantly different from theories whose role is to prescribe processes which do not exist. (Whether we want to call the latter "theories" will be dealt with in chapter 4.)

Psychologists also seek to establish empirical regularities between, say, motivation and learning, but a condition of establishing any such regularity is that the two be separate and independent entities. This separation presents conceptual problems for the psychologist, the resolution of which requires precision in definitions of "learning" and "motivation." These precise definitions make the meaning of the psychologist's "learning" and "motivation" somewhat different from the more diffuse and complex meanings proper in education. The educator's level of interest is such, however, that the question of how to make knowledge about the Industrial Revolution interesting to grade nine students tends to collapse any precise distinctions between the content, learning, and motivation. The educator cannot assume a stable body of knowledge about the Industrial Revolution which students are to be motivated to learn. The "motivation" has to be built into the way the knowledge is selected, organized, and presented. This seems, on the face of it, a somewhat different task from applying principles of motivation, of learning, of development to organizing content and teaching about the Industrial Revolution. At least there is some opaqueness here; the centrality for all educational questions of particular content and the meanings and values of that content makes the application of theories which abstract themselves from such matters problematic. However, let us return to this topic in more detail in chapter 5, at which point we will have accumulated some ideas to help clear up some of the opaqueness.

We may, in passing, use two metaphors to reflect on the function of a theory. We can see a theory as a kind of lens which brings a particular set of elements into focus. We can also see a theory as a kind of syntax; as syntax organizes phonemes into larger meaningful linguistic entities, so a theory organizes data into more general claims. As suggested above, when dealing with topics like learning, development, or motivation, psychological theories focus on a different range of phenomena from educators and also a different "level" of phenomena; the data organized by psychological theories into more general meaningful claims are likely to be different from the data organized by educational theories, as are the claims made by each. Because educators and psychologists both express interest in topics such as "development" or "motivation," the common terms tend occasionally to bewitch us into thinking that their commonalities are greater than is in fact the case.

II. LOOKING AT EDUCATION
WITH PSYCHOLOGICAL LENSES

A not uncommon effect of importing psychological theories into education is that, because of their apparently greater precision and scientific authority, they tend to displace the proper role of educational theories. This might be seen in people taking, for example, Piaget's developmental theory as providing aims for the educational process. At its crudest this results in situations where, as David Elkind puts it, "some 'Piaget-based' curricula aim at teaching the kinds of concepts (conservation of substance, liquid quantity, and so on) that Piaget has shown most children acquire pretty much on their own as a natural consequence of their active involvement with the environment."[4] A little more insidiously it leads to the not uncommon claim that the aim of education is to achieve sophisticated formal operations—the final stage of the cognitive developmental process which Piaget describes—and that the particular things taught and the methods of teaching are important to the extent that they help realize this end. This is to substitute intellectual skills for education, and psychological development for educational development. The former has to be encompassed by the latter; it may provide constraints or boundaries or variables that affect the latter—it cannot, as a part, provide an aim for the whole.

Piaget's theory focuses on a particular strand in the wide and complex thread of human development. Indeed, even within the strand of cognitive development, Piaget focuses on and highlights particular parts. As Flavell and Wohlwill put it, Piaget has been highly selective with regard to the phenomena he has focused on, and

> We should not be at all surprised to find some future theorist making an excellent case for the simply momentous cognitive changes that take place, say during the three-to-five-year-old span . . . Developmentalists would then say that some very important things happen between three and five and that some other things, quite different, but equally important, happen between five and seven.[5]

If we might expect to see quite different things from focusing on different aspects of the cognitive developmental strand, we might *a fortiori* expect the strand of educational development to have different characteristics, highlights, stage divisions, and so on. Or, at least, we must be open to that possibility. The danger for education in letting Piaget's theory focus our attention on the developmental process is that it will focus attention on phenomena of prime interest to the cognitive psychologist but of possibly only peripheral interest to the educator, and it may focus attention away from the phenomena of most direct interest and value to the educator.

Similarly with motivation: as mentioned above, education is properly concerned not so much with isolating and explaining a phenomenon called "motivation," but rather with how one engages children's interest in learning particular things of value. Importing the term "motivation" into education, while it may have more technical éclat than, say, "a study of children's changing interests," is mischievous. It is mischievous not just because it converts what is appropriate technical language in psychology into educational jargon, but because it shifts educators' attention away from childrens' interests toward trying to spin tenuous connections from ideas about "need reduction" or "extinction of orienting reflexes" to the behavior of groups of children sitting in classrooms. If we borrow psychology's theories we borrow also its focus of interest, and lose our own.

III. SHOULD PSYCHOLOGY'S DESCRIPTIONS CONSTRAIN EDUCATION'S PRESCRIPTIONS?

Psychology aims to become a scientific discipline. It seeks to handle its data of interest with the rigor and security of the physical sciences. That such rigor and security may be achieved in rather different ways in psychology and physics, and that such differences may be reflected in the theories proper to each field, is a reasonable expectation. Psychology at present seeks to describe certain processes and behaviors rigorously and explain them as far as possible. Piaget thus had the scientific aim of describing as precisely as possible what is the case about human cognitive development. He sought to generate a theory that has as general application as possible. Cross-cultural studies are designed in order to provide data that will help establish the general claims or will allow the theory to be revised in order to make it more generally applicable.

An educational theory might outline a developmental process which no one has yet experienced. But if it outlines a new ideal, and provides plausible practical steps whereby that ideal can be realized, it will tell us precisely the kinds of things we want to know in education.

A psychological theory like Piaget's is, we may say, properly descriptive, with the ambition of becoming explanatory, whereas an educational theory is properly prescriptive. We want an educational theory to prescribe a program that will lead to a particular end-product. We will not, of course, be satisfied with an educational theory that is purely prescriptive. We will expect it to make empirically testable claims, and we will expect its prescriptions to be made within the bounds of what a secure descriptive psychological theory tells us is possible. It is in this regard that Piaget's theory is considered by some educators to have its most important implications for education. Given the general differences between educational and psychological theories noted above, we might conclude that what psychology tells us are stages of cognitive development are not to be converted into *components* of an educational theory, but rather are to serve as *constraints* on what an educational theory may sensibly prescribe. Indeed, the developmental form of an educational theory might not be expressed in terms of Piaget's stages, but Piaget's stages might form a constraint on what can be prescribed for the process of educational development.

A problem for accepting psychology's descriptive theories as a constraint on education's prescriptive theories is that it is not altogether clear what such theories in psychology actually describe. If we consider, for example, the theories that are constructed, like some parts of Piaget's theory, on norms for the acquisition of certain concepts, it is not clear how far these norms are determined by a kind of genetic unfolding or how far they are determined by typical methods of educating and socializing in particular areas of the world at particular times. That is, in dealing with the human *psyche* or human behavior, it is difficult to separate nature and culture. To build a curriculum on the assumption that certain cognitive developments are determined by our nature, if in fact they are determined by the forms of cultural initiation we have used, is to seek to institutionalize a particular process of cognitive development which is caused by social and educational contingencies of a particular, now past, era.

For example, to assume, with reservations, that Piaget's developmental theory describes constraints of nature, is what is meant by treating it with due caution. No one would argue that educators should feel constrained by a psychological theory which is itself insecure. Being duly cautious means assessing carefully the status of the psychological theory from which one wishes to draw implications, and maintaining critical sensitivity about the differences between the scientific context of the theory and the complex field of practice in which the implication is to be applied. But if no one is making the argument against which the point is directed, the point is worth making here because it seems commonly to be ignored in education.

With these general differences noted, let us consider the four main educational questions mentioned earlier and try, in the process, to make these preliminary distinctions somewhat more clear and precise. Because of the interrelatedness of the questions it will be quickly apparent that dividing up the discussion around these questions is simply done for organizational convenience, and that the topics discussed under any one might often be equally appropriately discussed under one of the other headings.

Educational End-Products

AS STEPHEN TOULMIN has stressed, for the psychologist more than for the physiologist the stages that represent the developmental process have to be normative. "Whereas the physiological notions of 'maturity' and 'maturation' serve, in a quite innocent sense, as 'norms' of physiological development—being used to define the 'deficiencies' and 'deficits' that mark off the color-blind, the aphasic, and the spastic as 'abnormal' rather than merely different—the psychological notions of 'maturity' and 'maturation' also overlap normatively into the area of *ethics*."[6] This presents a problem for psychology's attempt to be objective or value-neutral in constructing its image of the developmental process in humans. Often some value-laden, but inexplicit, notion of the desirable end-product of the developmental process serves to determine what are the stages that represent progress, and to provide criteria for deciding how adequately individuals are moving toward the end of the process. Psychologists try to defend their objectivity by reference to "norms" based on as wide samples as possible.

That developmental psychologists strive to defend their inquiries against the accusation that they are infected by value-preference suggests ways in which educators are not even striving in similar directions. Educators are not trying to describe a process of development in a value-free way; they are trying to prescribe the best way of actualizing a range of preferred potentials. The value-laden nature of the end does not present a problem for educators; it is a part of the job in hand to deal constantly and explicitly with value matters. The developmental dimension of our educational theory, then, will not be primarily concerned with descriptive norms, but rather with prescribing how people can best be enabled to reach a particular, explicitly described end-state of educated maturity.

So the statement of educational maturity cannot be taken for granted, or remain implicit, to serve as a hidden guide or criterion for measuring progress through the process. It must be dealt with explicitly for the theory to be useful. We want to know what kind of educated person is likely to be produced if we follow the prescriptions of the theory.

In an educational theory the end-product is a kind of person. In Piaget's developmental theory it is a kind of thinking. In such a psychological theory the end-state is a relatively innocent terminus of the process. It just so happens that the process of cognitive development as dealt with by Piaget leads to formal operational thinking. This end-state is achieved by any individual more or less spontaneously—given an appropriate environment. Piaget's theory seeks to focus on spontaneous underlying processes of cognitive development and to exclude developments brought about by particular forms of cultural initiation. In an educational theory the end-product is an explicitly characterized ideal kind of person. Its achievement requires, invariably, hard work. The *value* of this end-product *justifies* the stages that lead toward its realization. Becoming a Spartan warrior justifies training in physical hardship; becoming a Christian gentleman justifies exercise in patience and humility.

Educators, then, will not seek to follow psychology's efforts to reduce the value-laden aspects of its theories. A value-free educational theory would be useless. What we want to know is how to produce a particular preferred kind of person; that is, we want to know what value decisions we should make at every step of the way. We want to know *what* we should teach in order to produce a person capable of enjoying and improving Western democratic social life and its culture (or that of some other culture); *how* we should teach those things to encourage the development of such a person; and *when* it is best to teach those things in those ways. Designing a curriculum to produce a particular kind of educated person requires answering these questions, and is a value-saturated and culture-bound task.

So, a general characteristic of our educational theory will be an explicit description of the preferred end-product of the process. This image of the end-product will provide criteria for judging the adequacy of progress through the process; the major steps toward achieving the most significant characteristics of this image will determine the stages which may be used to divide up the process—either for descriptive convenience or because they represent significant discontinuities in the normal pace of orderly advancement.

This suggests a choice for educational theorists. In explicitly describing the preferred end-product of the educational development process they must take account of the fact that humans are social and political as well as intellectual animals; that to specify a desirable educated person is to specify a desirable political, social, cultural context within which the particular set of desirable human potentials are actualized. One may either accept a particular "culture" as the ideal into which one is going to initiate the novice, and so this given culture may serve to determine the stages of development; or, one may propose the development of a range of human potentials which are appropriate for a better "culture" than presently

exists. In this latter case the educational theory is likely to be seen
as an instrument of change.

Either way—accepting the present culture or trying to rebuild it
closer to the heart's desire—we will look for reasons justifying the
theory's claims that the particular educational prescriptions will indeed bring about, or support, the preferred cultural forms. And, indeed, we will expect some justification for those cultural forms being
considered desirable. Which is to say that a comprehensive educational theory has to be, implicitly or explicitly, a social and political
theory as well.

Thus the developmental dimension of an educational theory is
hardly a psychological theory of development plus a normative component. It involves rather the selection of a set of preferred human
potentials and generating a program for their actualization. The more
or less natural and spontaneous cognitive developments which Piaget seeks to describe amount, at best, to a minor constraint on what
an educational theory may prescribe. Psychology, of course, makes
no claims to specify what human beings ought to become. At best it
might be claimed that it helps delineate something of the constraints
upon what human beings can become.

What Should We Teach?

THE WAY in which a psychological theory may be considered
to have implications for deciding what should be taught at any particular stage of a student's educational development is exemplified
in David Elkind's attempts to read from Piaget's theory to curriculum
content. Elkind discusses, for example, the appropriateness of some
of the topics and questions he found in an unnamed first-grade social
studies textbook. At the end of a section on "communities" the text
posed the question: "What religions do people have?" (One assumes
that the text previously discussed in some way that different groups
of people believed different things.) Referring to his own studies of
children's conceptions of their religious denomination he concluded
that it "is not really until adolescence . . . that children understand
what religion is about (because it involves the concept of belief, a
formal operational concept) so the question has to be empty."[7]

That is, certain topics may involve concepts that are not normally
comprehensible until much later in the process of children's psychological development. Thus it seems that a psychological theory
like Piaget's can give negative guidance, about what to avoid, and

some positive guidance, about the most appropriate stage at which certain concepts may be taught. Presumably, on the basis of Elkind's analysis he would caution that trying to teach about religion in first grade is hopeless.

To the educator reading that children do not understand what religion is about before adolescence, it remains unclear what implications follow for what should be taught. Are we to infer that "religion" should not be taught? Well, of course, this depends on what is meant by religion. We would hardly conclude that we should defer until adolescence to explain that there are different religions and that these tell their adherents different things about God and the cosmic story. Indeed we might sensibly argue that such knowledge, however superficial its initial meaning in the child's mind, is a necessary prerequisite to later, more sophisticated understanding. It is a condition of education that no topic is fully understood before maturity, if then, and the problem for educators is working out what constituent parts of any topic can be made meaningful at different stages, so that the various parts build toward a sophisticated coalescence in maturity.

Perhaps we might conclude that the contribution to education made by Piaget's theory with regard to this example is to tell us something about *how* we should organize knowledge about religion in the curriculum and in presenting it so that it is most meaningful to children. Elkind's own studies of how children's conceptions of their religious denomination develop may be expected to give us guidance here. (In passing, I might observe that the normal progression of his North American subjects seems unlike that experienced during my elementary school years in the north of England. There, religious denomination was a fundamental fact of social life, and a vivid part of one's consciousness. By age six all but the mentally maimed were sophisticated sectarian casuists. Our theological discussions, framed usually in terms of vilification while hurling stones, might have lacked something of the mystical insight of St. John of the Cross or the systematic elegance of St. Thomas Aquinas, but we apparently had a much sharper awareness than Elkind's subjects that there were various religions, and that these groups believed different things about God and the world and how to behave. This hardly throws into question the appropriateness of the Piagetian stages Elkind uses in organizing his subjects' responses, but it does raise again the question of just what these stages are measuring.)

Because the concept is the usual unit of inquiry for the cognitive developmental psychologist, this imposes another restriction on psychology's ability to tell us *what* we should teach. The educator is concerned with many other pieces of mental furniture in addition to concepts. This restriction to concepts, and indeed to a restricted range within the limited range of concepts, tends to lead to what I am tempted to call the "psychological fallacy." This involves observing a concept which is a part of a curriculum topic and concluding that the topic is appropriate to the age at which the concept is normally best understood. Let me elaborate this with an example.

Psychological research has shown that elementary school children normally lack some of the basic concepts that are necessary to make history meaningful—concepts of historical time, historical change, historical causality, and so on.[8] What implications does this have for whether or not we should teach history in elementary grades? Depending on our educational theory, we may use this knowledge to reach a wide variety of conclusions about the curriculum. I will consider three possible responses.

The first response embodies what I call the "psychological fallacy." Its prevailing influence is a tribute to the power of psychology over education, and to the theoretical poverty of education. It follows from the assumption that this knowledge has direct and obvious educational implications. It concludes that if children lack basic historical concepts, then it is a waste of time teaching history in elementary schools. This leads to an elementary school social studies curriculum innocent of any history and built around the expansion and elaboration of concepts with which the child can be expected to be familiar from daily experience—concepts like "families," "communities," and so on. The local environment increasingly provides the content of the curriculum. Children thus are to move "outward" along lines of gradually expanding concept associations from what they already know. This kind of "expanding horizons" curriculum expands from the set of local concepts which largely untutored experience seems normally to generate.

A second possible response to the knowledge that young children normally lack basic historical concepts is to conclude, on educational grounds, that historical knowledge is important and that within the constraints imposed by children's conceptual limitations as indicated by psychological research, we will teach as much history as possible. This second response, then, seeks an accommodation between claims about norms of concept development and what seems educationally desirable. So, on educational grounds, we might decide that it is desirable for young children to learn the broad outline of the history of the world. In order to find a way to teach this meaningfully, we might examine the kinds of stories that most appeal to young children and make an inventory of the kinds of concepts which children must have available to make such stories comprehensible.[9] These concepts then may be used to form an organizing structure for our history. So while we may accept psychology's general conclusion that young children lack a concept of historical causality, we may see that they clearly do have a concept of the kind of causality that holds stories together and moves them along; while they may lack a sense of historical chronology, they clearly understand "before" and "after," and "long, long ago," and "just a little while later," and so on; while they may lack an abstract sense of "kingship," or of interacting elements within political structures, they clearly understand power and weakness, oppression, resentment, and revolt, ambition and punishment; and while they may lack sophisticated notions of politically constructive or destructive behavior, they do clearly understand good and bad. Using the more simple concepts children do have available, and acknowledging the restrictions on their understanding suggested by psychological research, it seems possible to teach young children some history. An educational theory may well suggest that it is vitally important for children's educational development that they learn early something of the struggle for knowledge, freedom, and security against ignorance, oppression, and fear, which their history is largely about. It seems reasonable to believe that young children normally have available the conceptual apparatus to understand such aspects of their true story, and that the later, sophisticated understanding of history requires that this more primitive and basic understanding shall have preceded it.

A third possible response to learning that children normally lack basic historical concepts is to set about devising ways to teach whatever concepts are considered necessary. This response is not uncommon among teachers who maintain a large degree of skepticism about the findings of psychology when they seem to conflict with their observation. In their observation, introducing a new word creates a kind of semantic space which children strive to fill with appropriate meaning. Furthermore, proponents of this position believe that the use of supposedly meaningless historical concepts generates semantic spaces which the child can then be helped gradually to fill. Sensitivity and pedagogical skill may seem to such teachers the only tools necessary to allow them to teach any concepts at any time, constrained only by the logic of their subject matter. Implicitly they believe that Piaget and his followers are measuring the results of what teachers and parents have in the past been doing. If teachers teach different things and the forms of social initiation change, they assume that the data gathered by such researchers will be different. Such teachers consider it nonsense to be told that young children can only understand the local and concrete, when their imaginations grasp monsters, witches, princesses, and talking animals in exotic times and places; that children should be restricted to content built on a narrow range of concepts, when they have experienced in their purest and most powerful forms, love, hate, fear, joy, courage, cowardice, ambition, oppression, and so on.

What implications, then, follow for whether or not we should teach history in elementary school from a psychological theory which tells us that children at that age lack the basic concepts to make history meaningful? As pointed out above, for something to be meaning-*full* requires educational maturity; the purpose of the educational process is to fill concepts with meaning gradually. The only alternative to something being meaningful is not its being meaning-empty. Degrees of understanding are infinite, and the complexity of how we learn a subject is endlessly complicated. Should we infer that lack of historical concepts means that teaching history is hopeless, or that we can teach certain prerequisites on which later historical understanding is to be built, or that we can teach anything we want if only we have sufficient sensitivity and subtlety? What does such a theory imply for *what* we should teach?

An implication can be read from the theory to educational content only if one assumes the truth of what I have called the psychological fallacy: that the normal lack of certain concepts means that topics that normally employ those concepts cannot be successfully taught. If one does not commit this fallacy, I think it is clear that the theory carries no implications about particular content. Topics are amenable to being organized by many concepts in bewilderingly many ways. The psychological theory's insights about concepts normally understood at particular stages of a child's development may, however, seem to have clear implications for *how* the content should be organized and *when* it should best be taught.

When Should We Teach Particular Things?

ONE OF PIAGET'S great indirect contributions to education has been to remind those who have forgotten Plato and Rousseau that the developmental process involves passing through qualitatively different stages in order to reach maturity; that the child's thinking is not a simple microform of the adult's. As noted in the introductory section of this chapter, we may reasonably expect different stage divisions to characterize educational development from those that characterize cognitive development. The general process of educational development clearly reaches maturity by passing through stages during which individuals' interests in and understanding of the world and experience are qualitatively different. An educational theory, in order properly to answer the *when?* question, will have to characterize the qualitatively different stages through which a person must go in order to reach the particular kind of educational maturity the theory describes.

Thus if our image of educational maturity involves certain freedoms of expression in words, or music, or stone, or paint, or whatever, then we will want to know what qualitatively different stages lead to that mature freedom. We might reasonably expect, for example, that at certain stages particular kinds of disciplines and constraints are necessary. Similarly, if our image of educational maturity involves also a certain scholarly discipline, we might reasonably expect our educational theory to specify that at certain stages the development of a certain kind of romance and freedom are prerequisite to achieving that mature discipline. An educational theory that lacks a sense of qualitative changes in the process leading to educational maturity, and provides, say, merely a curriculum of accumulating content, has simply ignored the whole essential realm of development—has failed to address the *when* question.

In passing it might be noted how different are these kinds of educational considerations of freedom of expression and scholarly discipline, and their prerequisites, from the kinds of concepts Piaget's theory is concerned with. One result of Piaget's theory dominating thinking about educational development is that it focuses sensitivity on a restricted range of concepts at the expense of virtually all other developmental processes.

But, it may be claimed, cognitive development is a constituent of educational development, and so learning about cognitive development tells us something about educational development, as learning about cotton also tells us something about cloth. However minor a part of educational development is taken by the process of cognitive development, learning about the latter must have some implications for education. There are a number of problems with this claim. Perhaps most crucial here is that resulting from psychology's ambition

to be scientific after the fashion of the natural sciences. This leads
to psychological theories focusing as clearly as possible on the underlying natural processes of cognitive development. Piaget, for example, is not interested in those concepts which occur "artificially"
as a result of instruction, but rather in those concepts which *develop*
spontaneously or naturally as a result of normal interactions with
the environment. He is interested in what happens of necessity in
the development of cognition. An educational theory is concerned
with making value choices among a variety of possibilities. One does
not *choose* to do what is necessary. As quoted from Elkind earlier,
it makes no sense to try to teach concepts which develop naturally.
An educational theory, then, will not incorporate a psychological
theory of "natural" cognitive development, bur rather will possibly
accommodate to it. The value choices that constitute a sensible
educational theory will be made within the range of what is
necessary.

This may only mean that the implications to be drawn from
Piaget's theory to education are a little less direct. That is, if the kind
of understanding of a topic, possible at different stages, turns on
developments in these fundamental, teaching-resistant, spontaneously developed concepts, then a psychological theory about these
concepts must surely have implications for *how* topics should be
organized in order to be meaningful at any particular stage. I will
consider this in the following section.

Even allowing for the point made in the previous section—that
topics can be organized by a variety of concepts—surely we may say
that if one wants to teach in grade one a specific concept that Piaget's
theory claims does not normally develop till adolescence, then his
theory has obvious implications for *when* we should teach such
things.

A problem that complicates the move from psychological theories
of cognitive development to the sequencing of the curriculum—*when*
to teach particular things—is the difficulty of distinguishing logical
from psychological constraints on children's developing understanding. In all subject areas there are logical constraints on the sequence
in which things can be sensibly taught. One cannot, for example,
learn calculus before learning to count; one cannot develop generalized notions of historical change before learning some historical
facts. In that such logical analysis reflects in some sense constraints
of our nature we may say that it has implications for education. It
serves to delineate constraints within which our educational theory
must fit. A considerable influence on the sequencing of the curric-

ulum, then, will be independent of anything a psychological theory can tell us.

It may seem that there is no conflict of jurisdiction here between psychology and logic. Logical analysis may tell us about certain general sequences which subject matter presentation has to follow, and empirical studies based on psychological theories of cognitive development may tell us about more detailed sequences within the over-all structure which are most effective in practice. Or logical analysis may yield a fairly detailed picture of an appropriate sequence, and a theory of cognitive development may tell us during what periods of individuals' development particular parts of the sequence can best be learned. Logical analysis, for example, may be able to tell us that in learning a subject the concrete and particular should precede the abstract and the general, and a psychological theory such as Piaget's can tell us in more detail the sequence of substages through which, and the normal ages at which, children proceed from more to less concrete thinking, and from concrete to abstract thinking, and from less to more abstract thinking. It may seem that logical analysis and pyschological investigations go hand-in-hand in elaborating desirable curriculum sequences.

Now, obviously, a psychological theory which told us that some historical facts are normally learned before students formulate historical generalizations would leave us unimpressed. We do not require empirical investigations to confirm logical truths. One question to be raised before granting that psychological theories may have implications for the sequencing of the curriculum is how far logical necessity preempts whatever psychological theories may tell us. A second question is whether the kinds of things we learn from logical analysis are indeed similar to the kinds of things we learn from inquiries based on psychological theories, and do they both have educational implications?

The second question brings us to an observation already noted. Logical analysis can reflect something about constraints of our nature. In so far as it can do this, it has implications for education. It is not clear that any psychological theory can tell us about constraints of our nature. Piaget's theory claims to show a general move from concrete to abstract thinking, but we may remain unimpressed because this merely reflects a logical necessity.[10] Are the much more detailed claims about the substages of cognitive development equally incontrovertible? Are they telling us about something which is, first, necessarily the case and which is, second, inaccessible to logical analysis? The latter seems to be true, and if the former is also true we must acknowledge that Piaget's theory has implications for education. At the level of generality of this discussion, however, we cannot resolve that problem. In chapter 3 Piaget's theory will be considered in some detail, and empirical evidence that reflects on this issue will be reviewed.

One difficulty in answering these questions is that so far neither logical analysis nor psychological theories have greatly helped educators in deciding on the best sequence for, say, a history curriculum. It might at this point be worth considering a related issue that might help clarify these questions. This is the issue of recapitulation. It has become a rather murky topic since the early enthusiasms of evolutionary theory, and it has developed from the observation that the human fetus seems in its early growth to recapitulate the developmental process through the life-forms from which we have evolved. If I am arguing that it is a problematic step from psychological theories of concept development to educational practice, we may seem to need our seven-league boots to get from this observation to the sequencing of curricula.

Education's interest in recapitulation may be stated as the question: How far, if at all, does the individual's initiation into a culture recapitulate the *history* of how that culture developed? That is, one is asking whether education is properly seen as a process of acceleration through the stages of cultural development of our cultural group. Now, clearly, there are some crude ways in which this is generally true and ways in which it is obviously false. The relevance of the question for the developmental dimension of our educational theory is that, if it can be shown to be in certain ways true, we may be instructed by history how to organize our curricula of initiation into particular forms of knowledge. In the extreme case, if we could show the "recapitulation hypothesis" to be true, then our history curriculum would follow the pattern whereby historical consciousness was developed; our mathematics curriculum would be built on the stages of the gradual progress to current mathematical insight.

One advantage of pursuing this recapitulation hypothesis is that it would allow historical scholarship to articulate a fairly detailed curriculum, which would of necessity be a logically coherent way of initiating an individual into understanding a subject. Whether it would be the best way is one question; another question is whether it would be coherent with the process of cognitive development exposed by a psychological theory.

This recapitulation hypothesis is not a new idea, of course, and it presents a number of immediate stumbling blocks; not the least of which are its past proponents and their curriculum recommendations. My concern here is to see whether there is any sense in which we can establish the *plausibility* of the hypothesis, because if we can, its implications for our educational theory may be profound. And, it might be noted, we are drawn to reconsider this old hypothesis in a new way by Piaget's work, and by the intentional ambiguity in the name he has given to his focal area of research: "genetic epistemology," which can refer equally well to the growth of knowledge in the human species and in the individual human being.[11]

That what we are looking for will not be a literal and explicit recapitulation is evident from simple observation and empirical research. We would not, for example, expect an early stage of children's historical understanding to mimic that of the sophisticated minds of Herodotus or Thucydides, nor would we consider it sensible to teach historical knowledge bit by bit as it was discovered by the historians of our culture. Some of Piaget's own empirical research has shown in certain detailed ways how children's normal process of mastery of mathematical concepts inverts the historical sequence of their discovery.[12]

The fact that this inversion is noteworthy, however, suggests that there is a general sense in which children's growing mastery of mathematical understanding follows that of our culture, and this general similarity leads us to question whether there may not be a level of generality at which we may see the two processes as identical. In the case of the development of historical understanding, where the recapitulation hypothesis may seem initially absurd, a plausible argument can be made: if we focus on a level of presuppositions that determine the kind of meaning derived from historical knowledge we may then see a similar progression both in the history of historiography and in children's understanding.[13] In the sciences, too, the recapitulation hypothesis may seem initially absurd—we will not teach first an image of a Ptolemaic universe or teach alchemy as an introduction to chemistry. But, as with history, there may be a way by which children can more readily and meaningfully be given access to sophisticated scientific understanding through stages that recapitulate an aspect of the history of science. Perhaps a useful model for educators to explore is that of succeeding "paradigms," such as are described by Thomas S. Kuhn.[14] Educators might consider whether such paradigms have an analogous form in children's development of scientific understanding.[15]

Where does this speculation take us? Let us suppose we could construct a history curriculum based on the developing understand-

ing of the history we observe in our culture. We can say safely that
it will be a coherent way of initiating children into an historical
consciousness; though it is not at all clear how it is coherent with
logical and psychological models of development. What implications
for the sequencing of such a curriculum could a developmental theory like Piaget's have? Or, to return to the earlier questions, how far
does the discovery of a sequence of this recapitulatory kind preempt
whatever a psychological theory like Piaget's might tell us? One
aspect of a recapitulation curriculum is that it suggests the notion
of logical constraints in the sequencing of subject matter in a different
light. It suggests the possibility that the process of educational development may be articulated, not in terms of the age or stage-related
acquisition of Piagetian teaching-resistant concepts, but in terms of
time-related mastery of content paradigms, which are subject to
teaching. So we would see young children's inability to achieve
historical understanding as due not to some genetic constraint, but
to the prerequisite paradigmatic forms not having been mastered,
and this mastery of progressively more sophisticated forms takes
time. (And indeed, it seems not impossible that the kinds of conceptual developments exposed by Piaget are in fact determined by
the kinds of paradigms that may be accessible to conceptual analysis,
their possible isomorphism being culturally conditioned by historical contingencies. Or perhaps the reverse is true; Piaget's developmental process showing how knowledge and understanding are
necessarily built because the human mind is the way it is.) But all
this merely continues the speculation.

It is commonly assumed, however, that while a curriculum sequence may, from a logical point of view, be impeccable, Piaget's
theory could tell us at what ages the various parts of it should be
taught. That is, his psychological theory might carry the clear implication that children should not be accelerated through such a
curriculum but that, for the curriculum to be best understood, the
speed at which individual students move through it should be co-
ordinated with underlying cognitive developments. This, of course,
presupposes that there is an underlying process of cognitive development which is more or less independent of whatever is to be
taught. Whether or not there is such a distinct underlying process
is crucial to deciding whether, or the degree to which, Piaget's theory
carries implications for the sequencing of curriculum. This is, again,
a question which cannot be resolved at the level of generality of this
discussion and will have to be left until we review relevant empirical
evidence in chapter 3.

One might note here, however, that Piaget is only casually interested in the ages at which children normally achieve particular stages in the developmental process he details; primarily he is interested in articulating as precisely as possible the actual process in terms of its most fundamental logico-mathematical forms. So even if we were to conclude that the Piaget theory's main implication for education's *when* question was to tell us the ages at which children move through the various stages and substages from concrete to abstract thinking, we would have to acknowledge that the practical guidance of that knowledge was considerably restricted by the typical environments in which educators work. Given a considerable latitude between chronological age and the age at which individual children reach any particular Piagetian stage, and the difficulty of knowing with any precision "where" any individual is in the process, let alone knowing where thirty children are, this leaves the seventh-grade teacher armed with detailed knowledge of Piaget's theory arguably no better off than if armed only with that imprecise practical knowledge that results from experience. But this issue will also be returned to in chapter 3.

Educators want to know when in the sequence of the curriculum particular things should be taught. Although we may learn a considerable amount of this from the logical analysis of subject matter, it seems possible that Piaget's psychological theory may have implications for when certain concepts can be taught, and not taught, and it may have implications for coordinating a logically designed curriculum with age-related developments. In chapter 3 I will try to show that Piaget's theory does not have such implications, but a more detailed look at his theory and related empirical evidence is required to make this case.

How Should We Teach Things?

LET US consider under this heading things relevant to organizing and presenting material so that it is most meaningful to children at different stages of their development. Even if we allow that Piaget's theory has no implications for what content we should choose to teach, it is generally assumed that it has clear implications for how we should organize that content in order that children may best understand it. Piaget's theory should help us in the courteous task Bruner recommends of presenting the structure of a subject "in terms of the child's way of viewing things,"[16] of translating "material into his logical forms."[17]

Elkind has suggested a distinction between what he calls "the school curriculum" and "the developmental curriculum." The school curriculum is made up of the sequences of subject matter, whereas the developmental curriculum is "the sequence of abilities and concepts that children acquire more or less on their own."[18] It is this developmental curriculum which, in Elkind's view, Piaget has done so much to reveal, and which Elkind thinks can serve as a complement to the school curriculum by providing "criteria for judging whether any given set of curriculum materials is appropriate to the cognitive level of the children to whom it is being presented."[19] It is not a curriculum to be taught but rather a set of tools for the analysis of the school curriculum. One could surely go further and suggest that if the developmental curriculum provides criteria for judging materials already developed, it also provides criteria for use in designing developmentally appropriate materials.

A first reflection on the possible educational implications Piaget's theory may have is because of its focus on a specific range of concepts. Educators are interested in how to organize material so that it is most engaging and meaningful to children at any stage of their development. Application of "the developmental curriculum" as a tool of analysis can tell us at best only *whether or not*, according to its criterion, a set of curriculum materials is organized appropriately for a given stage of development. It cannot tell us which of the endless possible developmentally appropriate ways is best, or which would be educationally most valuable. It is precisely this, however, that we want an educational theory to tell us. Still, we will consider a psychological theory to have clear educational implications if it can tell us how to avoid making a topic meaningless or unnecessarily difficult through incorporating developmentally inappropriate concepts.

A second possible restriction on the implications of the theory for deciding how we should organize and present material will follow from the degree of doubt we have about the validity of Elkind's distinction between the school curriculum and the developmental curriculum, which is an expression of Piaget's distinction between learning and development, which is, in turn, the stumbling block we ran up against in the previous section. That Piaget's theory has implications for the organization and presentation of educational material turns on Piaget's claim that he is exposing a fundamental and spontaneous process of cognitive development which determines what can be learned and taught meaningfully at any developmental stage. Implications about the propriety of discovery learning, readiness, the organization of topics, and so on, hinge on this claim. I will argue in chapter 3 that there are good reasons to doubt the validity of Piaget's distinction between learning and development, but making that argument requires a close look at the theory and at the relevant empirical data.

Answering the question about *how* best to teach things, may seem a matter of more straightforward empirical testing than trying to draw inferences from a developmental theory. The area one might more immediately turn to for guidance is that which is concerned with establishing empirical regularities between kinds of teaching and degrees of learning: applied psychological research on teaching effectiveness which aims to generate a theory of instruction. One of the oddities of this research is the difficulty it has experienced in establishing any generalizations or principles which teachers may apply with confidence. The methodological approach used in these empirical studies seems, in some opaque way, to rule out precisely the matter of most concern to the educator; that is, the units of teaching and learning which the methodology requires the researchers to restrict themselves to, seem to be not educational units. That is, education is clearly a process in which something accumulates. To be able to do sensible research about education one must be sure that the thing one is researching is educational stuff—whose accumulation we recognize as education. That this very stuff of education, the unit of education, is not, say, "the fact" or "the concept" is clear because we recognize that the best educated person is not the one who accumulates in readily accessible form the most facts or concepts.

This is to say, a research program whose theory of instruction may be able to tell us about the best way to get children to learn a set of facts or concepts may still have no implications for education. What teachers have to teach, while involving facts and concepts, may be so significantly different in its basic units that the results of such research may not generalize to them. Again, at this level of generality we are unable to get beyond the conclusion that there is something opaque here. We will return to this issue, and consider relevant empirical research, in chapter 5.

Conclusion

I HAVE aimed in this chapter to clarify some distinctions between what educators want to know in order to do their job better and the kinds of things psychological theories, particularly Piaget's, tell us. Not surprisingly, perhaps, I have succeeded only in showing that what might commonly be accepted as abuses of psychological theories are of no help to education. I have, as it were, nibbled around the edges of the argument that psychological theories have no implications for education, and have had to leave the core of the argument for later.

In the process of nibbling around the edges, however, I think enough has been said about what educators want to know for us to identify Plato's theory as telling us a number of those kinds of things. In order, then, to set the stage for the later part of the argument, I will turn to considering in some detail Plato's and Piaget's developmental theories, and discovering what they can tell us about what we should teach, and when and how we should teach these things, in order to produce a particular kind of educated person.

2/ Plato's Developmental Theory

Biographical Introduction

PERICTIONE, wife of Ariston, gave birth to a boy, Plato, in 428 or 427 B.C. He was their third son. Both Perictione and Ariston came from families who had for generations been prominent in the political life of Athens. After Ariston's death, Perictione married her uncle Pyrilampes, who had been a close friend and prominent political supporter of Pericles. We may say that politics was in Plato's blood. In his youth he must have become familiar with the maneuvering and strategies of power politics during the feverish years of the Peloponnesian War. We know from a probably authentic letter written late in his life that he had had invitations to take part in the government of Athens while still a young man. But the constant attraction of active political life never led to Plato's actually holding office. The reasons for this include the combination of his peculiar intelligence and the influence on it of Socrates.

During his youth, Plato must have heard Socrates frequently. In the *Republic*, Plato's elder brothers, Glaucon and Adeimantus, appear as participants in discussions with Socrates. By the time he was a young man it seems that Plato had become largely persuaded of the rightness of Socrates' general teachings. In the *Apology*, Plato mentions himself as present at Socrates' trial and among those who tried to persuade Socrates to pay a conciliatory fine—the money for which Plato offered to provide. Socrates did not, however, lessen

the interest in politics which Plato's family life had stimulated—
rather, he redirected it.

It was characteristic of Socrates to think about problems ex-
haustively, to try to find a bedrock of truth. Usually he began by
demolishing the answers that were commonly given to what he perceived as the most important questions people had to respond to in
life, showing the superficiality and falseness of the answers that most
people accepted as adequate. These were not abstruse philosophical
questions, but the basic questions about how one should live. Few
Athenians took pleasure in being shown that the principles on which
they conducted their lives were wrong, crude, and superficial. Socrates was to pay for the accumulated resentments of his fellow citizens with his life, in 399 B.C.

To Plato, who grew up during the Peloponnesian War and who
became a follower of Socrates' way, it became clear that how one
organized a state affected profoundly the quality of citizens' lives.
His intellectual and political interests combined in trying to answer
two questions: How should one organize a state for the best; and
how can one bring such a state into being? A crucial part of the
answer lay in the form of education which would prepare citizens
to sustain something as close as possible to the ideal state. As Plato's
Socrates says in the Republic, "It is important that our best efforts
be given to the education of youth."

Some people see Plato's Republic as a utopian vision—"utopian"
being defined as something unrealizable and, therefore, useless. But
it is important to remember that Plato was closely involved with
practical politics in a variety of states all his life. He was not interested in merely describing an ideal—much of his energy went into
seeking ways of approximating the ideal as closely as possible in
reality.

During the decade after Socrates' death Plato seems to have trav-
eled widely, apparently despairing of finding any plausible method
of introducing into political and social life the ideals represented in
Socrates' teaching. On his return to Athens Plato bought land and
founded his Academy. The Academy was intended, in part at least,
for the education of future statesmen. He seems to have concluded
that one way to realize his ideal was to educate future leaders of
states so that they would, on achieving power, increasingly convert
their states to embody those principles Plato expressed in the Republic.

During the first decades of the Academy's existence Plato wrote
the Republic, influenced many prominent young men, and super-

vised the intellectual training of others who would later advise pol-
iticians and leaders. (Aristotle, who joined the Academy in 367 B.C.,
became the tutor of Alexander the Great.) By these indirect means
Plato hoped to encourage a gradual progress toward the ideal state.

Whatever effect he had on the conduct of political affairs and the
organization of states in the ancient world, his method remains influential. The tool he recommended for the amelioration of the world's
ills, and on which his greatest efforts were spent, was education.
Plato, perhaps more clearly than any other philosopher, understood
that if philosophy was to serve human life, its central focus must be
education.

It is often claimed that the perspective of history is necessary in
order to get a proportionate view of a great person. But the perspective of over two thousand years somehow does not help much in
taking a proportionate view of Plato. Perhaps our ways of thinking
and making sense of the world and experience have been so profoundly influenced by him that he has become a part of what we use
in trying to get a view of him. It's a little like trying to see oneself
proportionately. A common image of him is as the great rational
philosopher. But that must be tempered by the realization that he
was also one of the greatest mystical visionaries of the Western tradition. It was said that after being converted to Socrates' way, Plato
burned the tragedies he had written as a young man. Whether or not
he burned his tragedies he did not destroy his gifts as a dramatist:
Who can read the *Apology* without being moved to tears? What other
great philosopher has vivified his arguments by dramatizing them
so captivatingly? The advances of modern philosophy have not left
Plato behind, but have simply opened up new riches in his work
which had not previously been fully understood. In the introduction
to his anthologies on Plato, Gregory Vlastos notes that the recent
developments in logical and semantic analysis have led to "a higher
appreciation of [Plato's] stature," and that he has become for modern
philosophers, yet again, "a living presence."[1]

Plato's purpose was to help people to live in such a way that
they would not, in his phrase, defile their souls in the process. Having
characterized the nature of the state that would enable each kind of
person to live the best kind of life, and having characterized ideal
images of adults in that society, Plato turns to considering how one
can achieve those ends. He turns to the problems of education:

> Let us speak now of the manner of teaching . . . and the persons to
> whom, and the time when [the various subjects are] to be imparted. As

the shipwright first lays down the lines of the keel, and thus, as it were,
draws the ship in outline, so do I seek to distinguish the patterns of life,
and lay down their keels according to the nature of different men's souls;
seeking truly to consider by what means, and in what ways, we may go
through the voyage of life best.[2]

Plato's Theory of Educational Development

IN WHAT FOLLOWS I will focus on Plato's educational ideas
from the perspective of *when*, and see what his developmental scheme
tells us about *what* and *how* to teach. Plato wrote with an ancient
city-state in mind, whereas our interest is in producing prople for
modern industrial societies; he wrote in the intellectual context of
ancient proto-science and a largely ahistorical culture, whereas two
of the most prominent features of modern intellectual life are an
increasingly sophisticated science and a complex historical consciousness. Consequently there are a number of points at which it
would not serve our present, practical educational interests to dwell
on the literal details of Plato's recommendations. In such cases I will
make somewhat free with Plato's proposals, "translating" them where
it seems sensible into terms more directly useful to our different
circumstances. One is tempted to observe that Plato is too important
a thinker to be left to philosophers and classicists. Their typical
concern has been to clarify precisely what he meant by certain terms
within the context of his time. My concern, obviously dependent on
the scholarship of the philosophers and classicists, is to clarify what
uses the principles he established have within the context of our
time.

In Section I below, then, I will outline Plato's theory of the four
stages of educational development. In Section II I will first describe
quite briefly the particular curriculum Plato recommends to aid development through each stage, then I will indicate the principles
that underlie those particular curriculum recommendations, and then
I will consider what kind of curriculum seems to follow from those
principles for modern industrial societies. In Section III I will discuss
Plato's theory in light of the ideas developed in chapter 1.

I. FOUR STAGES OF EDUCATIONAL DEVELOPMENT

Having characterized his ideal of the educated person, Plato
turns to considering how such a person can be produced: "What

must they learn, and at what age should they take up each branch of study" (R.VI.502). To introduce us to his model of the developmental process he tells us to draw a line and to divide it into unequal parts. (Though he is not clear about the proportions, I interpret it as it seems most sensible to me.) The smaller left-hand side is to represent the world of objects, the concrete, sensuous world, and the right-hand side is to represent the world of thought, the abstract, intelligible world.

He tells us then to subdivide the two parts in similar proportions as the over-all division. The left-hand side of each subdivision is to represent a more superficial understanding than the right-hand side. The metaphor he uses suggests that we consider the left-hand side of each subdivision as if it were a shadow or image, of which the right-hand side is the reality; or the left-hand side as appearances, where the right-hand side is knowledge.

A similar appearance/knowledge relationship holds between the combined subdivisions on the left and those on the right. He uses an example to illustrate this. In the two left subdivisions people might learn some geometry by manipulating wood or drawn squares or triangles. In the two higher subdivisions people will realize that these are merely images or representations, and that knowledge of geometry is properly concerned with abstract forms, and these abstract forms are the reality of which the particular drawn shapes are mere imperfect representations. Plato concludes his brief outline of the four stages of educational development by naming them. We might summarize his model in the figure below.

Plato tells us that each stage of thinking orients the mind toward a particular range or set of objects; therefore in elaborating on this

Model of Plato's Developmental Stages

Stage One EIKASIA	*Stage Two* PISTIS	*Stage Three* DIANOIA	*Stage Four* NOESIS
Uninquiring acceptance of appearances	Common-sense beliefs of man-in-the-street	Abstract reasoning that fails to examine critically its own premises	Philosophical reasoning tha examines its own premise and reaches the most secur forms of knowledge
Concrete thinking about the visible world/opinions rather than well-founded knowledge (DOXA).		Abstract thinking; manipulating mental entities	

model I will characterize each stage in two parts. The first will deal with the kind of thinking; the second with the objects toward which that kind of thinking is oriented (i.e., curriculum content). Following Plato's general metaphor, we may see movement through each stage of thinking as representing an increasing clarity of knowledge and understanding and each stage of objects as representing an increase in their reality. That is, in Plato's view, the process of educational development involves proceeding from superficial thinking focused on a world of shifting appearances to profound thinking focused on the most real and stable things.

Stage One: Eikasia

Kind of thinking. The name of this stage is "etymologically connected with *eikon* = image, likeness, and with *eikos* = likely, and it can mean either likeness (representation) or likening (comparison) or estimation of likelihood (conjecture)."[3] Cornford suggests "imagining" as the least unsatisfactory translation. This is perhaps less satisfactory today because of the kinds of positive associations attached to "imagining," but it does serve to point to that kind of thinking which accepts uncritically what it imagines to be the case from the appearance of a thing. Thus, it would accept that the sun and moon are about the same size, and that the moon follows one along the street, because this is how they appear. It is a superficial kind of associative thinking that has a quality akin to what Piaget describes as "a sort of confusion between the inner and the outer, or a tendency to fix in objects something which is the result of the activity of the thinking subject."[4]

Objects of thought. The superficial aspects of things; whatever the senses suggest.

Stage Two: Pistis

Kind of thinking. Pistis means literally "belief." This stage is exemplified by that kind of thinking which accepts the dominant conventional beliefs about things. It is more sensible than the previous stage, being less accepting of appearances and apprehending objects in the world more clearly. It would accept, for example, that the sun is larger than the moon, but on the basis of being satisfied with the common opinion rather than inquiring further into it. It is concrete, practical, conventional thinking.

Objects of thought. The things of which the previous stage perceived only the surface images; the concrete entities that make up the world accessible to direct experience. The distinction from the previous stage may be clarified by reference to Piaget's concepts of "conservation." At the *eikasia* stage appearance is all, at the *pistis* stage the person is no longer taken in by the appearance but apprehends things more clearly—even though the "things" might be falsehoods.

Stages one and two: *eikasia* and *pistis*. Plato combines these two stages under the general heading of *doxa* ("opinions"). These are, he suggests, stages of cognition limited to opinions. They thus carry no guarantee of stability. They are rooted, not in fundamental principles, but concrete examples. If asked for a definition of justice, people at the *doxa* stages would respond by giving examples of things they consider just. Their concept of justice, then, would be bound up in the particular instances, and would thus be local, provincial, conventional. The "opinions" of these stages—the things people think with and think about—are not implanted by rational instruction but by persuasion and conditioning; equally they are amenable to being changed not by reasoning but by persuasion and conditioning.[5]

Stage Three: Dianoia

Kind of thinking. Dianoia means literally "thinking." At this stage the mind recognizes, for example, that diagrams, models, particular cases are merely representatives of things which are properly dealt with in abstract terms. A particular drawing of a triangle may be useful, but it only crudely represents the ideal triangularity on which geometric inquiries must be based. A particular law or custom is recognized as an instance of some abstract ideal of justice or social order. During this stage, people recognize the need to develop sophistication in dealing with this abstract realm in order to avoid being caught up with concrete examples. That is, the examples are understood to be examples of something else, and that something else needs to be formulated in abstract terms. Plato suggests that this is a kind of bridge from the concrete thinking of the *doxa* stages to the more sophisticated thinking of the next. *Dianoia* is discursive, rational thinking which has the imperfection of still relying somewhat on the concrete images it evolves from, remaining at least partially trapped by appearances, and of not consistently examining the premises on which its thinking is based.

Objects of thought. A somewhat impure mixture of concrete objects and the abstract ideas of which they are exemplars; hypotheses, as distinct from fundamental principles.

Stage Four: Noesis

Kind of thinking. *Noesis* means literally "intelligence," though Plato also once uses the word *episteme* ("knowledge") for this stage (R.VII.534). This is the highest stage, and Plato points at it rather than clearly characterizes it. The mind at this stage frees itself from the confusing ambiguities of the previous stage. It no longer relies on concrete examples, but can deal in a sophisticated manner with abstract entities. It also recognizes the inability to discover secure truths unless one works from fundamental principles. One establishes these principles by the use of the method Plato calls *dialectic.* That is, one pursues a topic with inexorable patience, by questioning and answering, and one shakes it and pulls it this way and that until all concrete appearances are shucked away, till all local and particular associations are eradicated. Once one gets rid of the contingencies and gets clear about first principles, one may then from this secure basis work back to decide the truth about any particular instances in the everyday world. It is the thinking of the ideal philosopher, represented by Socrates in Plato's dialogues; the person who will not be satisfied with appearances or easy answers, who will go on searching till he finds a secure basis for knowledge claims, if one can be found.

Objects of thought. In this highest stage the objects of thought focused on are what Plato calls the Forms, or Ideas—that is, the most abstract concepts which most precisely embody the reality that is being thought about. These Forms he considers the most secure kind of knowledge. We might modernize this notion by comparing Plato's Forms with the kinds of "laws" sought by physical sciences. They too refer to ideals (a body falling in a perfect vacuum) which never actually exist in nature, but the understanding of which enables one to account for particular natural events.[6] If, as in the *Republic*, one is discussing justice, the thinker at the *noesis* stage is the one who has reached an understanding of the essence or nature of justice and can refer back from this to resolve social conflicts in the everyday world. Plato does not suggest that he, or Socrates, had attained such understanding of any Form, or that anyone had or could. But, he says, this is a way of representing the ideal of secure knowledge *toward which* one should try constantly to move. The value of an ideal lies not in its practical attainability, but in how well it suggests the direction in which the educated person should continue to move. As Cornford puts it: "An ideal has an indispensable value for practice, in that thought thereby gives to action its right aim."[7]

II. CURRICULUM CONTENT

For Plato the path from *eikasia* to *noesis* is a difficult one. Children cannot be expected to launch forward with ease and speed, but must gradually "grow accustomed" to the next higher stage, taking the steps calmly one at a time. For each stage, he prescribes (mainly in the *Republic* and the *Laws*) the most appropriate kind of curriculum,[8] which will both satisfy the kind of thinking proper to any particular stage while developing the capacities that are prerequisite for moving on to the next.

In general terms, Plato sees the process of educational development as beginning in a world of sensations and the manipulation of concrete objects and leading by degrees to sophisticated abstract thinking. He represents this process from concrete particular to abstract generalization as a growing ability to see things as they really are. This is a paradox, but one with whose basic truth we may by now be familiar. The mind entrammeled in concrete entities is fettered as far as thinking is concerned. A sophisticated ability to plan and calculate requires becoming freed from concrete particulars in order to generate abstract concepts, which will allow the mind to manipulate the world in the mind's terms, referring the results of such abstract manipulation back to the concrete world.

Plato's curriculum, then, is designed to be one in which the "steadfastness of opinion has to be translated into logical consistency; the quickness and exactness of perception and fancy into the power of abstraction and reasoning; the love of things and persons into the devotion to principles and ideas."[9] The latter do not so much replace the former: the former serve, as it were, as the concrete templates for the development of their abstract counterparts. Having used the world to think with, the mind has generated concepts which can then themselves become the vehicles of thought.

Educational development for Plato is not only an intellectual task, it is also a moral enterprise. He believed that weakness of character inhibits a person's ability to achieve educational progress. Consequently his curriculum includes a sequence of activities that are calculated to develop strength of character. Indeed, Plato's concern is not merely with the development of an intellectual, but rather with what we might better characterize as a combination of scholar, warrior, saint, and athlete—with each aspect in proportionate harmony with the others.

Before looking at his particular curriculum recommendations, it is useful to recall that Plato did not set out to specify in detail an ideal curriculum. Rather, he wanted to establish a set of principles upon which such a curriculum should be built, and he resorted to particular recommendations only to clarify those principles. In describing his curriculum, then, I will not dwell on the particulars that seemed to him best suited to prepare a citizen for an ancient city-state but, after simply mentioning those particulars, I will try to characterize the principles he considered fundamental to an ideal curriculum that would help development from the stage of *eikasia* to *noesis*. I will then indicate in general terms the kind of curriculum content that seems to follow from applying those principles in our modern situation.

Stage One: Eikasia

Curriculum content. Plato recommends two major emphases in his curriculum for the first stage. One concerns the general cultural initiation of the child, and the other is concerned with what we might call physical education.

The main instruments of cultural initiation are stories. Plato believed that the stories a child first hears and learns are profoundly important—a conclusion echoed in somewhat different terms by Bruno Bettelheim.[10] Traditional myth-stories and the epic poems of Homer would form the staple. Plato, however, insists that only those stories which exemplify desirable patterns of thought and behavior should be allowed in the curriculum at this stage. The purpose of these stories is to bring the child to feel and learn to love those aspects of human character and behavior which it will be necessary for the child to develop later.

Hand in hand with learning these stories, the child would receive instruction in reading, writing, and elementary computations. These should be introduced using so far as possible concrete objects, and incorporating what is to be learned into games, the way, he says, mathematics is taught in Egypt.

Physical education will include, as well as the more expected activities, dancing and learning about diet. Physical education is seen as contributing to self-control, hardiness, and courage. It stimulates the spirited element in our nature. It is given so prominent a role in Plato's curriculum not simply because it produces healthy bodies, but because of what it can contribute to the development of a strong character.

Underlying principles. The following, somewhat overlapping principles seem to underlie his choice of the curriculum for the *eikasia* stage. They appear in no particular order.

The most careful attention and teaching should be spent on the very young, at the beginning of their educational development. The qualities that are later to constitute the ideally educated person must be established in embryo, and form as firm a foundation for later developments as possible. "The beginning, as you know, is always the most important part, especially in dealing with anything young and tender. That is the time when the character is being moulded and easily takes any impress one may wish to stamp on it" (R.II.377).

The problem in designing the curriculum for this first stage is how to make accessible to the child with this *eikasia* kind of comprehension—this conjecturing, this confusion, this ability to see only as through a glass darkly—the highest truths; in Nettleship's phrase about religious education: "how to express the highest truth in the most appropriate and least inadequate forms."[11] The task is to work out what is the best way to introduce children to, and begin moving them toward, the ideal he has identified. The child has not yet developed powers of reflection and logical reasoning, and responds to the world mainly in imaginative and emotional terms. Consequently the curriculum cannot be based on appeals to a kind of rational ability which the child lacks, but must be one which stimulates, persuades, and conditions. One conditions the child to prefer the morally good, the harmonious in music, the beautiful in literature. That is, one's initial instruction must be at an appropriate level for the child's understanding, but it must nevertheless present the child with a subconscious acceptance of true principles. Children, Plato believed, would come to admire and imitate the good, the true, and the beautiful; and that these desirable patterns of thought and behavior, "if persisted in from youth up," grow into habits "which become second nature" (R.III.395). As Nettleship puts it: "By presenting to the soul the true principles of human life in the sensuous material which it is able to assimilate, they prepare it unconsciously for assimilating them when presented at a later stage in a more rational form."[12]

There should be no difference in the education of males and females, either in their cultural or physical education. Plato may be considered one of the most radical of "feminists." Not only does he argue that both sexes equally require the development of the knowledge and character traits of his ideal educated person, but he argues that women should be trained for war in much the same way as men, differing only in developing particular skill with weapons best suited to their physique. Intellectually women are no different from men.

At this early stage learning should be a pleasure. He says, "there should be no element of slavery in learning. Enforced exercise does no harm to the body, but enforced learning will not stay in the mind. So avoid compulsion, and let your children's lessons take the form of play" (R.VII.536).

A prominent principle for early education is the establishment of harmony in the character. The foundation on which the educated person is to grow must be balanced and harmonious. Plato sees a danger in excessive emphasis on cultural education. It can lead, he says, to effeteness, to weakness, to a kind of narcissistic and consuming aestheticism which lacks generating vigor and energy. His curriculum during this stage is concerned, then, not primarily with the systematic amassing of knowledge, but rather with the development of an harmonious character. Physical education is designed to counter the tendency toward effeteness inherent in cultural education. Similarly, an excess of physical education, without the counterbalance of cultural education, he sees as tending toward brutishness and grossness of perception. In Nettleship's metaphor, Plato tends to see the character as a stringed instrument: tightening this string a little, slackening that one, till harmony is created in the instrument. It is the person who combines cultural and physical education in their proper proportions whom we may think of as the "musical person," in harmony with themselves and their world. Plato's prescription is to continue a Greek practice "which long experience has worked out" (R.II.377).

Applying these principles today. Perhaps the most obvious discrepancy between Plato's principles and modern practice is seen in the place of physical education in the curriculum. We tend to relegate physical education to an incidental role—in some vague way intended to keep children fit or to shake them out of a lethargy induced by hours of sitting. Our courses of study would be considerably affected if we were to allot to physical education the prominence found in Plato's curriculum, and if we were to aim consciously to produce self-confident and courageous people. We might introduce more competitive games, and we would put much greater emphasis on dance and movement, and diet, for all children. These activities would be designed so as to teach the value of, and help develop, self-discipline, self-reliance, courage, endurance. We would be concerned to teach the self-confidence that can come from the strength and grace of controlled movement.

A second major discrepancy is in the place given to traditional stories in the curriculum. Plato notes that there are two kinds of traditional stories—true ones and false ones. The true ones are better, but the "false" ones are useful in so far as they express the appro-

priate ideals. That is, children are introduced first to those elements
of their tradition which best exemplify the qualities to be developed
in them. Instead of a tradition based on legends and myth stories,
we have history. Following Plato's principle seems to me to lead to
a curriculum beginning for children with the true story of their civ-
ilization, in such a way that it emphasizes those qualities most desirable in the mature person. That is, history would initially be taught
as the story of our struggle for rationality against ignorance and
obscurantism, for freedom against oppression, for courage and her-
oism against cowardice and fear, and so on. Our elementary school
curricula at present typically ignore all this and concentrate on the
routines of the present world immediately surrounding the child—
as though children had access to nothing else.

A further principle if applied today would lead to a greater emphasis on moral education. Plato could be clear and explicit about
this, knowing precisely the kind of state for which he was educating
citizens. One of the products of a pluralistic society is a lack of
agreement about specific moral principles. There is, however, one
suspects, much greater general agreement about a range of moral
attitudes we would like to see inculcated in our young than is commonly acknowledged. Our commitment to pluralism has tended to
make us reluctant to deal with any aspect of moral education at all.
This reluctance has been increased by what seems a common confusion between moral education and religious training—many people assuming that moral attitudes are somehow necessarily dependent
on religious beliefs. If we can manage to clarify the proper relationship between religion and morality, and see moral education as something of no less importance to the atheist than to the religiously
committed, we might find it possible to work more consciously toward the inculcation of certain moral principles and attitudes in
something like the manner that Plato recommends.[13] We might, however, conclude that the school is not the best institution to take
primary responsibility for this moral education, though the curriculum might be designed to play a more conscious supporting and
reinforcing role.

Other principles seem to be incorporated in a number of modern
movements within Education—education of the "whole person"
(something whose meaning is more difficult to grasp in modern writings than in Plato's, because they do not characterize the "whole"
or the social structure within which that "whole" becomes fully
realized); designing games and stories to convey much of the curriculum content; suiting the curriculum to the child's level of un-

derstanding; equality of the sexes; and so on. There is an inescapable irony, of course, in seeing such proposals put forward today as new insights.

Stage Two: Pistis

When setting out his curriculum proposals Plato does not make clear distinctions between the *eikasia* and *pistis* stages, so I am to some degree inferring which proposals appear to fit better this later stage. Because he tends to deal with these stages together under the general *doxa* heading, I will be much briefer here, assuming that much of what applies to the earlier stage applies here also, and assuming that in general this stage is largely an extension and elaboration of the curriculum of the previous stage.

Curriculum content. Physical education continues to be important for the reasons indicated above. Dances and gymnastics that promote the desired qualities of character are practiced, and the students exercise with various weapons. They are, during this period, male and female alike, taken out with the army to war, and are given a "taste" of actual battle, while remaining protected some distance from the front lines.

They learn the use of the lyre for creating pure rhythms, and how to compose music. They learn model pieces of literature by heart, and how to recite them dramatically, but with civilized control.

They also learn much useful knowledge—preliminary information about geometry and astronomy. They will become increasingly familiar with the humane culture of their time.

Underlying principles. Plato's aim at this stage is to "make people more useful to themselves, and more wide awake" (L.VII.819). He concentrates on the development of a person versed in the various forms of humane culture, and who is also made hardier and more ready for war. The move toward "awakeness," however, is hard work. But this is the best time for it, he says, because "youth is the time for hard work of all sorts" (R.VII.536).

Students should learn the basic principles of a subject first, and these should be learned quickly. The more refined parts of these subjects may not be appropriate for everyone to learn and these can be taken up in a specialized way later. But a basic knowledge is proper for everyone, because it is disgraceful not to have a general preliminary knowledge of all subjects.

Many will find that the hard work of learning is not to their taste. Plato recommends a limited time for instruction in various things, and advises that the specified time should be enough for adequate mastery. If some people have not mastered the subject by then, they should not be driven. They simply will not master it, and should be directed toward things for which they have greater aptitude. This implies that many people will not get beyond the *pistis* stage, and will throughout their lives respond to the world in the manner characteristic of this stage, and find their minds engaged by the objects proper to this stage.

Applying these principles today. The impact of Plato's principles for this stage, if applied today, leads to a continuation of some of the differences noted for the *eikasia* stage. We would perhaps want to include much more music—insisting that everyone have some mastery of a musical instrument and knowledge of musical composition. The common lack of this in our public schools deprives so many people of treasures of experience that seem necessary to becoming properly educated. (Though, of course, Plato's meaning of "music" is different from ours.) We might also increase our emphasis on students' familiarizing themselves with their cultural tradition.

Stage Three: Dianoia

Curriculum content. The core curriculum at the *dianoia* stage will involve learning, in the following order, the subjects of mathematics, plane geometry, solid geometry, astronomy, harmonics. The progression in the studies is from a residual reliance on concrete objects of physical representations toward increasing abstraction.

The more refined mathematics of the *dianoia* stage may begin from the concrete apparatus used in the earlier stages.[14] That is, this is the stage during which abstract categories and forms of manipulation are being generated, but they are formed initially out of the student's reflection on past sensuous experience.

Plane geometry leads to the greater abstraction of astronomy, which is the study of solid bodies in ideal motions. But, Plato decides, solid geometry should precede astronomy, as a bridge between plane geometry and astronomy. Astronomy, while concerned with the most perfect and regular movements of bodies, is still concerned with objects within the world of senses. But the perfection of regularity in astronomical movements leads the mind's focus of contemplation away from the sensuous objects toward the study of the ideal proportions and ratios in the movements which they body forth—that is, toward a pure mathematical science of motion. Harmonics is in this respect similar to astronomy, except that its ratios and forms are detected by the ear rather than the eye.

The physical education of the students will continue and intensify to the point that for a period of a couple of years they will give themselves over exclusively to military training.

Underlying principles. In the study of, say, astronomy Plato is not concerned with the furthering of astronomical science. Indeed he seems rather scornful of those who see astronomy primarily as an empirical study. The primary purpose of such studies, for him, is that they can train the mind to think abstractly. So his discussion of these subjects is less in terms of what they contribute to our store of knowledge or add to our practical capabilities and more in terms of how they develop particular intellectual skills. His prime purpose during this stage is to move the student beyond dependence on the senses, to compel the mind to abstract from the particulars and confusions relayed by the senses to the intellect the idealized forms, which the particulars imperfectly body forth.

Despite the emphasis on the role of the curriculum content in developing intellectual capacities, Plato does not undervalue what he calls its "incidental advantages" (R.VII.527)—the powers it yields in dealing with practical matters in the world.

The understanding developed during the *dianoia* stage is not for everyone. A person who is to advance through this stage must have an "inborn disposition" to "take a reasonable delight in a task in which much painful effort makes little headway. And if he cannot retain what he learns, his forgetfulness will leave no room in his head for knowledge; and so, having all his toil for nothing, he can only end by hating himself as well as his fruitless occupation" (R.VI.486).

During this stage, too, the student will come to see how the primitive knowledge of computation, geometry, astronomy, and so on, learned during previous stages comes together in the connections perceived at the level of underlying abstract principles. Plato says: "The detached studies in which they are educated as children will now be brought together in a comprehensive view of their connections with one another and with reality" (R.VII.537). That is, a vision of unified science develops from growing familiarity with the underlying principles of each area of study.

This development of abstracting and reasoning power Plato sees as having what we might call considerable transferability. He sees it as quickening the mind for all kinds of mental tasks.

Applying these principles today. We would no longer think it appropriate to train all people for war, but I think we should recognize the continuing need to develop the qualities of courage, self-reliance, and self-confidence. We might search for different methods of exercising these same qualities—such methods perhaps as offered by the Outward Bound programs.

Plato's concern with intellectual development is to direct the student toward the securest forms of knowledge. He did not see the means to this security through the physical sciences, though he clearly recognized their utility. We may attribute this to the primitive state of science in his day, and, as I have argued above, we might sensibly substitute the physical sciences as best representing the kind of secure knowledge that Plato was aiming toward. So, for the *dianoia* stage in the modern curriculum we might include a heavy emphasis on the physical sciences for all students able to reach this stage of abstract thinking. The *initial* introduction to the sciences, however, would not involve the careful amassing of factual knowledge and accumulation of precise observation. Rather, the initial concern would be to move from particular observations and knowledge to general "laws," principles, and theories as quickly as possible. That is, the educational aim would be better achieved by moving the student rapidly from the sensuous entities with which the sciences deal to the abstract entities—concepts, theories, laws—by which the sensuous entities are made intelligible. This suggests an educational method which runs counter to much modern science teaching practice.

Stage Four: Noesis

Curriculum content. These subdivisions (i.e., "curriculum content," etc.) are less useful when it comes to the final stage. We may say, a little simple-mindedly perhaps, that Plato's "curriculum" for the *noesis* stage is constituted by the Forms of secure knowledge, which can be apprehended by proper application of the use of dialectic. This method of inquiry, however, yields its fruit only if the student has been properly prepared—that is, has passed through the previous three stages successfully. The fruit is that final perception of the fundamental principles upon which secure knowledge rests.

Underlying principle. The relevant principle seems to be an attempt to find what is securely knowable, what is real in the world, to see what is the nature of things uninfected with our beliefs, opinions, hopes, conjectures, and the distortions generated by our perceptions.

Applying this principle today. We would construct our *noesis* curriculum from any kind of content, but we would be more concerned with the method of scholarly inquiry used. That is, the *noesis* stage represents the pursuit of knowledge of what is true, excluding from our conclusions those distortions and infections that result from our perceptions and manner of thinking—as far as possible.

In the sciences we might recognize a modern distinction between the *dianoia* and *noesis* stages as between someone competent in the use of empirical or conceptual inquiry techniques and someone with similar competence augmented by a sophisticated understanding of the role of theory. That is, we recognize people who are competent in engaging in what Thomas Kuhn calls "normal science"—designing experiments within "paradigms" that suggest appropriate problems and methodology. In distinction, we also recognize people who are not only competent researchers in this sense, but who have what we may call philosophical sophistication—who appreciate precisely the assumptions they work with and the effects of these assumptions on the epistemological status of the knowledge they generate; who are also aware of the presuppositions underlying what they accept as "normal science" and who are open to discussion of the status and utility of these presuppositions. They do not confuse presuppositions with reality.

Similarly in the arts, there are those who recognize clearly that between our ideas or theories and reality there falls a shadow: that historical explanations or critical theories of literature have an epistemological status that is problematic in subtle ways. This philosophical sophistication we may associate with the *noesis* stage, and its lack in the journey-man scholars in these fields we may associate with the *dianoia* stage.

The *noesis* intelligence recognizes as an ultimate base of current knowledge claims some aesthetic, or utilitarian, or moral foundation; that one cannot apply to the foundations of a discipline the kinds of truth-tests that are properly applied within it. One applies rather tests of beauty, utility, or whatever. Our educational scheme, then, should be concerned to bring people to as clear as possible a view of such fundamental principles in their discipline. Plato suggests that such insights come not only from intellectual training, but from a refined intellectual training combined with the development of qualities to which we give vague names like courage and goodness.

III. PLATO'S EDUCATIONAL THEORY

Above, then, is a sketch of the developmental dimension of Plato's educational theory and a brief discussion of some of the educational issues it brings into focus. Plato does, of course, say much else about education, and some of his other ideas may become relevant as we turn now to look at his theory in light of the discussion of chapter 1. I have already indicated in passing various points which the researcher, curriculum designer, or teachers might find useful; what follows will be somewhat more explicit in addressing their interests.

The first points discussed in chapter 1 concerned the general nature and structure we might expect an educational theory to have. Plato's theory seems to conform with our first expectation: that an educational theory about development would be likely to differ radically from a psychological theory. He does not give us a distinct theory of development, in the manner of psychology, but rather deals with individual development *in terms* of the sequence of *what* should be learned and *how* the teaching might be conducted. That is, it is an educational theory with a developmental form.

Another general expectation concerned the degree to which the theory would explicitly characterize the desirable end-product of the developmental scheme, and would justify that end-product in terms of an appropriate and desirable social and political context. Plato is of course explicit about the qualities of an ideal citizen and an ideal constitution and how the one supports the other. In his text he does precisely what he recommends that his philosopher-despot should do in practice:

> He will take society and human character as his canvas, and begin by scraping it clean. . . . Next, he will sketch in the outline of the constitution. Then, as the work goes on, he will frequently refer to this model, the ideals of justice, goodness, temperance and the rest, and compare with them the copy of those qualities which he is trying to create in human society. Combining the various elements of social life as a painter mixes his colours, he will reproduce the complexion of true humanity, guided by that divine pattern whose likeness Homer saw in the men he called Godlike. He will rub out and paint in again this or that feature, until he has produced, so far as may be, a type of human character that heaven can approve. (R.VI.501)

Having established ideals of justice, goodness, temperance, and the rest, Plato argues step by step how such ideals can be embodied in a state, and in individual citizens. He is sensitive to the objection that his ideal state is unattainable, and argues that by converting the sons of hereditary rulers to these ideals there is some chance, however small, of moving states in the direction of the ideal. Thus, he concludes, "our institutions would be best, if they could be realized, and to realize them, though hard, is not impossible" (R.VI.501).

To the objection that the ideals could not be realized in individual people his response is the whole educational theory. It is an attempt to show "how men of this quality are to be produced" (R.VII.521) and "how we can make sure of having men who will preserve our constitution" (R.VI.502).

One point made in chapter 1 about the need for an educational theory to be explicit about its end-product was that we might readily decide whether or not we would find the theory useful. If we do not like, or want to produce, the kind of people for whom the theory is a prescription, then we will ignore the theory. Can we ignore Plato's theory on this ground? Do we want to produce philosopher-despots for ideal ancient Greek city-states? Put this way, of course we don't. But do we want to produce people with the character Plato specifies as proper for the products of his educational scheme—people who embody those qualities of wisdom, justice, goodness, temperance[15] and the rest, which he discusses at such length earlier in his book. An educational system that produced such people would surely be considered a source of great benefit.

But two other questions may be raised in objection to our accepting Plato's scheme as an appropriate guide today. Did not Plato see his scheme as one that weeded people out at every stage and led to very few achieving the desirable end? And, were not the citizens to be chained to the service of the state, serving merely as instruments of the state's purposes?[16]

As noted above, I have ignored all references to class distinctions in the educational scheme recommended in the *Republic*, blending the various discussions into a single ideal scheme. I think this is warranted for other reasons as well as my main one, which is simply to assume in our modern democratic way that everyone should have access to the highest good. Perhaps most obvious among the "other" reasons is that Plato seems at times to share our modern democratic notion. He does not really outline an educational system that is class-based; rather he seems to suggest that elementary education will be compulsory and that only those who show themselves able will go on to the next stage. That is, advancement is dependent only on the ability to benefit from the higher stage—and this is dependent on mastery of the lower stage. It is unclear how Plato intended the two main sections on education (in Books II/III and VI/VII) to fit together. Perhaps, as his argument developed and became more complicated, Plato found the earlier section on education inadequate to the burden of producing his ideal rulers and so he returned to the topic to buttress his educational program. He can hardly have concluded that different kinds of education were appropriate for different classes if ability and demonstrated mastery were to be the criteria for selecting who should go on to the next stage and thus form the different classes. No doubt those who did not show the ability to benefit from higher education would, *after* failing to show that ability, receive a different kind of education or training. Plato seems to assume that training to become, say, a cobbler is a fairly straightforward matter, but implicit in his model for the state is the notion that cobblers, too, will have elementary knowledge of their cultural heritage and some training in temperance and courage. However, it is not a matter Plato deals with explicitly, and is mentioned here only to establish that Plato's basic principles are not so removed from our own that we cannot use his theory. Indeed, for present purposes, it does not matter what Plato meant, so long as we can interpret his theory in a way that will allow us to use it.[17]

But yes, Plato did assume that few people would advance beyond the *pistis* stage, and that very few would achieve *noesis*. This is not, however, a situation Plato wishes to impose on people in order that his ideal totalitarian state may be achieved. Rather, his state is designed to be ideal in that it accommodates the varieties of people that experience shows us do exist. The state, then, is designed in light of what seemed to Plato a realistic assessment of the distribution of talents and dispositions among a typical population, along with a realistic assessment of the improvement that may be achieved by education and a constitution that best utilizes that range of talents and dispositions. His assessment of what proportion of the population might have the abilities to achieve the higher stages of educational development is probably little different from a typical modern assessment. In North America we might want to give a much larger proportion of the population whatever benefits they can derive from a college education, but no one imagines that any but a small proportion is able to achieve a profound understanding of the subjects they study. Indeed, Plato seems also to support the most idealistic modern view which sees the higher stages of educational development as accessible to everyone, if only techniques, resources, and a supportive environment were available for all. He notes:

> We must conclude that education is not what it is said to be by some, who profess to put knowledge into a soul which does not possess it, as if they could put sight into blind eyes. On the contrary, our own account signifies that the soul of every man does possess the power of learning the truth and the organ to see it with; and that, just as one might have

to turn the whole body round in order that the eye should see light instead of darkness, so the entire soul must be turned away from this changing world, until its eye can bear to contemplate reality and that supreme splendour which we have called the Good. Hence, there may well be an art whose aim would be to effect this very thing, the conversion of the soul, in the readiest way; not to put the power of sight into the soul's eye, which already has it, but to ensure that, instead of looking in the wrong direction, it is turned the way it ought to be. (R.VII.527)

This passage expresses as well as anything written, I think, the faith which properly spurs the educator on; that there is an art which will enable us to harness that interest which nearly everyone shows in something—whether that something be the paraphernalia of rock music, drugs, sadomasochism, or more generally admired subjects for human activity—and turn that interest onto subjects of greater educational value. It is not a matter of creating interest; it is a matter of engaging it in subjects that provide a greater return of human value, that give life and give it more abundantly. Our failure—recognized in the expectation we share with Plato that very few will achieve the higher benefits education gives—we prefer to see as a failure of technique, of our art, rather than a failure of nature to provide some people with the means of achieving these benefits.

It is also worth mentioning that Plato's scheme did not involve weeding out and somehow discarding those who could not achieve the higher ages. They were to be made as happy and secure as possible in their various social roles. Those who achieved the final stage of *noesis* were not to be happy as a result of being able to consume more of the state's products or to have privileges without responsibilities. Their greatest pleasure lay in what they were, not what they had. They were able to see and understand the world more truly than others. And for this benefit of education, they paid dearly in the burdens of administering the state, and were to lead a life of frugality.

As for Plato's supposedly totalitarian state, it depends how one assumes such an ideal would work out in practice. Those with a low estimate of "human nature" and little faith that Plato's educational scheme would lead to the ends he hoped for, tend to see such a state collapsing rapidly into a rigid totalitarianism. Those who have a higher estimate of human nature and a greater faith in Plato's educational scheme tend to accept that the state is well designed to facilitate the best expressions of the variety of talents and dispositions available in a typical population. Again, for present purposes, none of this matters much, as long as we can interpret Plato's proposals in a manner which does not fundamentally, and necessarily, contravene our general principles and ideals.

My concern, obviously, is not detailed exegesis of Plato's text, but selecting whatever may help our modern interests. If we had to answer "yes" to the question of whether Plato's educational scheme was necessarily wedded to a totalitarian system which weeded out and cast aside into some kind of servitude huge numbers of its citizenry, then we would have had to reject his scheme as useless for our present purposes. But I think it is clear that neither of these are necessarily the case, and that even if these totalitarian-tending ideas were in fact held by Plato, his scheme is open to interpretations allowing its use for different social and political systems. And indeed, it seems to me that there are sufficient reasons to believe that Plato's educational ideals are coherent with modern social democratic educational ideals.[18]

WHAT AND HOW SHOULD WE TEACH

In chapter 1 it was concluded that modern psychological theories of cognitive development told us nothing much about what particular content we should teach at particular ages or stages. What does Plato's theory tell us about when we should teach *what* particular things, and *how* we should teach them at particular ages?

Plato suggests that once a stage is entered it determines what kinds of objects are seen and how they are made sense of. At any particular stage a particular range of objects is "seized upon" (R.V.479) by the mind. This suggests an image of the stages as a kind of lens which, at different settings, brings a different range of objects into focus.

This image leads to a dissimilarity between Plato's curriculum and a typical modern curriculum. We tend to follow most subjects through from elementary to late secondary school, where we begin to specialize in one or a few of those subjects—it is a longitudinally continuous curriculum with few lateral discontinuities. Plato's theory, on the other hand, suggests a focus on different subjects at each stage—it has clear lateral discontinuities and longitudinally it is only weakly continuous. Along with basic mastery of the three Rs (taught largely through games) and physical control, his *eikasia* curriculum focuses heavily on traditional stories (which I have translated into history). It is to be primarily a conditioning or "accustoming" procedure. His *pistis* curriculum involves an emphasis on literature and music, with an elementary acquaintance with the sciences, and he seems to see this as a period of hard disciplined study. The *dianoia* curriculum focuses primarily on what I have translated into the sciences. The *noesis* stage is concerned primarily with a profound study of any subject area, but it should be done with considerable philosophic sophistication, using the method of dialectic.

The weakly continuing threads through this curriculum involve the increasingly rigorous physical, or perhaps more appropriately called, moral-character education; as well as the study of mathematics, whose educational function Plato considered crucial—something I will return to below.

So it would seem that Plato's theory claims that *when* should indeed have a profound effect on *what* and *how*. To him it is not a logical or psychological decision to teach, say, the sciences at the *dianoia* stage; it is an educational decision. That is, his particular educational aim determines what things should be learned, and how they should be taught, at the various stages—within, of course, the constraints of what seems psychologically possible and logically coherent.

We have seen in Plato's model of the developmental stages what he considered the general nature of the educational process. He believed that behind the diversity of material objects and the confusions about them which our senses report to the mind, there is an orderly, consistent, lawful world which is knowable by the properly trained intellect. The process of education is the process of coming to know this world with increasing security.

He seems to believe that the general dynamic of the process is an inborn disposition to prefer to know the truth, but he seems to see this as a weak impulse, easily overcome by the clamor of the assembly, the law courts, the theater, the camp, and "the present state of society" (R.VI.492) in general. He spends much effort on working out how the general dynamic might be enhanced by procedures that would stimulate movement from stage to stage.

Plato discusses at length just how one can get the process moving; how one can turn the eye from the concrete to the intelligible world. He wanted something that would show clearly how the senses offered the mind confusions which could only be cleared up by the operation of the intellect. Remembering that he is concerned not only with those who will go on to the end of the educational process, but also with those who will take up other occupations, he wants something that will incidentally be useful to all who learn it. "What studies will have this effect?" he asks Glaucon (R.VII.521).

He introduces his answer by indicating how some kinds of perceptions provoke thought whereas others do not—and our educational interest at this stage is in the former. Some perceptions, such as seeing a finger, raise no questions for the mind. Others, such as comparing fingers in terms of size, begin to raise problems for the mind. If we hold up, as he suggested to Glaucon, our little finger and the two next fingers, we might call the end finger small and our middle finger big. But the finger between them we might call big when compared with the little finger and little when compared with our middle finger. Our vision thus reports to the mind that one finger is both big and little. Such a confusion provokes thought to sort it out. It may stimulate thought on how we use "big" and "little" to differentiate objects in comparison to each other, and may lead eventually to conclusions about relativity. It serves, that is, to begin making the distinction between objects of perception and objects of thought. The ideal subject to make this distinction clear, Plato decides, is mathematics. Mathematical units have the quality of being able to refer to things in the world while being clearly distinct from them. No two trees are alike in the world, but in counting two trees we use units which are ideally equal. Quickly mathematics leaves behind the material things that may have formed the initial objects of calculation, and deals with purely intellectual objects—numbers, each of which is equal to all others. By concentrating on subjects that will begin moving the child toward seeing the world of intelligible objects, the move from *eikasia* to *pistis* may be encouraged.[19]

The dynamic that moves the student from the *pistis* to the *dianoia* stage seems to be stimulated by selecting those studies that show the student a level of abstraction at which a unity can be perceived underlying the apparent diversity of subjects. Plato recommends an almost casual teaching during the *pistis* stage of elementary knowledge about the subjects which will form the central focus of *dianoia* study. The means of moving the student to the higher stage seems to be by drawing together the scattered material learned during the earlier stage. The focus of teaching would appear to be on organizing principles, theories, "laws," and so on.

The dynamic that moves the student into the *noesis* stage seems to follow from mastery of the *dianoia* curriculum. With this mastery comes freedom from the mind's infection by or dependence on, the material world. When the mind has become freed from the material constraints of a subject, and has mastered the abstract language— theories, laws—by which the material is finally knowable, then the student is ready to engage in dialectical thinking.[20]

Plato's curriculum, then, is a series of stimulants toward *noesis*: stimulants designed to support and carry forward the weak inborn disposition to prefer to know the truth about things.

This theory may be interesting, but what use is it? What does it offer the teacher, the curriculum designer, and the educational researcher? I am tempted to introduce a discussion of its present uses by observing that, the present state of educational theorizing being what it is, we can use any help we can get.

Is it true? Is it true that if we do what Plato tells us we will produce the kind of person he describes? Is it true that his stages represent a logically and psychologically possible process of development? Is it true that the kind of thinking characteristic of the *dianoia* stage follows from that of the *pistis* stage? (Does this mirror Piaget's claim about the development of formal operations?) Is it true that certain kinds of curriculum material stimulate more sophisticated abstract thinking, and does this *dianoia* thinking "transfer" to other curriculum areas? These, and dozens of other questions, are raised by the theory, and provide fodder for empirical research.

Empirical research could no doubt help us revise and refine the theory at a number of points, and could certainly tell us something about the adequacy of the general model as descriptive of a possible form of educational development. But empirical research cannot tell us whether *eikasia* perception is more or less desirable than *dianoia* thinking. Empirical research may be able to tell us in a general way whether the curriculum content Plato recommends does indeed encourage the development of the intellectual capacities he wants. But it cannot tell us whether such knowledge is desirable, or more valuable than some other knowledge.

The major research activity that may help us decide whether Plato's theory is good or bad, useful or useless—or what parts of it are useful or useless—is conceptual. The most important questions are normative ones and inaccessible to empirical research. So we must simply sit and think about it. This sitting and thinking might usefully be directed toward clarifying empirically testable claims made by the theory, but should also be directed toward deriving practical help from the theory for present-day teaching and curriculum designing.

The curriculum designer—who may be a school-board member, a teacher, a government official, a school-district superintendent—cannot usually wait on the conclusive results of empirical or conceptual research before making decisions about the structure of the curriculum. Indeed, experience has suggested that conclusive results about the most important educational matters rarely issue from the vast industry of educational research. The most practical aid the pragmatic curriculum designer can have is a comprehensive educational theory—and few theories can more justly claim the curriculum designer's attention than Plato's. If one accepts the assumption that it is desirable to produce the kind of educated people Plato characterizes, and if one finds his general scheme (with appropriate modifications such as those sketched above) to be a plausible means of achieving this end, how does the theory help one reform a typical modern curriculum?

Perhaps the most obvious of the reforms Plato's theory would suggest concerns the need for harmony between the development of "character" and intellect. An academic program that leaves character development to chance would seem foolish to Plato; and an outdoor education program justified in terms of physical gratification or as romantic exhilaration would seem close to sacrilegious. Achieving the harmonious development of character and intellect would become a central concern that would inform the structure of the curriculum.

Plato's image of the educational function of character development makes modern discussions of moral education seem fatuous. Plato's synoptic vision of the role of physical training reduces the modern discussion of moral development—in terms of cheating in tests and verbal responses to moral dilemma scenarios—to a sterile, segmented part of a larger whole. Similarly, the virtually total separation of the literature on moral development from that, for example, on outdoor education suggests a bizarre compartmentalization of subjects that need to be dealt with together. Whatever our opinions about the appropriate social institutions to be given responsibility for "character" development—an educational curriculum cannot ignore this or leave it to chance. An "academic education" is not, in Plato's terms, an education at all; and a curriculum drawn from experience of the local environment is a formula for remaining a captive of *eikasia*. Plato not only raises questions, he helps us answer them.

We might usefully consider his claim that educational development is best stimulated by emphases on different subjects at different stages. We might want to amend the lateral discontinuities as a result of advances in the human and physical sciences since Plato's time, but we might well conclude that our "expanding horizons" or "spiral" curricula provide less adequate educational stimuli than Plato's. For the *dianoia* stage, which can be equated with the refinement of abstract thinking during adolescence, I have interpreted the principle underlying Plato's curriculum recommendation to mean that a strong emphasis on the sciences should form the core of the curriculum. At this stage the student engages and deals increasingly well with abstraction, theory, generalizations—the level at which diversity is drawn together by some underlying abstract scheme. Modern advances in the human sciences allow us to reinterpret Plato's recommendation so that we can include history, psychology, and anthropology. But this expansion of the content will be permissible only to the extent that it allows us to achieve what Plato requires at this stage. History, for example, may be justified only if it focuses on the study of general laws or patterns of historical development, or on developing ideologies or metahistorical schemes. Similarly, psychology and anthropology might be included so long as the focus remains on general theories in these subjects—most obviously theories about "human nature." It is by learning to manipulate this level of abstraction with increasing sophistication that students can achieve mastery over, and access to, the particulars to which this level of abstraction refers.

For the teacher, even though Plato rarely and briefly makes comments on teaching method, his theory is rich in suggestions on how to organize and present material at each stage so that it is most readily accessible to students and contributes to their further educational development. For elementary school years Plato recommends the constant use of games and stories in teaching. Drawing on modern analyses, we might note that games and stories are alike in that they have beginnings, middles, and ends; they limit the world to be dealt with; they involve a restricted set of characters, ideas, or events; they have clear rules or conventions that determine rigidly the *meaning* of their characters, ideas, or events; and they are the *forms* which most obviously and powerfully engage young children. Plato's recommendation is not simply that one plays games and tells stories; rather he suggests that we use the underlying form to teach whatever we want children to learn.[21]

As a general educational principle during elementary school years Plato recommends what I have perhaps misleadingly called "conditioning" procedures. It is misleading largely because of the associations the term has gathered as a result of its use by behaviorists. The word "accustoming" might be better. That is, one's teaching should help develop in embryonic form, those characteristics and qualities whose full development constitutes the ideally educated person. This is to be distinguished from the procedure recommended by the grandmother's sisters in *Remembrance of Things Past*, "that one ought to set before children, and that children showed their own innate good taste in admiring, only such books and pictures as they would continue to admire when their minds were developed and mature."[22] Plato is concerned to show us that the things to which children's minds are attracted are different from those which attract educated adults. The teacher's task is to select from the objects to which children's minds are attracted those which contain the qualities that are embryos of those that attract adults, and which will lead step by step in the direction of adult understanding. He tells us something about those qualities, and he helps our selection by showing us step by step the path from this initial *eikasia* perception to *noesis*.

I have already discussed the kinds of thing Plato recommends as appropriate in teaching at the *dianoia* stage. The objects toward which the *dianoia* mind is attracted are the powerful organizing ideas inherent in any subject matter. The message for the teacher is that these are the routes whereby students can find access to understanding these subjects. Whether this is true is in part an empirical question—and any teacher can test the claim by organizing teaching on the principles Plato recommends and observing the result. A much more complicated question is whether it is desirable to teach this way even if it proves successful in engaging interest and encouraging learning and remembering. Many educators dislike the tendency of adolescents with intellectual interests to develop ideologies and general schemes while at the same time being impatient with details. Plato seems to see this as a necessary stage in an individual's educational development. If it is necessary, we need not ask whether it is good or bad. It seems partly a question for conceptual research to determine whether this *dianoia* generalizing stage is in some sense necessary to the achievement of *noesis*. However, if we would like to have our students achieve *noesis*, and conclude that this *dianoia* craving for generality is a necessary step on the way, then we have clear guidance about how to teach students at the *dianoia* stage, so that knowledge is made meaningful to them, and useful to their further educational development.

A general contribution that Plato's theory offers to modern educators, and one which seems to have been largely ignored as a Grecian gift, is a sense of exactly what is necessary if one wants to generate an adequate educational theory. One might properly say *timeo Danaos et dona ferentes* (I fear the Greeks even when they bear gifts) when one of their gifts is a vision of the enormity of the task facing anyone who hopes to talk sensibly about education. If we hope to expand our sights across this area we might be wise to climb on Plato's shoulders.

Conclusion

I MAY REASONABLY be accused of a selective reading of Plato. Quite so. My selectivity has been determined by what seems to me of present use. Subjecting oneself to the criticism of excessive interpretation is at least a protection against Tom Paine's withering protest about Edmund Burke—that he pitied the plumage but forgot the dying bird. I have at least avoided the exegetical excess of admiring the plumage while starving the bird. No doubt I have been tendentious about what I would like Plato to have said, but so long as the resulting ideas are useful it scarcely matters what their source is (especially as Plato is not around to claim a share of the royalties). Obviously, I believe that all the points I have made can be supported from Plato's texts. I shall be less perturbed by someone pointing out that that was not really what Plato meant, than by someone claiming that the developmental scheme is useless. (I would be more perturbed by someone claiming that Plato's developmental scheme is useful but that my interpretations have rendered it useless—but at least my errors might lead to such a critic showing us the proper meaning and use of Plato's theory.)

Still, even following so bold a defense, I should acknowledge the degree of the tendentiousness of my reading. Plato's writings have in common with the Bible the richness and diversity that allow a multitude of interpretations. One may abstract a liberal democratic Plato, as I have done, only by ignoring much else that is indubitably present. One may abstract a moderate pursuer of increasing security in knowledge only by ignoring the passionate presupposition that absolute certainty may be gained in moral matters no less than in geometry. (But we must remember that the Platonic program for reaching secure knowledge outlined in the *Republic* is, in many ways, "little more than a tantalising prospectus,"[23] which Plato himself later modified, and which was modified more radically by Aristotle.) But, at worst, I have abstracted from Plato, not invented him.

A further word may be in order about what may seem to some an unsupportable "translation"—from Forms to Science. I realize that, given Plato's epistemology, modern empirical science suffers the same defects as ancient proto-science, so my substitution of science for understanding of the Forms is hardly legitimate as an act of straightforward interpretation. Plato's epistemology, however, was fashioned in the context of ancient proto-science; one could scarcely imagine him reaching similar conclusions in the context of modern science. This may involve drastic modernizing, but my conclusion seems less absurd, and more useful, than that which, in the hindsight of modern scientific consciousness, finds fault with one feature of Plato's epistemology, and then dismisses as worthless everything even tenuously connected with it.

I should add that the study of science by itself cannot replace study of the Forms. Though Plato is concerned with achieving as secure knowledge as possible—something we equate with the physical sciences—an integral part of his program involved acquiring secure knowledge of moral matters. I have separated these two, discussing the latter in terms of a richer sense of what we usually mean by moral education.

On the criteria sketched in chapter 1, it seems clear that Plato has given us an educational theory.

3/ Piaget's Developmental Theory

Biographical Introduction

JEAN PIAGET was born in Neuchâtel, Switzerland, in 1896. He has been one of the most prolific academic writers of our time, beginning his career of publication at age ten, and continuing until his death in 1980 with an unabated flood of material. Brian Rotman notes:

> When he was asked how he had had time to write so much, Piaget replied that fortunately he had not needed to read the work of Piaget. He admits a neurotic compulsion to write and describes how, overcome with unease and disquiet the moment he finishes a book, he has to start another. What is it that he keeps having to say? And is it always the same? Piaget encourages us to think that it is: "I fear that I have given the impression of a man who has touched many fields. But in fact, I have followed a single goal that has always remained the same: to try to understand and explain what a living development is in all its perpetual construction and novelty and its progressive adaption (sic) to reality."[1]

Piaget's precocious B.A. and Ph.D. were earned from studies in the natural sciences. He quickly became one of the most prominent experts on mollusks, having published, by the age of twenty-one, over twenty-five papers based largely on his careful observations of mollusks in the lakes around Neuchâtel. As Piaget has explained,[2] these observations led to his general image of biological development as a process of adaptation to the environment.

Increasingly he became interested, and then immersed, in the study of psychology. He worked for two years in Paris, beginning in 1919, with Alfred Binet, who was refining his standardized intelligence tests. Piaget developed little interest in Binet's concern with achieving accurate and reliable measures of intelligence; he was more interested in the wrong answers that children often gave on the tests. In the commonalities among the wrong responses more significance about children's intelligence could be found than in test scores.

In 1921 Piaget accepted the directorship of studies at the Institut J.–J. Rousseau in Geneva, and began his experiments on the intellectual development of children. Like the rest of us, he observed that although children are born apparently knowing nothing about themselves or their world, within a couple of decades they have developed a huge array of enormously complicated systematic schemes for making sense of the world and their experience of it. Unlike the rest of us, Piaget expended enormous ingenuity in discovering how this process takes place, and showed incredible fertility generating theories to account for a substantial part of that process.

In the 1930s Piaget began, like so many parents, keeping notes on the development of his children. Unlike other parents, however, Piaget soon began creating little experiments to clarify or check some observation. The fact that a child cried while his bottle was visible but stopped crying when it was removed from sight suggested that the child had no clear understanding that unseen objects existed; little games with hidden matchboxes might be played to confirm, or disprove, this observation; similar proto-experiments might be conducted to discover more and more precisely just what the child seemed to understand. Such informal methods of discovering what he wanted to know were then generalized and later tried on other children. What should be underlined here is that Piaget's "methodology"—if that is not too pompous a word—has always been subservient to what he wanted to know.

We might follow J. McV. Hunt's division of Piaget's earlier work into three main periods.[3] The first, from the early 1920s to the mid–1930s, involved studies of children's language and thought, judgment and reasoning, conception of the world and of physical causality, and moral judgments. During this period Piaget's method of research was almost entirely interrogation. This was much criticized. Piaget accepted some of the criticisms and increasingly began to invent experiments. The second period, from the 1930s to the mid–

1940s, involved most centrally his observations of his own children from their first movements to their acquisition of language. During this period he seems to have developed his most general theoretical formulations about the child's construction of reality as an assimilative and accommodative interaction with the environment. The third period, beginning in the 1940s and continuing into the 1950s, involved clarifying the developing structures of thought from the earliest years to adolescence and beyond. A huge array of topics was studied to elaborate Piaget's general theory of intellectual development. In the years following, Piaget and his co-workers conducted vast amounts of research—refining and elaborating further his basic theories—and he himself published an increasing number of works on methodology and philosophy.

Piaget's early training and work was in biology, and this played a significant role in the way he conceptualized and described the process of intellectual development. At a trivial level we may see the influence of biology in his adapting biological concepts for use in psychology. But this is only symptomatic of a much more profound influence his biological training has come to have on the study of psychological development, and on epistemology as well. Piaget's claim, and vision, is that a proper understanding of the nature, function, and epigenesis of thinking and knowledge requires seeing them as simply the forms of a particular organism's adaptation to its environment. This vision, and the enormous empirical elaboration he has provided for it, leads to a remarkably general and powerful theory which claims to unify developmental psychology, biology, and epistemology.

Piaget's theory of intellectual development, and his connected theories of learning and motivation, are different from most others currently prominent in Britain and North America because of the fundamental sense in which Piaget conceptualizes the human mind as an organism, rather than as a mechanism. This pervades every level of his theory. He conceptualizes concepts and mental structures as living organisms, and mental functions as biological processes. In textbooks about Piaget's theory we may find diagrams indicating some of his theory's developmental stages, but any kind of diagram tends to be inadequate in conveying an image of Piaget's theory, in a way which is less true for many other prominent theories. One can get a better sense of Piaget's theory if one thinks of its main terms as referring to entities like those moving, pulsing, dividing, and uniting microorganisms visible through a microscope.

An observation occasionally made about Piaget's work and style of reporting is that both, while having virtues now commonly recognized, are often abstruse and confusing in a curious way. The name he has given his area of study exemplifies the combination of insight, suggestiveness, and opaqueness that characterizes so much of his daunting output. "Genetic epistemology" is an enormously *suggestive* title, having an almost poetic ambiguity, but it is also that little bit impenetrably opaque.[4] Apart from the more obvious reasons for Piaget's international eminence, the curious difficulty of making sense of his writing may be another reason. There is always that slight, almost mystical opaqueness which leaves the reader with the sense of having to solve a puzzle as well as making sense of the text. His writing stimulates something like an active sense of personal discovery in the reader. This combination of opaqueness at the core of his work and the odd sense of discovery on reading him, helps to account for the incredible amount of exegesis Piaget's work has stimulated. Such books find a ready audience because many people clearly prefer the exegetical literature to Piaget's own writing. He is certainly more read about than read.

One should mention the irritation his writing commonly causes many of his readers. The vagueness and obscurity appear where there seems no excuse at all for them. It is not uncommon to read a report of an experiment that gives little information about what was said and done by the experimenter, who and how many participated, under what circumstances, and then to be presented with a general claim that could be no more than one dubious interpretation of the results reported, and, finally, to read a bald conclusion asserting: "That is what this experiment proves."[5]

Perhaps most striking among Piaget's scholarly virtues is the degree of his originality, along with the fertility with which he has expressed that originality. It is perhaps no coincidence that I have, intending no conscious comparison, used the term mystical about both Plato and Piaget. The mark of a great mystic, paradoxically, is the ability to see reality with a unique purity, even if only in flashes, even if only once long ago. Piaget seems to have had a mystical vision of the process whereby we grow from ignorance to knowledge. It has guided his hypotheses and theories and these have guided his research. The fruitfulness of his research might help us to see the value of this kind of mysticism as a component of a sensible research methodology. (This seems to me an important point, though I am aware many people may shrug it off with irritation as suggesting a return to mumbo jumbo and away from hard-nosed science. Perhaps there might be less resistance if the reader remembers that I am merely echoing Einstein.)

Comments on the Theory

IN THE previous chapter I sketched Plato's developmental theory and the curriculum he prescribes for moving people through its stages. I will not similarly sketch Piaget's developmental theory, because there are so many descriptions readily available: students of education today are more familiar with preoperational, concrete and formal operational stages than with those of *eikasia* and *pistis*. Nor will I outline the content of a Piagetian curriculum, because the connections of the theory with education do not yield a particular, elaborate curriculum. What I will try to do is to show in more detail some of the difficulties of moving from a psychological, or genetic epistemological, theory to education, and I will then try to generalize some of these points in chapter 5. I will consider the difficulties in moving from Piaget's theory to education first by considering the status of some features of the theory that are crucial to the connection, and then by considering some of the commonest educational practices that are justified by being implied by the theory.

Piaget claims that his theory describes a natural process whereby some aspects of cognition develop: it answers such questions as "What conceptions of the world does the child naturally form at the different stages of its development?"[6] As our bodies develop naturally in a certain typical pattern if they have adequate food, exercise, and so on, so the part of our cognition which Piaget's theory describes follows a regular pattern if it has adequate interactions with social, physical, and cultural environments. As different foods may affect our bodily growth patterns, so, too, different cultural environments may affect some aspects of our cognitive development. But these effects do not mean that we cannot distinguish the natural process of cognitive development from the cultural process of learning specific content. The fundamental cognitive processes, whose development Piaget claims to describe, are expressed in terms of logico-mathematical structures. These are "the natural psychological reality, in terms of which we must understand the development of knowledge."[7]

So the first question one might reasonably ask is whether Piaget is correct in his claim about what his theory describes. Does it really describe some real, natural development of logico-mathematical structures? It might seem odd to ask whether a theory describes what it claims to describe and indeed what it is articulated in terms of, but the difficulty in this case is due to the problem of separating some underlying, abstract, "natural psychological reality" from developing knowledge, language, skills or whatever. We do not have access to the psychological reality except by inference from performance on tasks or from other kinds of behavior. The problem then is, as Piaget puts it, that in the attempts to expose the underlying psychological reality it is "constantly fused with exterior data,"[8] and so it is not always evident whether a change in task performance or in understanding is due to changes at the profound level of logico-mathematical structures or whether such changes are due to more superficial learning.

This is a crucial question for education because if Piaget is right and his theory does describe a natural developmental process then it is something to which educational practice should attend and conform with. Piaget, confident that this is what his theory describes, can lay the blame for children's failures to learn on teachers who do not understand what structures have already developed and so cannot provide appropriate learning tasks: thus, "it is not the child that should be blamed . . . but the school, unaware as it is of the use it could make of the child's spontaneous development, which it should reinforce by adequate methods instead of inhibiting it as it often does."[9]

If, on the other hand, Piaget is describing a process which is informed by particular methods of social and cultural initiation, then educators will sensibly be much less interested in letting the theory affect their practice. This point is made plainly in the following quotation from the introduction to a conference report on school mathematics:

> It has been argued by Piaget and others that certain ideas and degrees of abstraction cannot be learned until certain ages. We regard this question as open, partly because there are cognitive psychologists on both sides of it, and partly because the investigations of Piaget, taken at face value, do not justify any conclusion relevant to our task. The point is that Piaget is not a teacher but an observer—he has tried to find out what it is that children understand, at a given age, when they have been taught in conventional ways. The essence of our enterprise is to alter the data which have formed, so far, the basis of this research. If teaching furnishes experiences which few children now have, then in the future such observers as Piaget may observe quite different things. We therefore

believe no predictions, either positive or negative, are justified, and the only way to find out when and how various things can be taught is to try various ways of teaching them.[10]

Whether Piaget is describing something necessary about human cognitive development, or something contingent upon educational and socializing procedures of particular times and places, or some mixture of the two, is obviously a question of importance to educators. If Piaget is describing a process determined by past social and educational contingencies, the inference that educators must conform with the process he describes leads to institutionalizing certain developmental norms determined by past socializing and educational practices. That is, accepting Piaget's psychological theory as describing constraints to which an educational theory must conform is to reinforce a process appropriate to past conditions.

A related, more particular, question concerns whether Piaget is describing cognitive developments or linguistic developments. Piaget seems occasionally to read through children's verbal responses to their cognitive structures with excessive facility. It remains unclear just what is the relationship between linguistic and cognitive development. The extreme case against Piaget here is the claim that what he is measuring is not the development of cognitive structures, but simply children's growing mastery of semantic rules that relate to the Piagetian tasks they deal with.[11] If, indeed, Piaget is describing something that merely reflects typical linguistic developments in modern Western societies then, again, this suggests to educators that his data need not greatly concern them. The data are not necessary constraints to which education must conform; they reflect the results of present methods of educating. Though the match of language and cognition may not be exact, the validity of the distinction between the two with which Piaget works can be sensibly doubted.

Piaget himself claims to be describing something necessarily true about the developmental process, something determined by our nature. He distinguishes often between what may be learned by teaching and "what the child learns by himself, what none can teach him and what he must discover alone."[12] This latter learning unfolds spontaneously with normal interaction with the environment over time, he claims; the search for equilibrium in changing circumstances ensures the developing, elaborating, diffusing, generalizing of schemata with constant assimilation and accommodation in a regular pattern.

In order to isolate the logico-mathematical structures which are, for him, the underlying psychological reality, Piaget distinguishes three kinds of knowledge: (1) innate knowledge; (2) the relatively superficial "figurative" knowledge that is stimulated by particular situations and which is, in sum, different for everyone; and (3) the profound "operative" knowledge that results from cognitive development, and which is the same for everyone as they progress through the unvarying sequence of stages. It is the relationship which Piaget claims exists between the latter two kinds of knowledge that makes his theory of most interest to educators.

While cognitive development requires experience of the external world, what *develops* as a result of this experience is knowledge of a different kind from that which is learned. The difference may be demonstrated by one of Piaget's examples. A four- or five-year-old boy sits with a set of pebbles in a line. He counts them from top to bottom and reaches ten. He then tries counting them from bottom to top and discovers that there are ten that way too. He then puts them in a circle and counts again. Still ten. The child feels that he has made a momentous discovery. What has he discovered? Whatever it is, it is not a property of the pebbles, or how to count, or any simple knowledge related to the particulars of the situation. Rather, the child has *developed* important knowledge about the action of ordering things in the world. He has discovered, among other things, that the sum of a set of objects is independent of their order. He has developed, that is to say, a fundamental category of thought which can be applied generally to other objects in the world.

Piaget claims that "learning is subordinate to the subject's level of development";[13] that "no sort of learning . . . is possible without logico-mathematical frameworks";[14] that "teaching children concepts that they have not attained in their spontaneous development . . . is completely hopeless";[15] that teaching must be "subordinated to spontaneous and psychological development."[16] Our final question, then, is in two parts. Before we ask whether what Piaget claims is the determining relationship between development and learning is true, we must ask whether the distinction itself is grounded in a distinction between kinds of behaviors and mental functioning. That is, we will first want to be sure that there *are* distinct processes of development and learning such as Piaget describes.

To summarize, we have three fundamental, related questions about the status of Piaget's theory: (1) What does it describe? (2) Is what it describes partly a linguistic or other cognitive development? (3) Is the distinction between learning and development valid? How can we go about answering such questions? A considerable analytic literature and a large number of empirical studies are available. We should review some of them.

CROSS-CULTURAL STRUCTURES

The logico-mathematical structures which Piaget's theory describes are presented as properties of our mind. As such they are obviously not open to direct observation. How then are we to have access to them? They are inferred from the logical structure of tasks that children perform. If the logico-mathematical structures are universally present and develop spontaneously through normal interactions with the environment and determine what can be learned at any stage, we would expect to find certain clear uniformities in task performance and learning generally in all people everywhere.

If, then, we all have in common a part of our minds which develops according to a particular sequence, we would expect some clear uniformity to be revealed whenever we could see this level at work underneath the superficial diversity of different experiences and learning. If, as Piaget claims, this is also the most important part of cognition, we would expect it to be fairly easy to detect this level of commonalty. This level is composed of what Piaget calls "the development of the operations and the logico–mathematical structures of intelligence." And, he continues, if his claims about the fundamental nature of these mental characteristics are true, "it would naturally mean a certain constancy or uniformity in development, whatever the social environments in which individuals live."[17]

Piaget's earliest studies were with a homogeneous population, and so it was difficult to establish whether the commonalties he was finding were the result of commonalties in the educational and socializing experiences of that population, or in the testing procedures he used, or whether, indeed, they were caused by an underlying developmental process such as Piaget postulated. Thus there was an interest in the results of cross–cultural studies which aimed to discover whether a similar developmental process was evident in different populations.

But it is not easy to see what kind of finding from cross-cultural studies would disprove Piaget's theory. One needs to remember that his is not simply a psychological theory; it is, rather, a genetic epistemological theory, which intricately mixes logical constructs and psychological claims. This is important to remember here because those parts of the theory which are logical constructs will guarantee a certain uniformity from empirical results. If, for example, one were to propose a theory that, among other things, claimed that children would learn addition and subtraction before calculus, or would learn historical facts before developing a sophisticated historical consciousness, one would not be altogether surprised if empirical tests confirmed this part of one's theory. The confirmation would not be due to the claims being obvious psychological truths: rather it would be attributed to their logical necessity. In the same way, the *general* sequence of stages as described in Piaget's theory does not involve psychological claims and is not an empirical matter. Of necessity, formal operations have to succeed concrete operations, because formal operations are defined as operations upon the operations of the previous stage. (This point has been made in a number of ways.[18]) That is, whatever we conclude about Piaget's theory, it is a matter of logical necessity that children will learn to perform certain tasks before they will be able to perform tasks which require the earlier tasks and then some additional skill.

So we will expect cross-cultural studies to provide some very general support for the sequence of stages. What is of more importance to our question about the existence of the underlying structures is whether a more detailed uniformity in sequence is evident from such studies. But, again, Piaget accepts that experience, environment, and social interactions will all affect the *rate* at which people develop these underlying structures, and will affect the extent to which the developments will occur.

Thus, before we conduct cross-cultural studies or look at the data, we are guaranteed a certain general uniformity by logical necessity and we are told to expect certain particular irregularities because of local contingencies. It is difficult to see, then, where we should look for evidence either for or against the existence of Piaget's operative structures. The general uniformity does not count as evidence for, and some particular irregularities do not count as evidence against. In addition, the problems inherent in any cross-cultural study— problems of cultural context, of communication, of meaning—are vividly evident in Piagetian cross-cultural studies. How are we to interpret whatever results we do get? If we find, for example, that most Australian aborigine adults fail Piagetian tests of the conservation of continuous quantity,[19] "are we to believe that aborigine adults will store water in tall thin cans in order to 'have more water'; do they think they lose water when they pour it from a bucket into a barrel?"[20] That these confusions are not evident in their culture suggest that the classic Piagetian task, in such a context, is yielding obscure data that possibly have nothing much to do with general intellectual capacity.

And yet this problematic area has attracted an enormous amount of research, and we are rich indeed in data—which confirm a general uniformity, of a kind guaranteed by logical necessity, and a great deal of local diversity.

Apart from the very general developmental sequence which logic guarantees, we might search for evidence concerning the sequence of substages Piaget postulates—such as the sequence in the acquisition of the conservations. Although some studies more or less confirm the Piagetian sequence, a number reject it.[21] I say "more or less" confirm it, because these studies report averages of test performance, and suggest that some individuals do not conform to the Piagetian sequence even in studies whose generalized trends form the empirical support for the theory. Whatever we make of these results they hardly support the existence of a universal, unfolding sequence of cognitive structures. Reviews of relevant research agree that "the research to date challenges the notion of invariance in the sequence of stage acquisition."[22] The data available so far cannot count as conclusive. They do not, however, offer any appreciable challenge to the claim that the kinds of structures Piaget describes do not exist.

CONSISTENT DEVELOPMENT

If we possess certain cognitive structures which in profound ways affect how we make sense of the world and which are basic determinants of the totality of our intellectual life, we would expect that once a particular structure had developed it would be evident in all our intellectual activity.

But even the early Piagetian experiments showed that the development of a structure, for example, that which enabled conservation of number, did not mean that the student could successfully apply that structure to conserving volume.[23] Empirical studies, however, indicated a regular sequence whereby the conservation structure became operative on different materials. It was discovered that among the children who formed the earlier experimental groups the "concepts of conservation are acquired in a constant chronological order."[24] Thus, such children on average could conserve mass two years before they could conserve weight, which in turn preceded conservation of volume by a further two years. These findings have been replicated without significant discrepancies on other children.[25]

These delays, or lags, in the structure becoming operative on different materials have been incorporated into the theory as Piaget's horizontal *décalages*.

With the recent proliferation of experiments that seek to test the theory in fundamental ways, rather than to elaborate it or replicate its findings, it is becoming clear that the ability to perform a particular task is a poor predictor of a child's ability to perform other tasks with the same logical structure in different circumstances with different materials.

A set of classic Piagetian experiments have produced the bulk of evidence for young children's supposed "egocentrism"—their inability to "decenter" like adults. In one of these experiments, for example, children are faced with a three-dimensional model of three, different-looking mountains. A doll is then placed to one side or another of the model and the children are asked what the doll can see. *Normally*, children fail to be able to work out what the doll would see from its perspective till about eight or nine years of age. Children under six normally identify what they themselves can see as what the doll can see. According to Piaget and Inhelder, children "really imagine that the doll's perspective is the same as their own,"[26] despite the fact that they know a view changes as one moves around. Similar findings from a set of similar experiments form the basis for the characterization of the mental structures which preoperational children are supposed to possess.

Margaret Donaldson reports a set of experiments which show that if one is sensitive to children's language use and the context of human purposes and intentions which are meaningful to them, one can create tasks which have the same logical structure as the classic Piagetian tasks but which can be routinely performed by young children.[27] Donaldson describes, for example, a study by Martin Hughes which uses the same logical form as Piaget's mountain task but substitutes a policeman doll and a child doll. In an apparatus consisting of walls in the form of a cross, the children have to work out at what points the child doll would be hidden from the policeman doll. There are positions in which the child doll would be visible to the subject but not to the policeman doll. Thus children would have to be able to work out what the policeman doll would be able to see from his perspective—the "decentering" which, according to Piaget, is impossible for young children because of their "egocentrism." In Hughes' study the vast majority of children had no difficulty in successfully performing the task; and, indeed, the ten youngest children in the study, whose average age was only three years nine months, achieved an 88 percent success rate.

Donaldson reports a series of other experiments which challenge the basis on which significant parts of Piaget's theory rests. The question here is what does Piaget's theory describe. That he has exposed consistent development in the performance of some tasks by some children is clearly true. Donaldson argues forcefully that the "egocentric" responses Piaget's tasks record are due, not to some specific structure of the mind not yet having developed, but simply to the fact that the tasks do not make sense to young children for different reasons. The classic Piagetian tasks are abstracted from any context of human purposes and intentions which children have learned to make sense of. Once Piaget's tasks are put into meaningful contexts with meaningful materials children's performance becomes much more like adults' and the characteristics which form the descriptive base for his cognitive structures are no longer evident.

There has been a considerable amount of discussion about what it means to be "in" a Piagetian stage. Related to this is the problem of how far being in a stage guarantees being able to perform all tasks whose logical characteristics conform with those of the structure which supposedly defines being in a stage. The fact that the structures are descriptions of competences suggests that their operation on different materials might be something learned over time. (This is as close as one comes to finding an explanation of *décalages*.) This leaves us, again, with some difficulties in working out how to gather clear evidence for or against the existence of these cognitive structures. If some materials and contexts are, for some unknown reason, more resistant to the operation of the structures, then the fact that the structure operates on one task but not on an identical task with different materials is claimed by Piagetians not to be evidence against the existence of the cognitive structures. Similarly, as a result of empirical studies, Piaget has incorporated into the theory the observation that as children approach transition points between stages their responses have a much less stable character than when they are more clearly "in" stages. Thus the fact that many children can perform one task but not another despite the fact that the tasks have the same logical structure is seen by Piagetians not as evidence against the existence of structures but rather as evidence that such children are at transition points between stages. Thus in a study concerning the conservation of continuous quantity, thirty-four children between ages five and seven were given tasks that tested whether they could conserve liquids and modeling clay. Fifteen children failed on the tasks and it was concluded simply that they had not yet developed conservation structures. Nineteen children, however, could do one but not the other task, or succeeded in a part of one of the tasks only. These nineteen were thus all classified as "intermediate."[28] Similar large proportions of subjects are consigned casually to intermediate status in most Piagetian experiments, when frequently fifty percent or more of the subjects do not display consistent operation of a structure across different materials. In addition, Piaget seems increasingly willing to acknowledge the role of experience in affecting students' ability to perform particular tasks.[29]

Thus, when a child's ability to perform a task with a particular logical structure seems to tell little about whether that child can perform a logically identical task with different materials, Piagetians can claim that these discrepancies can be caused by *décalages*, by the child being "intermediate," or by some extraneous experiential factor. One can only conclude that if the kinds of structures exist which are the core of Piaget's theory they have weak effects, and have only slight and wavering explanatory force. If such cognitive structures are the most important determinants of what can be learned and understood, their effects should surely not be so elusive in the available data.

Consider this task: Given the rule, "if the letter is sealed it has a five penny stamp on it," work out which of the following four envelopes has/have to be turned over to test the rule—the back of a sealed envelope, the back of an unsealed envelope, the front of an envelope with a four penny stamp on it, the front of an envelope with a five penny stamp on it. Of twenty-four subjects in one study, twenty-one succeeded in this task. When the same subjects attempted a logically identical task in which cards with letters and numbers were substituted for the stamps and envelopes—to test the rule "if a card has a 5 on one side it has a D on the other"—only two of the twenty-four succeeded.[30] If our ability to perform a task is determined by the possession of logico-mathematical structures, how do we account for the above kind of finding? What function do the structures perform? How can we tell whether such structures exist or not?

If we look at those surveys of empirical data from studies aiming to find evidence of consistent responses corresponding to the use of Piagetian cognitive structures we find conclusions such as the following: "one would become cautious about assuming 'conservation' to be a skill more general than it is content specific";[31] or, despite "progressive refinement of method aimed at removing from the experimental data all variations due to extraneous factors, the most striking feature of the results of these studies is the degree of inter- and intra-individual variety obtained";[32] or these "data suggest that the assignment to a particular stage seems to depend upon the task used as a criterion, and the implication of structure is that it should not";[33] or "in general, logical task structure does not seem to be a good predictor of behavior across situational variations."[34]

Piaget's theory over the decades has amassed a considerable bag-gage of *ad hoc* metatheoretical glosses, whose combined contribution is to remove the theory from the realm of the testable. If discrepant data can be explained away as a result of *décalages,* or of intermediate status, or experience, or learning, we are left to wonder what could count as evidence against the theory.

When it was a matter of accounting for the fairly consistent data about children's ability to perform tasks with the same logical struc- ture which was produced by the classic Piagetian tasks, then Piaget's theory provided a plausible explanation of those data. When it comes to explaining the degree of inconsistency and heterogeneity which is increasingly evident when tasks other than Piaget's are used, then his theory of determining logico-mathematical cognitive structures seems increasingly inadequate.

LANGUAGE OR COGNITIVE STRUCTURE

One of the difficulties in convincingly exposing and repre- senting abstract cognitive structures is that their existence is inferred from children's performance of various tasks and that performance is invariably tied up in complicated ways with language—the lan- guage used by the experimenter in giving instructions; the language children use in giving their responses; the degree of understanding and meaning shared by adult experimenter and child subject. A consistent criticism of Piaget's work has been the casual ease with which he has read through children's language use to their cognitive structures.[35]

How do we know when asking children to perform particular tasks that they understand what we say? If they fail in the task, if they give a wrong answer, how do we know it is not because they have misunderstood due to some linguistic confusion rather than because they have not yet developed the cognitive structure which would enable them to get it right? The problem for the researcher is posed well by Smedslund:

> During the prolonged debates about criteria for the presence or ab- sence of certain structures, notably conservation and transitivity . . . I

came to recognize a problem which seems to have no satisfactory solution within Piagetian psychology. In order to decide whether a child
is behaving logically or not, one must take for granted that he has cor-
rectly understood all instructions and terms involved. On the other
hand, in order to decide whether or not a child has correctly understood
a given term or instruction, one must take for granted that the child is
behaving logically with respect to the implications which constitute his
understanding. . . . There is a circular relation between logicality and
understanding, each one presupposing the other, and this constraint
forces the researcher to make a choice of which one to take for granted
and which one to study. . . . In so far as Piagetian psychologists focus
on logicality as a variable . . . they are making an epistemological error
and are out of step with everyday human life as well as with all useful
psychological practice. . . . It is a matter of historical record that children
who failed on tasks were often simply described as non-logical, and the
problem of criteria of understanding has received relatively scant attention in Piagetian literature.[36]

If Piaget and his followers are not adequately distinguishing among
reasons why children succeed or fail at certain tasks, it may well be
that a cause they are ignoring is responsible for what they attribute
to the presence or absence of a particular cognitive structure. The
data they use as evidence of the achievement of a particular cognitive
structure may be rather a record of children's normal age of mastery
of a linguistic convention which enables them to understand in a
different way what the experimenter means.

The Piagetian position on this seems initially straightforward.
Piaget asserts strongly that linguistic competence follows on, and is
only one among other expressions of, the development of cognitive
structures and the operations they make possible. "Linguistic progress is not responsible for logical or operational progress. It is rather
the other way around."[37] Children's language use and comprehension, then, provides only a delayed reflection of underlying cognitive
structures. Piaget also asserts that there is considerable murkiness
in inferring thought or cognitive structure from language. He notes
that language expresses cognitive structures only vaguely, and points
out that his inferences are based not only on language but also on
all the child's various behaviors in the experimental situation.[38] He
argues that "language is not thought, nor is it the source or sufficient
condition for thought."[39]

Yet despite the claims that language is determined by cognitive
structure and that it can provide only a hazy reading of present
cognitive structures, the experiments whose results provide the bulk

of support for Piaget's theory rely heavily on the experimenter's instructions and questions and on children's verbal responses. Indeed, when some training experiments seemed to challenge aspects of the theory, a major criterion enunciated for judging whether actual structural developments had taken place was "the child's justification of his answers."[40]

So if one looks at the classic Piagetian experiments one seems to see an assumption that language use clearly and directly can provide access to thought, or cognitive structures. If such were the case one might test the theory by seeing whether linguistic changes in the context of the experiments, while preserving their logical form, would produce significant increases in children's successful responses. If they did, this would seem to count as disconfirming evidence against the theory. But Piaget asserts that the path between language and cognitive structures is murky and complex, so it is not clear what the results of such experiments would show. That is, the metatheoretical glosses serve to protect the theory from easy testability.

Even the most general and apparently straightforward Piagetian claim about cognitive structure determining language is difficult to test. (This is especially the case when we consider the additional claim that language is partially figurative and partially operative, and that the operative functions seem to be generally ignored by Piagetians.) A recent attempt to test this most general claim, however, concludes that "a perusal of Piagetian literature on language acquisition, in conjunction with the data reported here, provides scant evidence for the contention that language skills are a reflection of more general cognitive operations."[41]

When a father phones home and asks his four-year-old son "What are you doing, Michael?" he should not be surprised to be told, in that tone of voice indicating the usual bewilderment and half-suppressed exasperation at adults' stupidity, "I'm answering the phone." If children were psychological researchers such common phenomena would no doubt contribute to a theory about human beings' increasing inability to "decenter" with age, leading to a characterization of adulthood as intellectually constrained by "egocentrism." Mildly funny as this may seem, there is accumulating evidence to suggest that it is precisely experimenter egocentrism that has produced a restricted understanding of how children think. Let us briefly consider some studies which show sensitivity to children's contexts of meanings, and see how the results impact on Piagetian claims about cognitive structures.

Donaldson notes three things which influence children's inter-pretation of what we say to them: their knowledge of the language; their assessment of what we intend (as indicated by our nonlinguistic behavior); and the manner in which they would represent the phys-ical situation to themselves if we were not present.[42] Research from a number of sources[43] confirms what any sensitive teacher or parent knows, that young children's responses to verbal commands, re-quests, and questions are often unpredictable. Understanding of par-ticular conventions of language which run counter to the literal meaning of the words ("What are you doing, Michael?" "Answering the phone") can determine behavior and responses in odd ways. How far a particular convention is understood, partially misunder-stood, mixed up by a bizarre association (hare/hair type confusions) is unknowable for any child at any time.

Among the classic Piagetian experiments that support the char-acterization of young children's inability to decenter are those which require children to compare a subclass with a class of objects. For example, if a bunch of flowers is made up of an unequal number of red and white flowers, children are asked, "Are there more red flow-ers or more flowers?" If there are, say, four red flowers and two white flowers, children under six will normally reply that there are more red flowers. Piaget claims that preoperational children respond this way because they *cannot* "center" on the whole class and on the subclass at the same time in order to make a comparison between them. The cognitive structure which enables this particular task to be performed successfully is assumed not yet to have developed in such children. Is this normal failure indeed due to children's lack of a particular cognitive structure, or due to the fact that they do not understand what the question is asking them to do? And if the latter, is it the case that this reflects something other than the development of the appropriate structure?

After pointing out that the question about comparing red flowers with flowers is unconventional and tends to confuse adults until stress is put on the unqualified second "flowers," Donaldson de-scribes an experiment devised by James McGarrigle to make the task less confusing. He used four toy cows: three black, one white. He laid them on their sides and told the children that they were sleeping. He then asked two questions whose logical forms are identical. First, he asked the classic Piagetian question, "Are there more black cows or more cows?" Twenty-five percent of the children answered cor-rectly. McGarrigle then asked, "Are there more black cows or more sleeping cows?" Here again the children have to compare a subclass with the class of sleeping cows. Forty-eight percent answered correctly. The addition of an adjective led to a significant improvement.

McGarrigle then experimented with emphasizing the contrast between the subclasses, trying to reduce what seemed like irrelevantly confusing aspects of the tasks. The tasks retained the same logical form, but they were gradually disencumbered of linguistic and perceptual confusions. The clearer the tasks were made, the higher the rate of successful responses became, until well over eighty percent of young children showed no difficulty in "decentering" and in casually comparing a subclass with a class.

A similar effort to see whether children's difficulty with certain conservation tasks was due to the artificiality of the classic Piagetian form was conducted by S. A. Rose and M. Blank. In the classic Piagetian test for conservation of discrete quantity, children are asked to judge whether objects in two rows are equal or unequal in number. The child responds, and then the objects are rearranged, and the experimenter poses the identical question again. Rose and Blank point out that, given typical school practice, when children are asked the same question a second time after having already made a response it is because the first response is wrong and they are being invited to revise it. Their test involved three groups: the first was given the standard form of the test; the second was asked to say whether the quantities were equal only once, after they had seen the rearrangement of the objects (that is, the condition for the second group was identical with that of the first group except that they were not asked to voice their judgment before the rearrangement); the third group was asked for one judgment but did not see the objects rearranged. The successful responses of the second group were significantly higher than those of the other two groups. Children from this group also scored higher one week later when they performed the classic Piagetian form of the test. This was taken as support for the assumption that the learned conventions of question asking and answering affect children's responses in often subtle ways. The experimenters conclude that their studies support "the notion that the implicit contextual cues which the child first encounters play a large role in determining the response he will employ on this and all subsequent related tasks."[44]

Donaldson reports a series of other experiments which proposed to make some of the classic Piagetian conservation tasks less confusing to children, and, again, once language conventions, contexts, and materials with which children were familiar were used, successful responses increased significantly, and sometimes dramatically. The results of these experiments are all consistent with the hypothesis that it is children's developing understanding of situations and linguistic conventions that determines their ability to make sense of the Piagetian tasks and to succeed at them.

But are these, and the multitude of similar results now recorded, necessarily inconsistent with the existence of cognitive structures developing as described in Piaget's theory? Consigning many of these children to intermediate status seems to offer little defense to the theory in light of the consistent improvement in the results; if large numbers were intermediate we would expect to see more random fluctuation in right and wrong responses. But clearly some defense is offered by the notions of *décalage* and resistance of materials to structures. Perhaps there is a *décalage* in moving from black toy cows to sleeping toy cows? More seriously, Piagetians might claim that the whole purpose of the unconventional and abstract tasks they employ is to ensure that they are measuing children's operative knowledge. By making everything so familiar, children may well be able to respond successfully by using figurative knowledge. The tasks, then, are measuring superficial *learning* rather than profound *development*. The whole purpose of beads and tables is their abstractness. If teddy bears and toy cows are used, then the results may simply measure children's memory and experience which are tied to these particular things.

Again, the metatheoretical glosses serve to defend the theory, but at the cost of removing it from the realm of the testable. One can only say that the theory increasingly explains less and less of the available data, and the metatheoretical glosses are called on to explain more and more. The problem with this is that the operation of these metatheoretical explanatory devices is called in arbitrarily. They are claimed to operate only when the theory is inadequate. How do we know that McGarrigle's experiments are measuring figurative rather than operative knowledge?

What does Piaget's theory describe? What evidence do the results of experiments such as those reported by Donaldson provide either for or against the existence of the kind of cognitive structures in terms of which the theory is articulated? Theories like Vygotsky's[45] seem more economically able to account for the array of data we now have about language and cognitive development than does Piaget's. Indeed, Piaget's theory seems able to accommodate much of the data only with much creaking and straining and with the support of a superstructure of metatheoretical glosses. The claim that language use is determined by the development of cognitive structures is a difficult one to sustain. If we doubt that such cognitive structures exist there is nothing in the available array of relevant data that asserts their reality. Given the role of language in the experiments that provided the basic data on which the theory was constructed, the assertion that the development of cognitive structures is responsible for language development is not a conclusion which itself rests on any data but is inferred from the truth of theory, which is presupposed.

LEARNING CONSTRAINED BY DEVELOPMENT

One of the most important claims made in Piaget's theory, and of special significance for educators, is that learning is constrained by development. Piaget concludes that "teaching children concepts that they have not attained in their spontaneous development . . . is completely hopeless." If Piaget is right about the nature of cognitive structures, which spontaneously develop, and their relationship to learning, then we might expect to find that learning cannot significantly affect the development of structures and that children cannot be induced to learn and understand any concept before the relevant underlying structure has developed. Once imported into education, then, Piaget's theory serves as a "readiness" model; it describes a sequence of developments which can instruct us about what a child is ready to learn.

Some of the experiments reported earlier in this chapter might be seen as disproving this claim. That is, some of them suggest that very young children can be taught, say, to conserve quantity if only the teacher/experimenter is pedagogically skilled and sensitive. But, as indicated above, much of this learning can be discounted as merely figurative. In Piaget's view, teaching or training of this kind "produces either very little change in logical thinking or a striking momentary change with no real comprehension."[46] What gives evidence of real comprehension is the child's recognition that what has been learned from such experiments involves not simple contingent or figurative matters (which may well be remembered and used in making responses) but rather their recognition that what occurred was a result of logical necessity. This is the major criterion by which we can measure whether operative/developmental knowledge has been acquired. "[T]his logical 'necessity' is recognized not only by some inner feeling, which cannot be proved, but by the intellectual behavior of the subject who uses the newly mastered deductive instrument with confidence and discipline."[47]

We have available results from a large number of "training studies" designed either to test or elaborate this claim of Piaget's theory. But, again, the difficulty of clearly exposing abstract cognitive structures, which are inferred from performances on particular tasks, leaves the results of these studies a subject of continuing dispute between Piagetians and their critics. Some of the earlier North American training studies (which sometimes tended to take a rather simplistic view of Piaget's theory and its claims about development and learning) were taken as refuting the theory if children could be taught, say, to conserve earlier than the theory predicted. In response to such studies, and more sophisticated ones which seemed to challenge the theory, Piagetians have attempted to spell out in more detail what kinds of things give evidence of real structural change, rather than of mere figurative learning. "In order to assess the operatory value of the progress obtained after training, the post-tests have to satisfy certain requirements."[48] They specify five main criteria:

1. At least two post-tests, the latter, at an interval of several weeks to establish the "stability of the progress."
2. The post-tests should include a more stringent replication of the pretests "to determine the potentiality of a subject's reasoning."
3. The subjects can generalize the acquired operation to materials other than those used in the training study.
4. The subjects can handle questions that require a different answer from those called for in the training study, though the additional post-test questions are of the same level of difficulty.
5. The subjects can handle "a problem whose solution requires a notion related, but not identical to, that treated during the training."

The difficulty in this area is not with any ambiguity in the training study results. Even before the above criteria were articulated there were considerable data from studies that seemed to meet these criteria and disprove Piagetian claims.[49] It is odd that the main Piagetian study of the subject, *Learning and the Development of Cognition*, systematically ignores all these studies, as well as all apparently challenging data in their discussion. The difficulty here is to resolve what exactly is the Piagetian claim, and what Piagetians will accept as a test of it. The earlier claim seemed clear. It asserted simply that the spontaneously developing cognitive structures determined what could be meaningfully learned. But the results of cross-cultural studies suggested that this simple assertion needed to be elaborated. If spontaneous development relied on interactions with the environment, then perhaps some interactions with some environments might well stimulate the developmental process better than might others. This would account for the considerable differences in the rate and extent of development exposed by cross-cultural studies. The present problem is compounded by Piagetians offering no explanation of why some interactions with some environments should so powerfully stimulate development, as in Geneva or New York or London, and other interactions with other environments stimulate virtually no development beyond the earliest stages, as in parts of Australia and Africa. If the nature of the environment and the subject's interactions with it can have such a huge impact on development one might assume that teaching which optimally organizes the environment to encourage cognitive development will be more successful than teaching which does not. Indeed, this is a tenet which guides much Piagetian educational practice, but the nature of its theoretical support remains hazy. Similarly, the ability of some training studies to induce significant learning of operative concepts has been acknowledged, but "operativity is malleable only within certain limits."[50]

The Piagetian training studies reported in *Learning and the Development of Cognition* have explored how far and in what circumstances learning could affect development, that is, what is the degree of malleability in operativity. The results of these studies have been taken as confirming the Piagetian hypotheses: "Under certain conditions an acceleration of cognitive development would be possible, but that this could only occur if the training resembled the kind of situations in which progress takes place outside an experimental set-up."[51] The odd part of this is that though we know little about how such cognitive development takes place in experimental set-ups, we know even less about how it occurs outside them; also, the use of "accelerate" presupposes a natural pace. Further, these studies indicated that progress was dependent on how close subjects already were to acquiring the cognitive skill being trained. This was taken as confirming Piaget's claim that if subjects

are close to the operational level, that is, if they are able to understand quantitative relations, the comparisons they make during the experiment are enough to lead them to compensation and conservation. But the farther they are from the possibility of operational quantification, the less they are likely to use the learning sequence to arrive at a concept.[52]

In addition, the studies are taken as confirming the importance, or necessity, of children being active discoverers in order that their interactions with the environment will stimulate developmental progress. "In terms of successful training procedures, this means that the more active a subject is, the more successful his learning is likely to be."[53] Unfortunately for the testability of this claim it is followed by the observation that children "can be mentally active without physical manipulation, just as [they] can be mentally passive while actually manipulating objects." Given the manner in which concepts develop, according to Piaget's theory, children's wrong answers, for example, failures to conserve, "should not be regarded as errors which need to be eliminated by suitable training." Rather they are evidence of "uncoordinated schemes . . . based on a preoperatory, ordinal type of reasoning . . . which cannot, and for that matter should not, be eliminated by coercion."[54] "Coercion" here refers to any method which contravenes the "natural" course of events, the "*necessary stages* of development."[55] This seems to involve the prediction that "coercive" methods—for example, telling children whether their answers are right or wrong—may lead to figurative learning but will not stimulate operative, structural development.

Let us briefly consider a few of the experiments that are commonly cited by Piaget's critics as disputing his claims about development constraining learning.[56] In the following brief review I will draw heavily on Brainerd's "Learning Research and Piagetian Theory." (However critical Piagetians may be of Brainerd's presentation of Piaget's theory, his articulation of problems for the theory that derive from the data cannot simply be ignored—as it so often is.)

In chapter 1 of *Learning and the Development of Cognition*, Inhelder, Sinclair, and Bovet report an experiment concered with training children to conserve quantity, using an apparatus of containers and water. They found that none of the children who failed the pretests succeeded in acquiring conservation, while 16 of the 19 children who were classed as "intermediate level" on the pretests showed improvement in their reasoning in one of the two post-tests and 10 even acquired conservation. Thus "the most striking finding was the existence of a close relationship between the child's initial level of development (pretest) and the types of reasoning he used in the training session."[57] The finding that none of those who failed the pretests learned anything seems to confirm Piaget's view that "teaching children concepts that they have not attained in their spontaneous development . . . is completely hopeless." In non-Piagetian terms these results suggest that children who know a fair amount about something beforehand manage to talk about it more sensibly and learn more about it than do children who knew nothing about it beforehand. That is, the most striking finding is one that would be predicted by any learning theory.

In a similar experiment Sheppard recorded different results.[58] The main differences in Sheppard's experiment were that his subjects were passive observers rather than active participants and that they were told whether their responses were right or wrong. In addition, *all* of his subjects failed the pretests for conservation. This combination—nonconservers in a passive condition given verbal feedback in responses (a "tutorial" method)—should, according to the predictions of Piaget's theory, lead to no progress at all. In fact, between thirty and forty percent performed perfectly on various of the post-tests and nearly all subjects showed some progress. The learning generalized to four conservation concepts—number, mass, length, weight—in which they were not trained, and the progress proved to be stable across a two-month interval.

The Piagetian experimenters' failure to achieve any progress with nonconservers was taken as confirming the theory's claim that developmental level constrains learning. But in an experiment conducted by Gelman, children who failed pretests for conservation of number, length, mass, and liquid quantity later performed perfectly in post-tests in the two areas in which they were trained—number and length.[59] They also gave correct responses about sixty percent of the time on post-tests in the two untrained areas. Murray conducted an experiment with children who had failed pretests for conservation of number, space, mass, liquid quantity, weight, and discontinuous quantity.[60] About 79 percent of these subjects learned conservation in all six pretested areas, and 81 percent generalized to conserve other areas not trained. Emrick trained four-year-olds on number and length conservation.[61] In post-tests for number, length, mass, and liquid quantity conservation two weeks after the training sessions, the subjects were successful on seventy-three percent of the items on the number and length tests. They generalized to perform successfully on forty-one percent of the items in tests for conservation of mass and liquid quantity.

Now, clearly, getting right answers on tests after such experiments is not what Piaget's theory is about. Neither are such experiments of any value in furthering knowledge of the underlying processes about which the theory is concerned. Their purpose is not to elaborate the theory but to try to find out ways to test it. We will consider the value of these, and the many similar experiments which report similar results.

First we might briefly consider the main experimental support for Piaget's belief that teaching conservation concepts to preconservers is completely hopeless. Apart from the Inhelder, Sinclair, and Bovet experiments referred to above, the other experiments commonly cited as supporting the Piagetian position are those conducted by Smedslund and Wohlwill.

Using tutorial methods, Smedslund[62] failed to train nonconservers to conserve weight. Hatano[63] has pointed out that Smedslund's equipment included a pan–balance and his procedures did not include any precaution to ensure that the young children in the experiment understood how it worked. In others of his set of experiments similar precautions were not taken to ensure that children understood what was happening—raising the dilemma between comprehension and logicality which Smedslund has since so precisely pinpointed. By eliminating these confusions, and performing experiments demanding the same logical task from the subjects, Gelman succeeded in achieving impressive improvements in number and length conservation. Hatano and Suga[64] similarly substituted a somewhat different experimental set-up which avoided the potential confusions inherent in Smedslund's. They succeeded in training sixty percent of their subjects to successful number conservation; there was successful generalization of the ability, and stability over time. Similarly, design flaws were identified in Wohlwill's experiments[65] which might well have been the cause of their subjects' failures to learn to conserve. Once such flaws were eliminated, similar procedures without the complicated apparatus have succeeded in training significant numbers of preconservers to conserve.

In addition to these there is now available massive evidence that "developmental concepts" can be taught. These studies would seem to show with overwhelming force that Piagetian claims are simply wrong, and that developmental stage as they characterize it does not constrain what can be undstood by children. But of course no Piagetian accepts this. Much dispute has focused on what is commonly called the "criterion problem." That is, what criteria do experimental training results have to satisfy in order to count as "real learning," as changes in cognitive structure? Whenever Piagetians have spelled out criteria, some training studies have met them. However, this does not prove the inadequacy of Piaget's theory to Piagetians; it proves only the inadequacy of the statement of criteria, or the simplistic way the, usually North American, experimenter has interpreted the criteria.

The American training studies which attempt to test Piaget's theory focus on those parts of the theory which seem to yield clear empirical claims. We have seen already how so much of the theory is either untestable, or it is difficult to interpret the test results. Piagetians seem so strongly to presuppose the general truth of the theory that they display some irritation at these American training experiments. Piaget saw them simply as part of what he called "the American question" of how fast one can "accelerate" the (natural) developmental process. That learning is constrained by development seems almost a *definitional* matter to Piagetians; that is, learning effects are identified by their following the development of a particular cognitive structure. The idea of testing to see whether this is the case seems to strike them as bizarre, and as *prima facie* evidence that such experimenters cannot understand the theory. The nonpsychologist reading Piagetian and North American studies is (or at least this one is) struck by the lack of engagement of discussion. My view is hardly unbiased by this point, I suppose, but the main hindrance to such engagement seems to lie in the degree to which Piagetians look at the data "through" the theory, rather than use the data to reflect back on the theory's predictions.

Piagetian defenses against the accumulating mass of apparent counterevidence remain in place. First, we have the assertion that the American training studies are achieving only figurative knowledge in their subjects. The fact that this knowledge meets all the criteria that Piagetians state for real comprehension only means that the criteria have not been stated, or interpreted, strictly enough. Indeed, what are interpreted by critics as confusions in Piagetian experimental situations, are to Piagetians tests of logicality; it is precisely such things that subjects who have developed the relevant operatory structure can work out, and subjects who have not, fail to work out. Another defense employed by Piagetians is simply to redraw the characterization of the preoperational stage to include more skills than is at present allowed; this would be merely a part of refining the theory in light of new data. Alternatively they may point out that, in their attempts to find some clearly testable part of the theory, North Americans have fixed on the stage concept and interpreted the whole thing far too literally. That is, American critics tend to see the stages altogether too crudely as exemplified in success or failure on particular tests. As Karmiloff-Smith expresses it:

Stages were initially used by Piaget as a *heuristic* for seeking far from obvious developmental links across widely differing conceptual domains. From the onset, Piaget's stage distinctions were not based on success or failure per se, but always pinpointed intermediate, oscillatory levels. . . . The stage concept can only remain a valid heuristic today if the stages described represent more than an analytic tool for the observer and are shown to be *psychologically functional for the child*. In other words a shift of emphasis is suggested from conservation-attainment to the psychological function of conservation-seeking.[66]

Thus if a child fails a conservation test, what is more important for assessing developmental level is to analyze responses "in terms of whether they represent powerful heuristics in development or merely shortcomings to be surmounted later."[67] If one presupposes the truth of the theory then *it* might provide a reference which would allow one to carry out such analyses. But it leaves even more obscure the problem of how someone might find out whether the theory is articulated in terms of real cognitive structures or not.

One difficulty in comparing Piagetian research on the theory with that of North America critics is that the former is concerned with elaborating and refining the theory, presupposing its general validity, and the latter are concerned to test its validity. A further difficulty, indicated above, is that Piagetians seem to interpret American training studies less as tests of Piaget's theory and more as some kind of unnatural scheme aimed, futilely or dangerously, at accelerating the natural process of development. Thus, Karmiloff-Smith concludes the paper cited above: "Well-meaning learning theorists who train small children to ignore perceptual cues, to sidestep misconceptions by reciting verbal rules, and so forth, are doing these children a great disservice. They seem to lose sight of the fact that there is a profound psychological importance in being a nonconserver."[68]

It is worth considering this passage briefly. The Piagetian learning experiments referred to above were indeed concerned with how best to help children develop operative knowledge, and they concluded, as predicted by the theory, that active self-discovery methods are best and other methods are useless. American training studies are trying to test the validity of the theory's predictions; they are not, as Karmiloff–Smith seems to think, exemplifications of preferred pedagogical methods. The nefarious training activities referred to— conditioning children to ignore perceptual cues, and so on—can be described in these terms only if one presupposes the truth of the theory and all its predictions, suggestions, and implications; in this particular case, not correcting children's false belief that the quantity of water changes when poured from a fat, wide container into a long, narrow one. Those who think that one might sensibly point out to young children that the quantity of water does not change are accused of doing children a "great disservice." There is no evidence to support this wild claim. Nor do those who think it sensible to point out such errors to children "lose sight of the fact that there is a profound psychological importance in being a nonconserver"; rather they are properly assuming that no such "fact" has ever been established.

Whatever resolution comes about on the "criterion problem," and however well Piagetians build further defenses for the theory against what appears to be massively accumulating counterevidence, our present concern is with the reality of the cognitive structures which are supposed to determine what can be learned. The mass of data now available from Piagetian and other training studies does nothing to challenge the claim that such structures do not exist.

The fact that we cannot find any evidence to support the belief that we have in our minds cognitive structures of the kind Piaget claims does not of course mean that they are not there. We have been looking for evidence for or against their existence because nearly all the implications derived from Piaget's theory to education require them. The differences between the two kinds of knowledge, operative and figurative, and between development and learning, suggest two distinct processes that educators must take careful account of.

Our search for a clear empirical basis for the distinction, and for the existence of the conceptual structures, has not been successful. And if we look at Piaget's writings where the distinction is developed we may find enormous theoretical elaboration of the separate kinds of knowledge and their sources and their development. When we search this writing for some basis in reality for the distinction we find a simple anecdote such as the one recounted above of the boy discovering that the ordering of stones was independent of their perceptual qualities. We are then told that this kind of logico–mathematical knowledge is not preformed and is not the same as trivial learning of facts. On this simple observation the vast baroque theoretical edifice is then elaborated; and all empirical findings are interpreted in terms of this distinction. It need hardly be said that one can account for differences in kinds of knowledge in many ways. The point here is simply that this massive theoretical structure does not rest on any evident empirical ground, and is built from a simple distinction in kinds of knowledge that is somewhat arbitrary.

Competing views of cognitive development, views which are not built on a distinction such as Piaget's between two qualitatively distinct kinds of knowledge, seem increasingly better able to account for the presently available array of data—data which we owe to testing Piaget's prodigious theory. Trabasso, for example, outlines a very simple alternative:

> Cognitive development, under this view, may be seen as continuous and qualitatively similar to the target, adult mode. The growth of a child's capacity for immediate, short-term and long-term memory is likely to be gradual and quantitative. If the processing of information occurs within the limits of these systems then the upper limit of this capacity is also continuously rising as one stores more information from a variety of task experiences, learns more and better ways for coding and chunking information, acquires symbol systems such as language, etc. Certainly at some age, a child will be able to perform operations involving class concepts before he is able to perform propositions since the latter involve relations among the former and hence are more complex. The added complexity may approach his then current limit for handling several classes simultaneously.[69]

In contrast to Piaget's view of the relationship of learning and development we have the more complex image presented by Vygotsky and elaborated by Luria and others. This theoretical position summarizes the mass of data we have on cognitive development as follows:

> There is no "natural" human thinking and no one direction in which it should inevitably develop in the course of its ontogenesis and cultural and historical development. Rather, different kinds of theoretical activity produce different modes of verbal thinking that are necessary in creating (or generating), acquiring, and using . . . the respective modes of cultural texts.[70]

It is no part of my task to explore and evaluate alternative theories to Piaget's, even if I could. The purpose of these comments is simply to point out the slender theoretical basis and the lack of empirical basis for Piaget's development/learning distinction, and the fact that his distinction is not, as some Piagetians seem to suppose, obviously true or the only way to think about how human learning proceeds. A theory, put most generally, is a thing to think with. If we use Piaget's theory to think about development and learning, we must see it in a particular way. But we can also, with greater difficulty, use the world to think with, in order to reflect back on our theories. By applying this "making/matching"[71] process, we may conclude

that the world of empirical data about cognitive development suggests increasingly that Piaget's theory does not adequately describe
it. In Flavell's judgment Piaget's theory is in serious trouble. If this
is an accurate reflection of the psychological state-of-play (and I have
tried to give some reasons for thinking it is) then this has obvious
implications for those educational practices and programs which
base themselves on the theory.

It may be objected that I have ignored all the evidence which
supports Piaget's theory and his learning/development distinction,
and that I have focused only on data which are discrepant with the
theory. We test theories by working out what they predict, and we
seek predictions in areas where falsification is most likely. We do
not test theories adequately by constantly replicating the same set
of studies or by assuming the general correctness of the theory and
seeking to elaborate some detail of it. The crucial test of a theory is
not how much of the data it can account for, but rather whether it
fails to account for significant data. The phlogiston theory still accounts for most of the available data; its inadequacy is shown by
those significant data it fails to account for. Similarly, Piaget's theory
is not disconfirmed by most of the data we have about cognitive
development—indeed, it is responsible for unearthing much of them—
its inadequacies are being exposed by the increasing accumulation
of data which it cannot account for. I have focused on these accumulating anomalies, from the theory's point of view, to indicate the
validity of Flavell's judgment and to argue that one of the very weak-
est and least supported parts of the theory is precisely the point on
which the connections with education rely.

Piaget's Theory and Educational Practice

THEORY AND IDEOLOGY

First a general matter. In examining claims about Piaget's
contributions to education, it is perhaps worth noting immediately
one of the major influences already evident. This is not one of the
more detailed types which follow from drawing particular implications from his data or psychological theories, but is, rather, of an
ideological nature. Piaget has been most enthusiastically adopted by
groups of people in education who ally themselves with general
notions such as the following: "The ideal of education is not to teach

the maximum, to maximize the results, but above all to learn to learn, to learn to develop, and to learn to continue to develop after leaving school";[72] or, "if the aim of intellectual training is to form the intelligence rather than to stock the memory, and to produce intellectual explorers rather than mere erudition, then traditional education is manifestly guilty of a grave deficiency."[73] These are fairly typical expressions of Piaget's general view about the purpose of education.

These kinds of statements may not be surprising from a psychologist whose major interest has been the development of logical forms, independently from any content; especially if he believes that learning content depends on those psychological developments. There may, however, be some surprise to read that an aim of education is to help the student "to develop," when at other times Piaget seems to etch so strong a distinction between development and learning— the former being supposedly resistant to educational interventions and occurring more or less in response to normal interaction with the environment. It is also difficult to sort out exactly what Piaget does mean in these kinds of general statements. His infamous opaqueness, or suggestive ambiguity, is particularly evident in the second quotation above. One wonders whether Piaget sees "intellectual training" and "education" as synonymous, or whether traditional education has been deficient in one of its branches, that is, intellectual training, but not deficient in another branch, that is, producing mere erudition—but, then, the production of mere erudition seems to be considered a possible aim of intellectual training.

From his description of development, Piaget and his followers make prescriptions for teaching and learning:

> It is absolutely necessary that learners have at their disposal concrete material experiences (and not merely pictures), and that they form their own hypotheses and verify them (or not verify them) themselves through their own active manipulations. The observed activities of others, including those of the teacher, are not formative of new organizations in the child.[74]

Teaching which does not cohere with the laws of development as he has exposed them is considered useless: "Teaching children concepts that they have not attained in their spontaneous development . . . is completely hopeless."[75]

Active discovery-learning methods must thus form the staple of useful teaching because they are seen as the methods which best mirror the kind of activity which is the dynamic of the developmental process. Thus we must discount "the older methods [which] set a premium upon passivity and receptivity" and encourage "free activity as a means of growth."

To anyone familiar with the rhetoric about schooling in North America over the past half–century and more, there will be something familiar about these ideas. Indeed, the concluding quotations in the previous paragraph, which could have been taken from Piagetian writings, are from John Dewey.[76] The claims of Piaget and his followers in education about the educational values of discovery-learning methods and active involvement with the environment seem to the outsider virtually indistinguishable from those we have heard for more than half a century. Many Piagetians are conscious of the echoes: "so much has been said about the subject over so long a period of time probably with few beneficial results."[77]

If this is so, we are justified in asking what is the difference between it and the Piagetian neoprogressives' notion of discovery learning. "The difference is that we have a theoretical design and some empirical data supporting its validity to explain the stages and processes whereby the child's intelligence presumably develops."[78] This claim is precisely the one we have seen as becoming increasingly insecure. More importantly, however, we must question the role played by Piaget's theory if the major implications derived from it are in practice indistinguishable from those recommended in the literature of progressivism for more than half a century. Piaget is used in education as a scientific support for what we may call neoprogressivism. Having learned something of the insecurity of the support, we should now consider some of the practices that find their support in the theory.

ACTIVE LEARNERS AND THEIR DEVELOPMENT

The most prominent implication for educational practice commonly derived from Piaget's developmental theory is that for learning to take place, children must be active. According to the theory, it is by children's action on their environment that disequilibrium is introduced, which then forces accommodation of the schemata, leading to ever more complex and adequate structures. It is children's actions and interactions in their social environment which lead to those accommodations that enable children to escape from the prison of their own viewpoints. Objectivity, according to Piaget, "is constructed on the basis of, and in proportion to, the activities of the subject."[79] It is in action that the roots of logic and intelligence lie and it is by action that we come to know the world—knowledge that is later reflected in language, but is most profoundly embedded in action. These claims are commonly cited as justification for the propriety of the discovery-learning methods of teaching, which include encouraging children's social interaction in the classrooms, and basing particularly early learning primarily on action and experience rather than words. Thus, learning in schools should follow the developmental pattern from actions, to representations, to verbal formulations.

Consider the derivation of this recommendation about active learners in its move from psychological theory to educational practice. The stimulant Piaget proposes to internal equilibration and the elaboration and differentiation of schemata is the child's active manipulation of things in the world and observation of what happens to them as a result. Thus, Piaget claims, it is important for development that children have opportunities for such active manipulation, and, as learning depends on development, he then claims that it is educationally important to provide opportunities for such activity in order for learning to take place. To justify the educational recommendation we might expect empirical support for the claim that these developments are indeed causally connected with active manipulation, as well as data indicating, for example, that children who engage in more active manipulation become generally better learners as a result. There are no such data. What seems to be true are the common-sense observations that a minimum of active manipulation of the environment is necessary for proper development and that given roughly equal amounts of such manipulation some children learn better than others.

The educational practices that mirror this activity are practical, concrete manipulation in early schooling and, in their later intellectual forms, discovery learning or discrepancy and conflict techniques. These latter involve inducing the student to become mentally active in discovering something or in sorting out some apparent discrepancy.

There are a number of difficulties in testing the Piagetians' claim that one implication of the theory is that these are the most effective ways of stimulating development. We have discussed the problem of determining whether or not the very structures, which are keys to learning, do exist. We have noted also the acknowledgment that physically passive students may be mentally active, and vice versa—making it difficult to know whether success or failure on any test is achieved by an active or passive student. As with so much of Piagetian literature, we become lost in trying to sort out a clear test of the claim, and may reasonably fear that the claim looks a little like a simple definitional one. The students who succeed are active. This does not help us sort out what the qualities of activity are in education.

The main empirical support in Piagetian literature are the Inhelder, Bovet, Sinclair experiments cited above. We saw a number of problems with them. A further difficulty with moving toward education is that the experiments referred to stimulating *structural* change, whereas in education we may often be concerned with "erudition," with cultural knowledge. We do not have any data to suggest that the procedures which are supposed to be most effective—if they are—in stimulating *developmental* changes are also most effective in stimulating figurative *learning*. This seems to be assumed by Piagetians.

Nondiscovery-learning methods of teaching have been used in a host of recent experiments which have successfully taught conservations and other operational concepts to children who on the basis of pretests were classified as preoperationals. Many of these experiments have used verbal feedback and simple rewards, like candy, for correct responses. In addition to learning and retaining the concepts over a period of time, children's explanations of their judgments were improved and their new abilities transferred to additional conservations not taught in the experiments.[80] Children have also been taught conservation concepts successfully by means of observation of live models, and of models on film.[81]

So far little direct experimental comparison between teaching by discovery-learning methods and teaching by other methods is available. In one of the few experiments that does provide some kind of test of the Piagetian claims that active discovery-learning can be the only really effective method of teaching "developmental" concepts, groups of children in "active" and "passive" conditions were compared. The passive group simply watched in silence from about a ten-foot distance the active debating group. There was little significant difference between the amount of learning in the two groups, the passive group showing a slightly greater improvement.[82] The Soviet psychologist, Gal'perin, has shown that children's learning is improved by observing a concrete demonstration of some task and verbally anticipating the teacher's steps before doing it themselves. The practical activity unrehearsed mentally seems actually to inhibit thinking and learning.[83] A. A. Williams has observed that, in his experiments, children watching others trying to solve practical problems showed greater insight into what was going on.[84]

If one compares the amount of learning achieved in Genevan experiments using discovery-learning methods with recent North American experiments using other methods—not a very reliable kind of comparison—one sees that the amount of learning achieved in the North American experiments has been much greater. It should be noted that because the Genevan experimenters assume the correctness of the predictions Piaget's theory makes about learning, the Piagetian experimenters only attempt to teach children who already show some signs of being at a transitional stage with regard to the concepts to be taught. North American nondiscovery methods have produced, unlike those of Piagetians, substantial learning of concepts of which the children previously showed no grasp at all. That is, these North American experiments have routinely taught by non-discovery-learning methods operational concepts to children who on pretests have failed all tests for operational concepts. According to the predictions of the theory, this should be impossible.

The degree to which these data fail to provide a convincing argument against the Piagetian claims seems equivalent to the degree that the Piagetian claims resist being empirically tested. As a claim about our nature—human learners learn better when active, in the Piagetian sense—it must be said that it lacks both a distinct conceptual character and to the degree that we can devise something testable it lacks empirical support.

Now clearly there are times when it is educationally valuable to use discovery-learning methods—particularly at points when children have almost grasped some general principle and we can design some activity in which their performance will clarify the principle for them. But such occasions are, relative to Piagetian claims, rare.

A related pedagogical principle derived from Piaget's theory, as outlined by Marilynne Adler, is that: "You must motivate the learner less with extrinsic rewards and more with the internal push of cognitive *discrepancy,* inconsistency, 'perturbation.' Motivation will probably be greatest when the discrepancy is large enough to be interesting, but not so large as to be beyond the child's scope of understanding."[85] Let us pass over the tautology of the second sentence. This pedagogical principle follows from the theory's assertion that the dynamic of the developmental process lies in the constant disequilibration of schemata by new experience which cannot be assimilated and so demands accommodation. It requires acceptance of the further assertion that learning must follow the same pattern as the distinct process of development. (Oddly perhaps, this should present more of a problem to the Piagetian than to the person who finds the Piagetian learning/development distinction improper.) Accommodation, it is claimed, is optimized when something occurs which is discrepant with the expectation generated by the current equilibrium state. Such conditions heighten motivation, and entail greater learning.

From an educational point of view, there are two main problems with these pedagogical implications. The first is that they are derived from a part of the theory that is increasingly insecure. The available evidence suggests that this technique of discrepancy-learning is inefficient compared with other instructional techniques.[86] The second is evident to anyone who tries to use the technique in a classroom to teach, say, social studies or language arts or mathematics: the technique can hardly ever be used. The point has already been well made by Charles J. Brainerd, and I may as well quote him:

> For conflict teaching to work at all, it is clear that children must possess certain beliefs which run counter to whatever it is we are trying to teach them. There are some special cases in . . . arithmetic . . . in which contradictory beliefs will be held by most children. But surely these cases are exceptional. I submit that children have no opinion one way or the other about the great preponderance of things they learn in school. Most of the information they encounter in subjects such as geography, hygiene, communication skills, history and so on are novel. To illustrate this flaw in the conflict approach, consider two things that most of us learned in elementary school, namely Columbus set sail for the New World in 1492 and "sheep" is the plural of "sheep." Try to imagine a conflict method of teaching either of these things.[87]

The result of experiments showing that "passive" watchers learn as much if not more than "active" doers, need not perturb the Piagetian. As a prelude to their own experiments, Genevan researchers point out that a child "can be mentally active without physical manipulation, just as he can be mentally passive while actually manipulating objects."[88] Is the claim that only through their own active manipulations can children learn to be read as a kind of metaphor? It becomes not an empirical claim but a tautology. There is no way to separate "activity" from "learning" in order to test whether the latter can take place without the former. The additional line of defense against testability—and falsifiability—is the frequent assertion that learning produced by other than discovery-learning methods is a matter of "coercion,"[89] and does not constitute "true learning."[90] We are reminded that "one may induce the appearance of learning but true understanding takes time."[91] True learning, of course, is learning produced by the correct methods. That is, there is a tendency in this literature to suggest that nothing is as important as using the proper method. There is thus no way of testing whether other methods may not be as good or better at producing learning because even if they seem to be—as they do—the resulting learning is not "true learning"; it is a product of "brainstuffing."[92]

A difficulty in dealing with this issue is due to the inaccessibility of those things in terms of which Piaget's theory is articulated—the operatory structures. Their existence is inferred from performances on various tasks. A certain logic is inferred as descriptive of an operatory structure from a description of the logical characteristics of certain tasks. Success or failure to perform tasks with certain logical characteristics is then explained in terms of the subject either having developed or not yet having developed the appropriate operatory structure. The obvious danger of circularity involved in this kind of mental model need not be succumbed to. There is nothing inherently illegitimate in inferring mental characteristics from ability to perform certain tasks. The danger becomes acute, however, when the model is reified and given a prior ontological status to performance on tasks—from which the model's very existence is inferred. And this is precisely what is happening when Piagetians reject certain performances as not exemplifying true learning on the grounds that such learning did not induce "actual structural change," or that these changes fail to reflect what would happen "during the natural course of events," or that they fail to resemble "the natural mechanism."[93] The achievements of the American training studies challenge whether there is such a thing as structural change in the Piagetian sense; whether there is such a natural course of events such as the theory claims; and whether there is such a natural mechanism. It is bizarre to question the results of these studies, and to continue to reassert the superiority of preferred methods of teaching, on the grounds that the correctness of the theory leads to such conclusions. It is the correctness of the theory that these results challenge.

Discovery-learning and associated "active" learning methods are rarely discussed as one among a series of pedagogically useful methods. Rather we are presented with a Manichaean world in which we may choose discovery-learning or "traditional" forms of education. "In the traditional schools, said Piaget, adults are the source of all morality and all truths. The child merely obeys the adult in the moral

realm and recites things in the intellectual realm."[94] In these traditional schools we do not have active discovery-learning because it
is accepted that "for the teacher to state some fact or principle is to
teach it."[95] Similarly, our choice apparently is between discovery-
learning and "active doers" or "traditional" methods and "passive
recipients."

"Passivity," we are told, "is the enemy of intellectual and social
development. It is everyone's enemy. . . . The effort against it must
be energetic and unrelentless (*sic*) if the mind is to be free to act
upon the environment of the school. It is less important to concern
ourselves with the accumulation of a bcdy of information than it is
to sensitize teachers to the way children think and to the way thinking develops."[96] We may be energetic and relentless in our efforts to
extirpate this enemy, but how are we to know whether the apparently
passive, well-behaved child is not at that moment having a wonderful
idea? What should we have done to Socrates standing in a puddle,
trancelike with thought? The point is that no one is against all these
desirable things, the serious problems lie in knowing how to further
them. The Manichaean rhetoric that now is uttered by Piagetian
neoprogressives, as it recently was uttered by Deweyian progressives,
simply does not help.

Further evidence that Piaget's theory is not being treated as a
theory in education, but rather as a sacred text, is available in the
kinds of absolute claims constantly made about what children and
teachers must and must not do. We are told that for learning to take
place "looking and listening . . . are not good enough";[97] that children must "interact *directly* with the subject matter and not merely
read or hear about it";[98] that social cooperation is "an imperative
necessity of modern education";[99] and that "you cannot further understanding in a child simply by talking to him."[100]

The first observation the educator not immersed in Piagetian
theory and Rousseauian ideology should make about these kinds of
absolute statements is that they are nonsense. Assertions like these
are usually made in the context of implicitly contrasting "Piagetian"
methods with "traditional" methods. If we take the Piagetian claims
at face value we must assume that traditional methods have never
taught anything to anyone. Of course one can promote understanding
by talking with children; social cooperation, in the Piagetian sense,
may obviously be desirable in some circumstances but is obviously
not an "imperative necessity"; if we can deal only with subject matter
that children can interact directly with, then we wipe everything
outside the immediate environment from the curriculum; that "look-

ing and listening" are inadequate for effective learning is demonstrated to be false every moment of the day.

Obviously these Piagetians would claim to be saying something much more sophisticated than these out-of-context quotations suggest. The sophistication, however, involves their articulation in terms of Piaget's theory's claims about learning. But it is these claims which, this section has argued, are not supported by the available evidence.

READINESS

Being "ready" simply means that children have available the cognitive abilities which are prerequisite for mastery of some new skill, concept, or knowledge. As an educational concept it has had, and continues to have, a strong tendency to tautology: "Those children who were ready did very well."[101] For the notion of readiness to serve as a useful explanation of learning or failure to learn requires that it be tied to a scheme that outlines a necessary sequence in which things must be learned. Piaget's developmental theory is claimed to be just such a scheme.

One obvious use of the theory would be as a guide to the teacher in knowing what and how to teach children at any particular age. "The task of the teacher is to figure out what the learner already knows and how he reasons in order to ask the right question at the right time so that the learner can build his own knowledge."[102] The teacher may thus be armed with detailed knowledge of the developmental stages, and the theory of the developmental process. Moving from the precision with which it may be stated in a book, and from the clarity achieved while sitting at one's desk learning it, to the reality of standing among thirty different little human beings, undermines somewhat the utility of the theory's precision. One may know that optimal learning occurs if one presents a concept some part of which the child can assimilate but some part of which will require accommodation. Unfortunately, some children respond better when there is a relatively large amount to accommodate, others when there is only a little. Also, of course, the teacher cannot know with any precision "where" the children are at any particular time. And, if one is teaching social studies, it may not be very useful to know that twenty-five percent of the class have just acquired conservation of number, fifty percent have acquired conservation of weight, and the remainder have acquired conservation of volume.

This may seem to suggest too restrictive a view of the theory's possible guidance. It is rather, I think, a way of trying to clarify a restriction in the guidance the theory *can* offer. This is a restriction touched on in chapter 1 where the psychological focus on certain kinds of concepts was noted. It is necessary to consider here how Piaget's theory focuses on only a very restricted range within this restricted focus. It seems to me most important to bear constantly in mind the nature of this restriction when trying to extrapolate from his theory to education.

For children from about age five and up, Piaget's theory deals mainly with the development of formal logico-mathematical thinking. It needs to be remembered, in the face of the generality Piaget claims for this slender strand in the complex thread of children's thinking, that it represents only a small part of the intellectual equipment children bring to making sense of the world and their experience. Indeed, for preadolescent children, it seems to be a very small part of the way they derive meaning from the world, and does little to account for what they find interesting. Logical abilities play a more significant part in thinking during adolescence and later, but even then they are only a small part of our thinking apparatus, and make only a restricted contribution to how we compose meaning in the world.

One pernicious effect of Piaget's theory when imported into education is to exaggerate the importance of these formal logical tools which children have available for making sense of things. The constraints on young children's formal logical abilities are read very frequently as general constraints on their thinking. The typical result of the overemphasis on these formal logical skills—an overemphasis encouraged by Piaget's off-stage rhetoric rather than his descriptive theory—is conclusions about vast ranges of human knowledge and experience that are judged to be beyond children's understanding.

The foregoing is an argument about the proper interpretation of Piaget's theory, but there is a prior question still to be dealt with, one we had to leave aside in chapter 1. Even if the teacher standing among thirty children cannot use the precision the theory potentially provides, we must nevertheless allow that the theory does offer some useful guidance about an important level of constraints and abilities of children's thinking. Even if we are only willing to grant that the utility of the theory for the practicing teacher amounts to suggesting that abstract concepts and prolonged teacher verbalization are likely to be ineffective with young children, then this is of value. It tells us something about what and how children are ready to learn. In addition, we must surely accept that in planning various kinds of teaching activities even more precision can be extracted from the theory, and that it provides guidance in the analysis of the appropriateness of already available materials and methods. For even so little to be granted, however, the theory must obviously be accurate in its claims about the stages, and about the necessary sequence by which children progress gradually through them. Particularly, Piaget's claim that children's thinking progresses by the coalescence of sets of schemata into larger systems and groups which determine the general manner of thinking at any particular stage has to be true. The main individual differences the educator has to be concerned with are simply the differences in the time taken to pass through the stages. As we have seen, recent empirical tests put these claims in doubt.

Another foundation of Piaget's theory as a readiness model is his development/learning distinction, and we saw earlier the insecurity of this. What, then, are we left with? When hearing novice teachers being taught about Piaget's assimilation/accommodation model, I am reminded of the old-fashioned teacher's tired advice to the novice, before disappearing behind his newspaper, "Don't make it too hard, and don't make it too easy."[103] This, too, might come as an apparently valuable insight in judging children's readiness, but, standing among those thirty active and different young people, it is not at all clear what counts as too easy or too hard, nor is it clear what they have assimilated or what they can accommodate. What we seem to be left with is some technical language turned jargon, and a dubious set of implications based on a dubious part of an increasingly insecure theory. That it is inappropriate to teach certain things in certain ways to children at certain ages is clear—what is not clear is that Piaget's theory can tell us any more than can observation and experience informed by theories as old as Plato's. It is also clear that uncritical use of Piaget's theory can and does seriously mislead educational practice by persuading teachers that sets of children are not "ready" for particular knowledge.

CURRICULUM DESIGN

"The first and most general principle of curriculum planning should be to respect the sequence of development of children in general, and of individual children in particular."[104] This represents what we may call the weak claim made by Piagetians. The stronger form is represented in claims like the following: "the teacher must understand the sequences of development before he can further them."[105] Now clearly such claims overlap with some of those considered in the previous section. The use of Piaget's theory in designing a curriculum involves decisions about what curriculum content children are ready to learn at different stages of their development. But additional issues are brought to light by considering attempts to construct general curricula based on Piaget's theory. Below I will consider the uses of the theory in designing curricula for the average range of children, and then for very poor learners.

Respecting the sequence of development in individual children is a principle one can hardly criticize in general. The problems arise when we see specifications of just what is meant by development—development of what?—and how respect is expressed. Typically in Piagetian literature on curriculum design respecting development means restricting what one teaches to conform with the logico-mathematical conceptual constraints detailed in Piaget's theory.[106] Development means the development of those logico-mathematical capacities when uninfluenced by systematic teaching. Given even this minimal elaboration of the principle, a number of the points raised in previous sections become relevant here as objections.

We have considered some of the weaknesses of Piaget's distinction between learning and development. From that discussion we may conclude that a respectful waiting on the spontaneous development of Piagetian cognitive capacities involves a degree of non-interventionism that seems educationally counterproductive. We have seen evidence concerning the teachability of Piagetian developmental concepts. Given this, it seems appropriate to consider the systematic teaching of such concepts or the waiting for their more or less spontaneous development as a curriculum decision to be made on educational grounds. We have seen that Piaget's theory is descriptive of a developmental process that is to some significant degree influenced or determined by forms of education and socialization. To the degree that this is so, a curriculum which is respectful of Piaget's stages is designed to reproduce forms of development influenced by, and appropriate to, a past social and educational context. We have seen that the individual's progress through the stages is not as regular or predictable as the theory asserts. A curriculum respectful of the theory will thus impose a uniform pattern on individuals whose educational development might better proceed by diverse paths. We have seen that the speed of individual development through Piaget's stages is only one of the huge range of individual differences the educator has to take account of. A curriculum respectful of the theory will recognize poor learners only as being at an earlier stage in the developmental process, and will restrict remediation to finding an individual's stage and trying to work up through the stages from there. We have seen that Piaget's logico-mathematical concepts are only a portion of the mental apparatus the child brings to making sense of the world and experience. A curriculum respectful of Piaget's stages views these logico-mathematical concepts as prescribing constraints on what can be learned, and as providing the basis on which the curriculum can be built.

Now, of course, typical teachers will not have this disproportionate respect for the theory, even if they know much about it. But the design of curricula is influenced by those who often are committed to the truth of some theory. And certainly there is no shortage of "Piagetian" curricula being designed and implemented. Some are general. In some cases the influence of the theory is felt in more particular revisions of an extant curriculum. We can see how parts of the theory can lead to general curriculum changes in such inferences from the theory as the claim that it "is important to avoid premature accommodations," and that implementing this principle may "require the complete absence of symbolic forms until such times as the child asks questions which indicate a readiness for the next stage, or such times as a Piaget developmental test indicates that his concrete understanding is firm enough to risk a new accommodation."[107] This is, needless to say, a remarkably bold recommendation running counter to what has usually been considered educationally desirable.[108] One would not expect such a recommendation to be based on anything but a bedrock of hard evidence.

This kind of disproportionate respect for the theory, and for implications for educational practice which seem to follow from the theory, is most evident in the apparent assumption that Piaget's logico-mathematical concepts constitute the sum or center of children's thinking. Encouraged by Piaget's own rhetoric, in which education is posited as ideally a subsidiary aid to the development of these conceptual capacities, Piagetian curriculum designers tend constantly to see the curriculum as an instrument for helping children achieve ever higher levels of Piagetian concepts. That is, the curriculum becomes an instrument for the development of this restricted range of concepts.[109] There is something odd and surely confused here. The development of these logico-mathematical concepts is supposed to take place spontaneously without educational intervention, and Piaget often waxes eloquent about the independence of this natural process.[110] He waxes equally eloquent, however, about the purpose of education being to "learn to develop." This ambiguity, this confusion, pervades Piagetian writing about curriculum design.[111] The argument that this is an abuse of the theory, and not a proper target for serious criticism, would be reasonable if the abuse were not so pervasive. The argument against this tendency to substitute psychological development, as described in Piaget's theory, for education is simple but devastating: "If Piaget in his developmental experiments demonstrates that at a certain age a certain operation exists, it does not have to be taught anymore. However, if the child does not yet have the operation at his disposal it cannot be taught."[112]

Another side of this abuse is evident in applications of Piaget's theory to mathematics curricula in particular. Piaget and Inhelder have argued that by early school years the typical child has developed the concepts upon which much Euclidean geometry is based.[113] This leads many Piagetian curriculum designers to conclude that Euclidean geometry *should* be introduced into the elementary mathematics curriculum.[114] Needless to say, this is an educational decision properly made on other grounds.

Mathematics is the curriculum area where Piaget's theory seems to promise clear and direct educational implications, and it is probably the area in which the theory has had most influence and in which most work has been done. A careful look at these curricula recommendations, however, shows the tenuousness and insecurity of the connections to the theory, and justifies Sullivan's conclusion: "There are no clear guidelines in Piaget's theory which indicate the steps that one must take in achieving certain concepts in arithmetic."[115]

The first principle of Piagetian curriculum design is to match the curriculum and forms of instruction to the child's level of development. The individual child's level of development is measured in terms of tasks a child can successfully perform alone. Teaching a curriculum is typically done in groups with the teacher continually providing support and assistance to understanding. This raises a problem which may be shown by use of Vygotsky's distinction between what he calls "actual developmental level" and "zone of proximal development." Vygotsky notes:

> In studies of children's mental development it is generally assumed that only those things that children can do on their own are indicative of mental abilities. We give children a battery of tests or a variety of tasks of varying degrees of difficulty, and we judge the extent of their mental development on the basis of how they solve them and at what level of difficulty. On the other hand, if we offer leading questions or

show how the problem is to be solved and the child then solves it, or if the teacher initiates the solution and the child completes it or solves it in collaboration with other children—in short, if the child barely misses an independent solution of the problem—the solution is not regarded as indicative of his mental development.[116]

Imagine two children who, when alone, can perform on tasks used to measure mental development at a level equivalent to, say, a normal eight-year-old. When working with a teacher who in some way or other uses pedagogical skills to help the children, one child is able to deal with problems up to a nine-year-old and the other one up to a twelve-year-old level. The zone of proximal development "is the distance between the actual development level as determined by independent problem solving and the level of potential development as determined through problem solving under adult guidance or in collaboration with more capable peers." In addition, Vygotsky notes, "psychologists have shown that a person can imitate only that which is within her developmental level. For example, if a child is having difficulty with a problem in arithmetic and the teacher solves it on the blackboard, the child may grasp the solution in an instant. But if the teacher were to solve a problem in higher mathematics, the child would not be able to understand the solution no matter how many times she imitated it." Further, he points out, "When it was first shown that the capability of children with equal levels of mental development to learn under a teacher's guidance varied to a high degree, it became apparent that those children were not mentally the same age."[117]

Even if Piaget's theory is correct in detail, and even if we could develop assessment instruments from it allowing a precise placing of any individual child at some particular step of the developmental process, we would still lack a crucial datum of major importance to the educator. That datum may be expressed in Vygotsky's terms as some index of the child's "zone of proximal development." That is, given two children, or indeed thirty children, who may be at the same step of a Piagetian developmental scale, we know only a little therefrom about how good they are as learners, and how well they may be able to perform under skilled pedagogy. In a group of thirty children performing independently at, say, an eight-year level, we may expect their zones of proximal development to vary from eight years to maybe fourteen years. This notion of a zone of proximal development may seem somewhat exotic, but it represents something I think teachers will recognize immediately.

The most evident result on educational practice of Piaget's claim that learning is constrained by development is the systematic under-estimation of what children can learn. Piagetian curricula are curricula of constraints; their designers' eyes are ever open to what children supposedly cannot do; their implementers are concerned with making sure that supposedly prerequisite developments have taken place, and they are somewhat fearful "to risk a new accommodation." In Vygotsky's words: "in normal children, learning which is oriented towards developmental levels that have already been reached is ineffective from the viewpoint of a child's overall development. It does not aim for a new stage of the developmental process but rather lags behind this process. Thus, the notion of a zone of proximal development enables us to propound a new formula, namely that the only 'good learning' is that which is in advance of development."[118]

We have good reason to doubt Piaget's learning/development distinction. Curricula which assume its truth must constrain learning to developmental concepts which have already been achieved.[119] This is precisely what Vygotsky argues, with good reason, is "ineffective from the viewpoint of a child's overall development." In Vygotsky's scheme, learning does not have to wait on development; rather "it creates the zone of proximal development."[120] This notion is akin to that briefly sketched in chapter 1: whether one sees teaching as generating "semantic spaces" or "zones of proximal development" into which the developmental process is absorbed, such theoretical positions conform better with common experience. In terms of designing curricula, theories of zones of proximal development or semantic space generation leave us with a degree of imprecision that is perhaps little improvement upon "don't make it too hard and don't make it too easy." They say only that one should keep some way ahead of the child's level of achievement, and insist that "level" is rather vague, somewhat elastic, and may be extended by good teaching. But they do help to highlight the fact that the precision promised by Piaget's theory is a gift educators accept at their peril.

The educational poverty of Piaget's theory is perhaps most evident when we consider individual differences among learners. Despite the rhetoric of Piagetians, the theory describes very poor learners only in terms of their unusual slowness in developing through the unvarying sequence of stages and substages. The options for attempts at remediation, then, are restricted to trying to help such poor learners move step by step through the sequence. Thus, the Piagetian curriculum for very poor learners is the sequence of activities and concepts in terms of which Piaget describes the developmental process: for example, "The developmental stages and substages suggested to the authors ways of delineating a curriculum that would move children step by step through the natural developmental course. A framework for a preschool curriculum for disadvantaged children was, therefore, derived from Piaget's theory."[121] The sequence of activities in such curricula is designed precisely to stimulate children to move from sensorimotor experiences to "foster the development of representative imagery which could then be the referents for spoken words and later for written language."[122] The aim of such curricula is a "firming up," "filling in," or properly establishing sensorimotor or preoperational achievements whose prior skipping or only partial mastery is presumed to be the cause of poor learners' general inability to learn.

A first objection to such programs may be made by extending Vygotsky's previous argument. In the 1930s he wrote:

> Formerly, it was believed that by using tests, we determine the mental development level with which education should reckon and whose limits it should not exceed. This procedure oriented learning toward yesterday's development, toward the developmental stages already completed. The error of this view was discovered earlier in practice than in theory. It is demonstrated most clearly in the teaching of mentally retarded children. Studies have established that mentally retarded children are not very capable of abstract thinking. From this the pedagogy of the special school drew the seemingly correct conclusion that all teaching of such children should be based on the use of concrete, look-and-do methods. And yet a considerable amount of experience with this method resulted in profound disillusionment. It turned out that a teaching system based soley on concreteness—one that eliminated from teaching everything associated with abstract thinking—not only failed to help retarded children overcome their innate handicaps but also reinforced their handicaps by accustoming children exclusively to concrete thinking and thus suppressing the rudiments of any abstract thought that such children still have. Precisely because retarded children, when left to themselves, will never achieve well-elaborated forms of abstract thought, the school should make every effort to push them in that direction and to develop in them what is intrinsically lacking in their own development. In the current practices of special schools for retarded children, we can observe a beneficial shift away from this concept of concreteness, one that restores look-and-do methods to their proper role. Concreteness is now seen as necessary and unavoidable only as a stepping stone for developing abstract thinking—as a means, not as an end in itself.[123]

A second objection is that while such curricula may claim to be based on Piaget's description of the natural course of development, the theory offers no support to the expectation that one can remediate learning difficulties by, as it were, going back and teaching early cognitive developments. A third objection is that there is no good reason to suppose that all poor learners' difficulties are due to their somehow having skipped or scanted some early developmental substages in the sequence followed by those concepts Piaget's theory is about. Obviously anything which might help in the training and education of very poor learners is worth trying. There is little point, however, in laboring the scientific contribution Piaget's theory can make to this persisting problem. Such curricula attempt to mirror in instruction parts of the theory which are increasingly dubious, and they are, in any case, connected to the theory by gratuitous assumptions. The disappointing results of such curricula to date are a matter of regret to everyone, but of surprise only to those faithful to the ideology which Piaget's theory is used to serve when imported into education.

Although few comprehensive Piagetian curricula have been in operation long enough to have undergone adequate testing, the Messianic claims frequently made for what will happen if we use such curricula seem unsupported by the evidence available so far. Given the extremity of typical Piagetian claims about what is educationally necessary and about the destructive confusions inherent in "traditional" forms of schooling, one would expect evident improvements in children's learning after a few years of Piagetian schooling. Yet, as Brainerd concludes in an examination of the data available from evaluation studies of the four major Piagetian programs: "The evaluation data . . . have failed to show any differences between Piagetian instruction and other curricula."[124] And, indeed, in the case of one of the two Piagetian schools that have undergone detailed evaluation in comparison with a traditional school, Brainerd notes that "those few comparisons which revealed differences tended to favor the traditional group."[125]

Conclusion

HOW IS Piaget's theory used as a guide to educational practice? My answer has been that it does so by reducing educational development to the development of the particular cognitive capacities Piaget's theory purportedly describes. In the process we see a constant deformation of education. We are told such things as: "The goal of education is not to increase the amount of knowledge, but to create the possibilities for the child to invent and discover."[126] Creating possibilities for the child to invent and discover may form a useful pedagogical technique to be employed in achieving educational goals. To suggest that a single pedagogical technique should be the goal of education is, of course, grotesque. But even when we move beyond the logico-mathematical structures we read definitional statements such as: "To educate means to adapt the individual to the surrounding social environment."[127] We might possibly consider this, with qualifications, as a goal of socialization, or perhaps indoctrination. The context of Piaget's theoretical work and the centrality of the notion of adaptation, leads readily to such claims. They are claims which, if acted upon, reduce and deform the process of education. This deformation of education seems to me the commonest result of Piagetians' common practice of accepting Piaget's theory as though it carried clear implications for education. That this "psychological fallacy" leads to a deformation of education might reasonably be expected, since Piaget's theory is, properly, concerned to exclude precisely the realm of cultural attainments which, again properly, forms a central focus for education.

One of the most interesting general questions remaining about Piaget's theory is: what is it describing? That it is not a description of some natural, necessary, developmental process—development being distinguished from learning as Piaget claims—seems increasingly clear. It does not, we might say, describe a constraint of our nature. The logico-mathematical structures are not descriptions of some "natural psychological reality"; indeed, the inadequacy of the characterization of the structures has led increasingly to accepting the tasks themselves as operational definitions of the stages.

More sophisticated Piagetians may consider much of my discussion of Piagetian practices aimed at straw men. Some will claim that Piaget's theory indeed offers only, say, guidance in the analysis of the appropriateness of curriculum content, or in evaluation, or in dealing with learning disabilities. That is, in the massive educational literature that claims Piaget as some kind of source, there are many different and occasionally conflicting claims about what the theory implies for education. The brief discussions of Piagetian practices are not aimed at straw men. Many real-life people are writing and teaching the kinds of things I have criticized (and, it may be noticed, quoted). Piaget's theory is commonly taught to teachers in training and there are courses, or parts of many courses, devoted to the theory in departments of education throughout the Western world. So while some of the claims of some Piagetians embarrass other Piagetians, it should be noted that the kinds of practices and claims I have criticized are commonly advocated. The more radical part of my argument is, I think, aimed appropriately at all attempts to read from Piaget's theory to education—however refinedly or sophisticatedly.

All the above criticism aimed at Piaget's theory and Piagetian educators' use of it, should be concluded with a note about the importance of the theory. Criticism is appreciation. If Piaget is occasionally inconsistent and plain wrong, and if his narratives occasionally stumble and mutter incoherently, we remember that we do not expect geniuses primarily to be clear, consistent, and right. We can teach almost anyone to be clear, consistent, and right. We expect geniuses to practice that magic which pulls new ideas out of the air. We need only recall the common image of cognitive development before Piaget's work to see how well he has fulfilled such expectations.

4/ Educationally Useful Theories

Two Theories: Similarities and Differences

IN THIS chapter I will use Plato's and Piaget's theories to reflect on issues raised in the previous chapters, and learn whether we might reach some firmer conclusions about what kind of theory is good for educational practice.

Because it is the differences between the two theories that are of most interest here, we might note similarities briefly and generally. Both Plato's and Piaget's theory present an image of children's development that involves progress through a series of stages during which understanding of the world is qualitatively different. The most general feature of this process is the move from concrete, perception–dominated forms of thinking to a kind of abstract, formal thinking that frees the thinker from confusions and distortions inherent in the previous stages. Both developmental theories are couched in terms which involve claims about learning and motivation at the various stages.

In considering differences between the two theories it may be as well to begin by discussing differences in the treatment they have received in the previous two chapters. They have hardly been dealt with equally. It may appear that Plato's theory has been treated to an expansive generosity of interpretation, while Piaget's has been subjected to a mean and narrowly critical attempt to undermine any connection between it and what are claimed as Piagetian educational practices. The same interpretative generosity applied to Piaget's theory would surely have endorsed all the Piagetians' educational claims which have been criticized as theoretically or empirically baseless? The interpretation of Plato's theory, however, is not an interpretation *from* his theory *to* educational practice, because his theory is couched *in terms of* an educational program. The interpretation, based on his clearly expressed educational principles, is from educational practices appropriate to an ancient city-state of primitive scientific achievements, to a modern postindustrial democratic society. The interpretation Piagetians make from Piaget's psychological theory to educational practice is, I have tried to show, a different kind of leap altogether.

A more fundamental inequity may seem to follow from my not focusing attention on the metaphysics and epistemology which form the backing for Plato's educational prescriptions. If I had, it may be claimed, I would have found that Plato's metaphysics have no more implications for education than Piaget's abstract theory. Plato, after all, did not draw his developmental model out of the air: there is a whole ontology, theory of mind, and a psychology underlying, and *informing*, it. Indeed, Plato's developmental scheme rests on a psychological theory, so how can I accept his as an educational theory and dismiss Piaget's as having no implications for education? Anyone can assert an educational developmental model, prescribing a proper set of stages, so why should we take Plato's seriously?

First, let us dispense with the objection that Plato's educational prescriptions, no less than Piaget's, are based on a psychological theory. The stages of Plato's educational program do not represent a psychological theory in the sense meant today. He is not concerned to describe what is the normal or necessary course of human development along one of its dimensions. His scheme is a prescription which, he clearly thought, is within the bounds of what is psychologically, and logically, possible. It is not a prescription *based on* a psychological theory, nor a scheme resulting from drawing implications from a psychological theory.

But if the prescription does not depend on a psychological theory, it depends on an articulated metaphysical position and an epistemology which, for present purposes, play an analogous role to that of Piaget's psychological theory. The prescription is to do certain things in educating people because the world, reality, is conceived to be a certain way. If reality is not that way—if Plato's metaphysics are wrong—then can we not criticize his educational prescriptions on grounds analogous to those on which I have criticized Piagetians'?

Do we take Plato's educational recommendations seriously because of his epistemology, ontology, and metaphysics? I certainly do not. Indeed, I know little about his epistemology, ontology, and metaphysics. We should take Plato's educational recommendations seriously, it seems to me, because he describes an end-product which has desirable qualities and prescribes a plausible and practical curriculum for gradually constituting that end-product. The claim that we should take Plato's educational recommendations seriously *because* they are based on a complex metaphysical position, or that we should refuse to take them seriously because there is something wrong with that position, seems to me analogous to the error of seeking educational implications in a psychological theory. If the latter is the psychological fallacy, the former is the philosophical fallacy. I would be more readily open to criticism if I were doing to Plato's theory what I condemn Piagetians for doing to Piaget's.

So this is to acknowledge an inequity in the treatment of the two theorists. It is not because of the epistemological status of the supposed "backing" for the educational prescriptions that we do or do not take them seriously. My general claim in this book is that an educational theory is not something which can exist only as an appendage to a psychological theory or a metaphysics. The reason for taking Plato's prescriptions seriously is that they are couched in the context of an educational theory—necessary constituents of which I will explore further below. The inequity in the treatment is due to the fact that Plato provides an educational theory and Piaget and his followers do not. I have been concerned to show in the latter case that the lack of an educational theory means that prescriptions which are supposed "implications" from a psychological theory deform education.

Further, it might be thought that Plato's prescriptions are of practical value only to people intent on setting up a society such as the one described in *The Republic*. But, again, it seems simplistic to see Plato's educational scheme as merely instrumental to the support of his social system. The social system also reflects his estimate of the best way to support what he clearly considers to be the best kind of person. That is, he does not start with an ideal social system and then manufacture different classes of people to fit it. It is as sensible to say that he started with a realistic image of what was educationally possible for different kinds of people, and fashioned a social system that would best support each group. Clearly both these views are simple-minded. Plato has worked dialectically, designing a system that could optimally support the best forms of human life and in turn be sustained by people living those various forms of life. In abstracting his educational scheme, then, one is not merely abstracting something that has meaning only if one wants to produce guardians; Plato clearly considered *noesis* to be the most worthwhile educational achievement regardless of the particular social system.

But is this worthwhileness not also tied inextricably to Plato's ontology and epistemology? Are Plato's prescriptions about how to educate people to be sensitive and courageous in their search for secure knowledge made irrelevant by our not sharing his image of the securest form of knowledge? Although this may not make his proposals irrelevant, it is equally not irrelevant that the *noesis* stage represents the end of a training program designed to enable its products to search for a kind of knowledge which we think does not exist. The methods of inquiry, therefore, are designed for a purpose we would consider fruitless, and consequently we should have no interest in the prescriptions. This, too, seems rather simple-minded. The practical value of Plato's educational scheme is independent of ontology and epistemology. As with the social system, Plato does not start with an epistemology and ontology and infer his image of human beings and their best education from these. Rather, he works dialectically; so in abstracting his educational scheme, one is not abstracting something that has meaning only as a part of his epistemology and ontology.

These are complicated issues, and I want only to suggest that Plato's educational scheme is not just something that is *implied by* or *instrumental to*, his political philosophy, his epistemology, and his ontology. It is equally sensible, or simple-minded, to see his political philosophy, epistemology, and ontology as supporting his educational scheme. The move from an epistemological scheme to an educational prescription is complicated; the former can never simply imply the latter. The move is similar to that claimed for the educational implications that are supposed to follow from Piaget's psychological theory, or other theories of learning, motivation, and so on. The move is far from obvious and the educational schemes that result can never be claimed as valid on the ground that they are implied by the psychological theory or the epistemological scheme, nor can they be casually rejected because some claimed theoretical support is undermined. The move from psychology or epistemology to education is never simple. That is, the educational scheme has to be considered in its own right; so we may consider Plato's educational scheme in its own right, abstracted from the epistemology, ontology, and political philosophy with which it was designed in concert.

A first difference between the two theories, then, from the point of view of our educational concerns, is that Plato's developmental theory is couched in terms of an educational program; Piaget's in terms of certain psychological forms. Piaget seeks to describe *what is the case* about the development of certain psychological forms; Plato describes *what ought to be done* to produce the best educated people. For Plato, his image of what is the case represents only one of the constraints within which he can prescribe what ought to be done. For Piaget, the description of what is the case represents the end of his inquiry. Piaget's enterprise is scientific; Plato's educational, social, and political. Another way of indicating this difference is to say that a psychological theory such as Piaget's is about phenomena that exist in the world; there are psychological processes and patterns of behavior that the researcher may seek to describe and explain. The process Plato describes can exist only if one follows his prescriptions and brings it into existence. There is no such thing as a natural educational process out there which we can discover, describe, and explain. The problem for the educator is not to discover the nature of the process, but, rather, to prescribe what one should do to create an ideal or good process of education.

A second, related, difference between the two theories concerns what they view as necessary to reach their final stages. Piaget views the achievement of formal operations as occurring routinely as a result of appropriate interactions with a reasonably rich physical, social, and cultural environment. Plato views the achievement of *noesis* as occurring rarely and as a result of a long and disciplined program of study.

Thirdly, we may note a series of differences in the way we can view the ideal end-products of the two processes. The end-product of Plato's developmental process is an educated person; of Piaget's a person with formal operations. An educated person is able to think in a sophisticated way and exercises these thinking skills on a range of topics and problems of immediate and persisting importance; knowledge of what constitutes such topics is a part of erudition— knowing what it is worthwhile to think about. A person who has developed formal operations may entirely lack erudition, and so lack any sense of how best to use those thinking skills. The end-product of Plato's developmental process is a kind of person; of Piaget's, a kind of knowing or thinking. Plato provides a conception of an ideal person in an ideal society; Piaget provides a conception of how scientific truth is normally rediscovered or reinvented (or learned) by each individual.

Plato's *noesis* stage, however, while in one sense an end-product of the process, is so only in the limited sense of being the stage at which proper inquiry may begin. It is the starting point for activities which justify the educational process that leads up to it. That is, the process is not necessary except in so far as one wants to achieve the particular end of *noesis*. Formal operations in no sense *justify* the preceding stages. It just so happens that this is the final stage of a process which is necessary in its sequence. The end-product is not an aim, in the sense that there may be alternatives which might rather be aimed for.

What and How Should We Teach?

WITH PLATO's theory we have little difficulty deciding *what* we should teach at each stage. A function of the theory is to tell us. Plato provides us not only with examples of appropriate content, but with a set of principles which enable us to decide on other content. These principles are sufficiently adequate, I think, to allow us—two thousand years later in unimaginably different circumstances—to construct a distinctively Platonic curriculum.

Piaget's theory offers the educator no guidance in deciding appropriate curriculum content for each of his developmental stages.

Plato rarely discusses explicitly the pedagogical methods appropriate for his different stages. He does tell us to incorporate what is to be learned by young children in stories and games, and recommends the use of concrete materials. For the *noesis* stage there is no shortage of examples of the dialectical method he recommends. But apart from these, he seems to assume that sensitivity to the different needs of different age groups, as characterized in his stage model, represents as much as can sensibly be said about pedagogical techniques. Perhaps he considers appropriate techniques to be so dependent on differences in individual teachers' personalities that detailed prescriptions about such things are pointless. Different teachers, because of their personalities, will have success in teaching the same material using widely different pedagogical techniques. (And it might also be concluded that the modern stress on pedagogical techniques and environments—usually in the absence of educational theory—is fruitless.) Plato's main conclusions about *how* we should teach are embodied in his characterizations of the different stages children go through in becoming educated. Technique is summed up in having, as Bruner puts it, the courtesy, and, one might add, the self-interested good sense, to translate knowledge into the appropriate form to be meaningful and interesting at the appropriate stage. That is, the developmental form of the theory *is* a set of recommendations about *how* we should teach. At the educational level we can see again how psychologically distinct topics like "development" and "motivation" coalesce.

Piaget's theory has no implications for how we should teach. Even the recommendation that children be active discoverers, while having obvious educational merit in certain circumstances, can hardly be claimed as an insight indebted to Piaget's theory. It did not escape Plato, nor the Egyptians before him, nor Montessori, Dewey, Susan Isaacs, and many others. The novel aspect of the general educational recommendation that we *can* trace to Piaget's theory—via Piagetians' "implication"—is a dogmatic claim about the necessity of active discovery which, we have seen, is neither logically connected to the psychological theory nor has it empirical support.

The Nature of an Educational Theory

I. PSYCHOLOGY AND CONSTRAINTS OF NATURE

It has been claimed that Piaget's theory has no implications for education, that his enterprise involves the scientific aim to describe what is the case about individual cognitive development, and that what is the case about individual cognitive development provides one of the constraints within which an educational theory may prescribe what ought to be done. There may seem a contradiction between the first claim and the other two. If Piaget's theory tells us what is the case, and this is a constraint within which educational theories must function, then surely his theory provides guidance to the educator? This returns us to the fundamental difficulty faced by psychology's ambition to be more rigorously scientific.

Those areas of inquiry that we call the human sciences, of which psychology is one, have constantly to acknowledge a fundamental insecurity, compared with the physical sciences. The physical sciences have achieved some success in describing what is the case about various natural phenomena. Psychology has had the ambition to emulate this success by describing what is the case about human behavior and the human *psyche*. It has claimed some successes in generating laws of behavior. These, to be accepted as properly scientific, should describe what are constraints of nature. The problem is that the more secure-seeming laws of human behavior so far formulated are not interesting; they do not impinge on those complex realms where educational discourse focuses. Piaget, at least, is telling us things that are interesting about some part of the human behavior. But if triviality is psychology's Scylla, Piaget is being sucked into its Charybdis of insecurity.

The inconvenience of human behavior for psychology's ambition to be scientific after the fashion of physics is that it assimilates into its essence the history of the culture to which it accommodates. The history of a stone is irrelevant to the physicist's ability to describe the laws by which it behaves, but the history of an individual *psyche*—its personal history or experience and that of the cultural group which shapes it—is a profound determinant of behavior. (We will return to this topic in detail in the next chapter.)

This returns us to the point touched on a number of times in the previous chapter. What is Piaget describing? If indeed he is describing constraints of nature on the development of certain forms of cognition, we would have to acknowledge that there may be some limited lessons the educator should draw from his theory. But one of the current fascinations of the theory concerns the degree to which it is culture-bound. It seems clear from cross-cultural studies that Piaget is not describing a pure constraint of our nature. Given that he is describing something in some degree determined by culture, it would be foolish for educators to accept the description as something to which they should seek to make children conform. For Piaget's theory to be able to have such an influence on education we would want to know not only what is the case in certain circumstances, but what is necessarily the case, and why.

The apparent contradiction indicated at the beginning of this section is resolved in the conclusion that Piaget's scientific ambition to describe what is the case about cognitive development is at present unfulfilled; he does not provide us with knowledge of a constraint of nature to which education must conform. This is not, of course, to accuse Piaget of some failure of which he was unaware—the point is to indicate what conditions are necessary before educators need be constrained by the claims of his theory, and to indicate that such conditions have not been met.

This is not to say, obviously, that there are no constraints to which educators must conform. There are some clear logical constraints in the way subject matter can be presented, and we can accept, with qualifications, as a psychological constraint, the move from concrete, perception-dominated thinking to abstract, formal thinking. It is this common observation that Plato incorporates into his theory, adding some refinement as he does so, and we are probably justified in accepting this normal development as a fairly secure general guide. An educational theory, then, should probably include a concrete-abstract continuum, but otherwise may feel a certain confidence in human plasticity and a consequent freedom to prescribe what seems logically prerequisite to the achievement of the desired end-product.

Therefore, converting psychology's *is* into an educational *ought*, especially when that "is" does not describe a constraint of nature, is not only logically illegitimate, but is educationally destructive.

II. EDUCATION AND CULTURE—BOUNDEDNESS

The end-product of the educational process Plato prescribes is a kind of person, compounded of thinking skills and erudition, who is a competent social and political agent. In prescribing an educational program, which is what an educational theory does in telling us what to teach, when, and how, one must deal with the social and political context for which the child is intended. Educational theorizing is in part a political activity. This does not mean that educational decisions must be made on political grounds, but rather that an educational program must be informed in some sense by the *polis* the child is being prepared to inhabit or change. Indeed, in prescribing an educational program there may be some conflict between the interests of a culture which encourages individual variety and expression of that variety, and a social and political structure whose smooth working requires a certain conformity. That Plato's program seems designed to reproduce an idealized version of Plato, does not distinguish it from Rousseau's program which seems designed to produce an idealized Rousseau, nor from any other theorist's program. Educational theorizing seems inevitably to involve a portion of covert autobiography.

The two points here—that educational theories involve social, political, cultural, aesthetic, and other considerations, and that they involve attempts to produce idealized versions of the theorist—are related in the observation that the end-product of the process prescribed by an educational theory is a kind of person.

The psychologist who isolates so far as possible for study, say, the development of logico-mathematical forms, separating these from all other forms of thinking, and from the context or erudition on which these logico-mathematical forms may be exercised, and even more so from the social and political contexts within which they may be exercised, is taking a necessary step toward secure scientific inquiry, as it is presently practiced in psychology. This isolating of a topic for inquiry is necessary for psychologists to do their job properly. The separation of thinking skills from erudition is pointless and destructive in education; it undermines educators' ability to do their job properly. (This is obviously not to claim that the distinction between thinking skills and erudition cannot be made in education, but rather that given the job educators have to do, it is not a very interesting distinction.) Psychology's general influence over education, and Piaget's particular influence at present, has, as we have seen, resulted in dichotomies such as thinking/erudition being imported into education with destructive consequences. The aim of an educational program cannot sensibly be merely a kind of thinking, it has to be a kind of person. And this means dealing as well as we can with the multifarious complex combination of things that are involved in becoming an educated adult. This in turn does not necessarily mean giving equal attention in our educational theory to every aspect of human life. We do not have to produce an ideal republic as an adjunct of our outline of the best way to produce a cultured person. But we cannot ignore the fact that our product's culture involves, and needs to be informed by, a social and political context. This is to say that the product of our educational theory must be recognizable as a person; rather than merely as a restricted set of thinking skills, or a catalogue of knowledge, or a moral agent. And our educational theory, to be useful will have to be, to some degree, culture-bound and *polis*-bound.

III. EDUCATIONAL THEORY AND EMPIRICAL TESTING

If an educational theory prescribes a process which, possibly, no one has yet gone through, it makes the question "What is its empirical basis?" rather complicated to answer. Such a question may initially mean: "Is there evidence suggesting that the theory recommends things which are impossible?" A "theory" offered in psychology without a substantial empirical base would be considered mere speculation. Should we, then, talk of educational speculations, rather than educational theories? Is Plato's an educational speculation?

We might note first that informed speculation, even in the natural sciences, may perform an important programmatic function. And, it is not entirely irrelevant to add, in education the program is the point. The line between theory and speculation is not as clear as the words' usual positive and negative associations suggest.

If our model for educational theory is psychological theory, whose model in turn is natural science theory—however far short of its model each may fall—then what I have called Plato's educational theory may seem like nothing other than a set of more or less arbitrary recommendations, lacking empirical support. How can we test such a theory?

Minimal requirements for an educational theory, thus far indicated, are that it characterizes its ideal product in terms of a recognizable kind of person, and that it tells us what things we should teach, when and how, in order to produce a person of this kind. So our educational theory will make at least one empirical claim: if you teach these things in this order in these ways then you will produce a person with these characteristics. How can we test such a claim? We might try the program and see what happens. This is not, of course, altogether satisfactory. Plato suggests that his scheme will probably work for only a few people who have the prerequisite innate capacities, and that most people, apparently, can be expected to achieve only some fraction of the desired characteristics of the ideal end-product, or, indeed, just some of the prerequisites. The general empirical test of such a theory seems to require implementing the program recommended by the theory, but human things being what they are, we may expect no conclusive results from such a massive test.

Can we instead abstract from Plato's scheme a series of smaller-scale empirical claims? When he tells us that young children should learn through games and stories, this seems like an empirically unsupported recommendation. We may be sure that it is not based on Plato's experimenting with young children, even in the fashion of the early Piaget. Can we convert such recommendations into empirical claims: that if we put material into game and story forms it will lead to more interest, more efficient learning, better mastery of later logically related material, greater transfer, or whatever? Such tests, even if they support the claims, hardly produce a convincing test of the theory. (They may, of course, help convince us that the program, or some part of it, is worth implementing.) But Plato may want to argue that it is irrelevant whether or not learning is made more efficient by the use of games and stories. His educational reason for insisting this method *ought* to be used is that such methods are prerequisites to achieving his ultimate ideal. That is, an educational theory may systematically eradicate the relevance of smaller–scale empirical claims, and propose a program whose justification at every step is tied to the end-product. So its only empirical claim is one that is, given the complexity of the phenomena, virtually impossible to verify or falsify.

Obviously, one might expect an educational theory to be a bit more generous than this in making empirical claims. I am, however, trying to sketch an austere, extreme case in order to clarify something about the nature of educational theories. A theory which makes only one empirical claim of such generality that its falsification is enormously difficult is still, of course, open to conceptual tests—of coherence, consistency, plausibility, and so on. The point, however, is that such a theory, if we desire its promised end-product and think it looks a plausible way of bringing it about, is educationally useful. Indeed, it tells us exactly what we want to know.

Now this criterion of formal falsifiability does not follow from some notion of what scientific theories are, nor from a reading of some Popperian ideas about the function of theories. It follows from my attempt to get clear on what kind of theory—or what we can reasonably call "theory"—is educationally useful. One role of a theory, which seems to be as appropriate in education as anywhere else, is that it predict probable outcomes. In education, a theory would predict that if one teaches these things, these ways, in this sequence, then you will probably get this kind of person. That is, if an educational theory implies, or embodies, a curriculum, then the curriculum is to be causally responsible for the product.

If we are dealing with assembly lines, or physical processes, this is fine. But in matters educational, it is much more complicated. Whatever and however one teaches, some will learn better than others. And yet a prescribed curriculum that makes no prediction about the result of following it is clearly useless. So the "falsifiable" part of my criterion simply alludes to the need of an educator for some kind of prediction about outcome being built into the theory; the "formal" part simply acknowledges the enormous practical problems involved in actually falsifying such a general prediction. Such a criterion in the physical sciences would be pointless, given the need to be able clearly to falsify a theory (though even here the problem is more complicated than it might on the face appear). But in education a theory which has no more restrictive criterion may provide precisely the kind of thing we want.

The claim that one can have a theory which is not empirically testable in practice may well be enough for some people to reject my argument out of hand. But that constant "in practice" is important. It suggests that our evaluation techniques are at present inadequate for the task. There is no point in reducing the task to the point at which presently available techniques can deal with it, because the degree of reduction required radically transforms the thing to be evaluated. One may squeeze some impressive-looking results from such a procedure, but they will not tell us what we want to know. Only by recognizing the inadequacy of presently available techniques to handle it, will we avoid the folly of measuring something different in place of what we want to know, and we will also have the stimulus to develop more sophisticated techniques. The current preference for rejecting claims such as are embodied in this notion of formal falsifiability in favor of reducing the phenomena to fit available technique—smashing the phenomena and looking only at isolated bits—is the kind of activity that gets empiricism a bad name. I am not proposing a withdrawal to obscurantism, out of the sunlight of empirical science: I am proposing an advance toward dealing with educational phenomena in their proper complexity— a theme of the next chapter.

The study of education is engaged in so that we may construct better educational programs, and prescribing how to construct such programs is the function of educational theories. Such theories are clearly unlike theories in physics or psychology, and we might well debate whether the differences are so great that the term "theory" should not be used to refer to them. Whether or not they are to be called theories seems to me a pragmatic question which has already been decided. Philosophical analysis may properly chart *a posteriori* the similarities and differences among meanings of "theory" as used in physics, psychology, and education, but cannot reasonably hope to decide the pragmatic question of whether the things vaguely called theories in education are to be so called. Our immediate concern here is to attach a little more precision to what "theory" should be used to refer to in education. One way to approach such a question is to try to work from meanings of the term in the human and natural sciences toward some definition of the nature of theory, and then try to see how such a thing might perform with regard to education. The problem with such a procedure seems to be a tendency to sketch a set of characteristics derived from the nature of theories in the natural and human sciences as definitional of what a theory must be and then prescribe *a priori* that an educational theory must have some or all of these characteristics. The usual result of this procedure is a rather vague image of what an educational theory ought to look like, and when the field of education is searched with this template in hand, typically nothing is found to fit it.[1] The procedure I have followed, however, is to look at what kinds of things we want an educational theory to do and tell us, and as long as the result falls roughly within the semantic area covered by the term theory, even if it means spilling over the side a bit and having to stretch the normal semantic area to cover the spill, then we might feel reasonably comfortable calling "educational theories" those things which prescribe what to teach, when and how, in order to produce a particular kind of educated person. The character of theories in physics, psychology, and education may reasonably reflect the different functions they perform in these different areas and reflect differences in the phenomena they tell us about. Educational theories may involve a greater degree of speculation than one would expect in psychology and they may not *explain* anything, unless one wants to speak very loosely about explaining how to produce a particular kind of person. We may accept that they need to be formally falsifiable—we would want to rule out programs that claim success if a particular procedure is followed regardless of its results—but we may acknowledge that empirically falsifying the most general claim of such a theory may be practically impossible.

We will want to regret all this apparent sloppiness only if we have the ambition to make educational theories the same as those in the natural sciences or psychology, and believe that designing educational programs should involve the same kind of activity as describing the causes of the French Revolution or of accounting for the behavior of subatomic particles. These activities share the use of reason, but the phenomena to which it is applied are enormously different. The kinds of theories that best help educators do their job may or may not share certain characteristics with those of physicists or psychologists. The practical job in hand is the proper determiner of the nature of the theories we require in education. Borrowing theories designed to study different phenomena and tell their students different kinds of things about those phenomena, has had a destructive influence on educators' ability to do their proper job effectively. It has also brought the whole necessary realm of theory in education into disrepute among those with a firm sense of the realities of educational practice, and has diverted the attention of those who might be providing educational theories away from the phenomena out of which such theories must be composed.

STRUCTURES OF MIND OR
STRUCTURES OF KNOWLEDGE

Is the characterization of the stages of educational development in Plato's theory presented in terms of the mind or in terms of the structures of knowledge? These seem to be the two poles on which educators have been persuaded to focus. In recent decades Piaget has persuaded us to look at development in terms of the mind; Bruner, in terms of structures of knowledge. Neither, of course, looks at one to the exclusion of the other, and there is an odd sense in which the terms we use about the one seem to refer readily to the other. This need not be surprising, however, as we know the mind mainly through what it does with knowledge. It is a kind of transparent organism whose forms become apparent only when it goes to work on some visible content—what remains difficult to see, however, is how far the transparent organism adapts itself to the structure of the content and how far it makes the content conform with its structure. Does Plato's characterization of *eikasia, pistis, dianoia,* and *noesis* seek primarily to describe the structure of the mind or of knowledge? And toward which should an educational theory properly be focused?

Our educational concern is of course with both mind and knowledge. Plato's characterization of his stages seems to be in terms of some *tertium id* between the two, or perhaps of the interaction between the two—that ambiguous, or ambispective, realm where the mind's development is spoken of in terms of knowledge, in terms of which, in turn, we know the mind. This curious and complex realm seems the appropriate habitat for educational theories, and we need to be explicit about the educational value of seeking out this middle way. Focus toward the mind tends to lead toward psychology and to the kind of educational vacuousness we have explored in chapter 3; focus toward structures of knowledge tends to lead toward philosophy, and to the educational vacuousness to which, it seems now commonly accepted, the search for structures of knowledge in the curriculum has led.

A prominent, indeed the dominant, image of how to study or research to improve education runs counter to this recommendation. Education, according to Kohlberg and Mayer requires "the method of philosophy" and "the method of psychology," each providing knowledge that will guide the educator in prescribing a curriculum.[2] Peters sees educational curricula being composed from philosophers' findings about knowledge and its forms, augmented by psychological research.[3] In an article referred to in the previous chapter, Deanna Kuhn urges on us a program of cooperative research in which developmental psychologists will outline a sequence of development better suited to the content of various disciplines.[4] That is, there is a common assumption built into a very large part of the present study of education that psychologists and philosophers—and no doubt sociologists and others—should provide us with knowledge about children and subject matter, and all kinds of other things, which will then enable us to design better educational programs. Thus Piaget and Paul Hirst, for example, can tell us about children's development on the one, psychological, hand, and about forms of knowledge on the other, epistemological, hand, and the curriculum person can then come along and shuffle these into a program of study that will produce optimally educated people. Such a program of "educational" research seems able to offer something of psychological or philosophical interest, but it is educationally sterile. This dominant approach to education—whose study is dominated by psychologists and philosophers—assumes that education is inarticulate; that educational praxis has no other resources to draw on.

So while education does not require a psychological theory of development on which to articulate a curriculum, it does need as a part of an educational theory some characterization of the developing psyche. This may seem paradoxical. But consider Plato's developmental model. It is not what one would call a psychological theory, yet it is a characterization of a desirable and possible developmental sequence. It is within the constraints of what is necessary, but these constraints, given educators' purposes, can remain opaque and distant. They become relevant only if there is a danger that an educational prescription contravenes what is possible.

THE NECESSITY OF EDUCATIONAL THEORY

Psychology has generated much knowledge that is properly of interest to education. Knowledge by itself is mute, however; it is made articulate by being organized into a theory. A theory is a kind of syntax; as the latter organizes phonemes into meaningful sentences, so the former organizes knowledge into more generally meaningful claims about certain phenomena. Knowledge about the psyche, about learning, development, motivation, or whatever, becomes psychologically articulate when organized by a psychological theory. The same knowledge may become educationally articulate only by being organized within an educational theory. This is not, I think, a trivial point. It means that apart from an educational theory no knowledge and no theory has educational implications. Even knowledge about constraints of our nature becomes educationally useful only when it has become incorporated within an educational theory, or an educational theory accommodates to it.

This suggests that every consideration relating to education—whether the organization of furniture in the classroom or matters of local policy-making, so far as these are educational rather than socializing matters—must be derived from an educational theory. That is, there can be no such thing in education as distinct lower-level theories—whether of classroom design or instruction or motivation or whatever—but only general, comprehensive educational theories with either implications for things like classroom design and instruction or direct claims about such things and about learning development, motivation, and so on.

If one wants to design an educational curriculum, the thing that will tell one how to go about it is an educational theory. One can obviously compose a curriculum made up as a result of "input" from diverse groups of people, as though decisions about educating were the same as decisions about socializing in a democracy. Only by chance will the products of such a curriculum be educated. Our schools have some clear social objectives, and guided by these can achieve some success in socializing. Their curricula, however, seem to lack the guidance of any systematic and comprehensive educational theory and consequently lack coherent educational objectives. Not only is an educational theory the most practical thing one can have in order to design a curriculum, it is a prerequisite to a curriculum that can reasonably claim to be designed to produce educated people.

Conclusion

IN LOOKING at the differences between Plato's and Piaget's theories it has been possible, I think, to get a little clearer about the nature and function of educational theories. The function of an educational theory is to tell us how to design a curriculum which will produce educated people, or, rather, to lay out such a curriculum. Such a theory must tell us what content we should teach to produce such people. The content can never be merely instrumental to achieving other goals, like "how to develop," because the educated person is in part constituted of the content learned. The theory must tell us how we should teach such content, because in education the medium forms some part of the message, and because learning that best promotes educational development requires that the learner be interested in the content being taught. The theory must also tell us when we should teach particular things and how we should teach them at the different stages of educational development, so that the content is most engaging and meaningful at each stage of the process. It must tell us also what kind of person will be produced if we follow its prescriptions about *what, how,* and *when.* This image of the end-product must *justify* the detailed prescriptions, making the latter causally responsible for the former. The theory must make at least one formally falsifiable empirical claim. The theory will be culture-bound and value-saturated, and will involve claims about desirable political and social structures.

It would be pleasant, for oneself, if one could prescribe meanings for terms. One might say that, given the job educators have to do, an educational theory which has the characteristics indicated in the previous paragraph best helps them do that job, and that such a thing looks somewhat like what are commonly called "theories." Therefore, we may legislate that "educational theory" refers to those things which have those characteristics. Clearly such legislative prescription lacks compelling force. Still, language, no less than territory, is an arena for imperialist aggression. One can invade a term, and then see whether anyone comes along.

5/ Psychology and Education

Introduction

WE STILL have some way to go to clarify the argument of this book (even if it's false). This is not because the argument is so complicated—indeed it can be put in the form of a simple syllogism:

Major premise. Psychological theories can have implications for education only if they describe constraints on our nature.

Minor premise. No psychological theory at present describes constraints on our nature.

Conclusion. Psychological theories at present have no implications for education.

The extension of the argument can be stated even more simply: Implications for education can properly be derived only from educational theories with the characteristics described in the previous chapter.

There are also a weak sense and a strong sense of this argument. The weak sense is expressed in the syllogism. The strong sense can be expressed by substituting "can describe" for "at present describes" in the minor premise.

The terms I use in the syllogism may seem odd. As I mentioned in the Introduction, I am neither a philosopher nor a psychologist, so my choice of terms may be rather facile. By "psychological the-

ories" I mean not only well-articulated theories, but all research that
aims at generating or supporting the kind of theories that conform
with the presuppositions of scientific psychology. And within "scientific psychology" I include all psychologists who presuppose that
they are using scientific methods in establishing empirical regularities about psychological phenomena—the distinctions between, say,
radical behaviorists and various kinds of cognitivists—between, say,
B.F. Skinner and Jean Piaget—which no doubt loom vast within
psychology, seem fairly insignificant from the perspective of my
educational concerns. My argument, that is, is intended to apply to
each equally well. By "constraints of nature" I mean simply things
that are true about human beings and their behavior.

We still have some way to go, however, because the premises of
the syllogism run counter to what is *presupposed* by so many people
in education and psychology. From William James and John Dewey
to Jean Piaget, B.F. Skinner, Jerome Bruner, and the massive industry
of educational psychology, it has been taken as obvious that the
science of psychology can help improve the practice of education.
(Even current arguments within educational psychology about why
it has evidently failed to do so are almost entirely about strategies
of research and barely ever question this basic presupposition.)

When something has been taken as obviously true for so long by
so many people it is difficult to make clear why it might be false, if
only because many of the terms one uses in the argument have become semantically colored to match the presupposition one is arguing against. It is the kind of difficulty one faces if one wants to
point out that the meaning of "instruction" in psychology is quite
distinct from the meaning of "teaching" in education, or that the
meaning of "learning" in psychology is quite distinct from its meaning in education. Educational psychologists who presuppose that,
when they borrow learning theories from psychology, they are dealing with what is properly meant by learning in education carry psychology's meaning across into education. In this way, unless education
asserts its autonomy, psychology's meaning of "learning" invades
education and usurps the proper place of education's meaning, with
the result that what has been meant in education by "learning" is
collapsed to what is meant in psychology. A kind of semantic Gres-
ham's law operates. This does not add precision to education's meaning, rather it deforms and impoverishes it. And this, of course, is no
small matter in practice. It means that the notion of learning that
gradually invades schools is inappropriate and impoverishing—as,
for example, when what is measured by instruments composed in

accordance with psychology's meaning are taken straightforwardly as evidence of children's "educational" achievement, and instruction is then designed to induce the kind of learning that psychology's instruments measure. Again, this is not to argue that there is anything impoverished or inappropriate in psychology's use of the term— simply that accepting this as the only meaning blinds one to the more complex meaning that is proper to education. One could, however, argue that psychology's claim that such theories are about "learning" is presumptuous, since the ordinary meaning of this term covers a great deal more than any psychological theory presently deals with. A similar presumptuousness and lack of a sense of distinctions have led to impoverishment of education's proper meanings of "intelligence" and "creativity." More restricted and technical terms would seem at this point more appropriate, and less confusing. As it is, one might note, to use Petrie's words, that:

> Learning is inextricably bound up with standards of correctness, with getting things right, with norms. If psychologists want to investigate mere processes of change of cognitive variables without regard to the normative feature, then they owe us an argument to show that what they are doing has anything whatsoever to do with our ordinary concerns with learning.[1]

In order to clarify my argument and clarify, so far as possible, where and how I am right, wrong, or confused, it is necessary to begin by showing that the particular argument mounted against Piaget's theory may be generalized to all current psychological theories. I will try to do this by stating in theoretical terms the grounds on which the argument may be generalized, and the two premises of the syllogism supported. I will then try to show how this generalized argument applies equally to some other areas of psychology commonly seen as having implications for education. I will try to show why the syllogism leads us to conclude reasonably that a range of research which is assumed to be archetypal educational research has no implications for education.

It might seem that all the talk of constraints of human nature is evidence that I have a strange idea of what goes on in psychology. These abstract arguments might be all very well, but they do not even approach saying anything about the kind of guidance which research in educational psychology gives to day-by-day educational practice. Much of that research is unconcerned with attempts to generate theories about what is necessarily the case about human nature or behavior—even the language is alien—rather, it is aimed at elucidating certain practical problems, indicating trends, regularities, or generating theories with limited and local applicability, which provide knowledge that is not supposed to constrain educators absolutely, but is knowledge that might well prove useful in constructing curricula, in teaching practice, or in whatever else they want to do that involves changing people's behavior and thinking. It may appear that my argument so far has been aimed only at what is generally acknowledged to be an error—at the attempt to move directly from "basic" research to practice without the intermediate "applied" or "engineering level" research. That is, even if some people might be willing to grant the minor premise of the syllogism, they consider the conclusion false because the major premise is false. In supporting the major premise, however, I will indeed be arguing that this "applied" or "engineering level" research—if based on psychological theories, at whatever remove—can have no legitimate educational implications.

Grounds for Generalizing the Argument

THE CHOICE OF PIAGET'S THEORY

How can the particular case made against Piaget's theory of cognitive development be generalized to a case against seeking implications from any psychological theory for educational practice? And why choose as an example of a psychological theory one that is, according to some, in a process of unraveling and is, besides, so atypical that some prefer to classify it as other than a psychological theory?

The main reason for choosing it to exemplify this argument is simple. Apart from the reason given earlier (that it is commonly assumed to have many clear implications for educational practice), I chose it because, despite its outstanding oddities, in terms of typical North American psychological theorizing, it has had an enormous impact largely because of the remarkable range and nature of its counterintuitive claims which have been routinely replicated when even vaguely similar experimental procedures have been used. In this it is unique among psychological theories. Usually the slightest change in experimental procedures, or stimulus materials, produces different results. The reasons why it may be seen in process of unraveling, or in process of revision and renewal, are reasons which,

I hope to show, illustrate why psychological theories in general yield no implications for educational practice. That it is atypical, and that some people find it difficult to classify as a psychological theory, seem unexceptional conditions of its being more sophisticated than other psychological theories. It is more sophisticated both in terms of the complexity of what it seeks to account for and in the theoretical apparatus it brings to bear on the problems which that accounting runs up against. That it is, in part at least, a psychological theory, seems beyond sensible question.

A colleague who read a draft of this argument complained of the choice of Piaget's theory because, he wrote, Piaget is as much an epistemologist as a psychologist, and I would be wise instead to try to exemplify my case against the use of psychological theories in education by means of Robert M. Gagné's theory. In response to the first point one might suggest that being an epistemologist, or being somewhat familiar with epistemology, should be a prerequisite for doing research in "psychology of education." That a familiarity with epistemology seems rare among psychologists, even among those dealing with human learning and development, can lead to confusions such as that which sees Gagné's theory as a more typical, or a less problematic, psychological theory than Piaget's. Gagné's theory of learning hierarchies seems to me a straightforward conceptual or logical enterprise, in which Gagné checks the adequacy of his conceptualization by empirical tests with children. The empirical checking is obviously a good idea in so complicated an area, but how the hierarchies are constructed is not an empirical matter—it is a conceptual or logical matter. That is, Gagné's theory does not seem to me a *psychological* theory at all,[2] in the empirical tradition of scientific psychology, that is. Like *parts* of Piaget's theory, it does not tell us about the *logos* of the *psyche* so much as the *logos* of *episteme*.

In considering other learning theories as exemplars for my general argument, I faced various problems. The "harder" theories achieve their relative security at the expense of reducing "learning" to something their available methodology for securing knowledge can deal with, and that something is so far removed from anything that is properly meant by "learning" in education that a large part of my task would be simply in clarifying these differences. Pointing out how certain improvements in particular skill acquisitions and improved memorization of certain kinds of facts and concepts according to some instruments of measurement have nothing much to do with what properly interests educators about learning (a point to be amplified below), would not allow me to generalize my argument in

the way suggested by the syllogism above. The notorious and fundamental problems inherent in S-R (Stimulus–Response) theories—
the problems for explanation and meaning that result from being
unable to specify an R independent from the S that "causes" it—
make Piaget's theoretical foundations seem less insecure by comparison. In addition, much of this area shares a form of the epistemological confusion indicated in the above reference to Gagné's theory:
what are taken as discovery of psychological regularities are in part
analytic truths—a point to be explored below in terms of Bandura's
theory. That is, learning theories in general labor under such a degree
of vagueness and insecurity[3] that pointing out the folly of accepting
direction from them would not allow me to generalize my argument
very far. Similarly, theories of motivation, as they exist at present,
have difficulty specifying even what are the phenomena they are
supposed to account for. That is, if I could show the inappropriate-
ness of drawing implications for educational practice from these
relatively primitive theories, it would still not allow me to generalize
my argument very widely, whereas if I show that it is inappropriate
to draw such implications from the most nearly adequate psychological theory (from an educational perspective) then I might more
easily be able to show how what holds in this case holds *a fortiori*
in the cases of less adequate theories.[4] But it will be necessary to
show, of course, by some examples, that the main reason why Piaget's
theory has no legitimate implications for education is the same reason why other psychological theories, and the "educational" research based on them, have no legitimate educational implications.

SCIENTIFIC METHODS AND PSYCHOLOGY

We do not need to asphyxiate ourselves mentally in the refined heights of philosophy of science—if you will forgive the man-
gled metaphor—in order to make the observations that are adequate
for my argument here. What we call the methods of science have
proven fruitful in securing knowledge about the physical world. It
is appropriate always to use the plural—"methods"—as inquiry into
various natural phenomena has led to rather different methods, and
indeed even in research on particular phenomena different scientists
sometimes ask somewhat different questions and use different methods in seeking answers. In a trivial sense one can even characterize
somewhat different national methods of doing science on specific
phenomena—differences more apparent at the practical level in international research facilities than in the more standard form of re-

porting findings in scientific journals. The methods of science have been worked out in interactions with a set of phenomena and a set of questions about these phenomena. These methods are not static: as the phenomena and questions change so there are changes in the methods of research.

No one has been able to characterize some general "scientific method" as an abstraction from the multitude of changing methods used fruitfully in various physical sciences. It needs to be remembered that scientific methods are in some sense a reflection of the phenomena with which they were in interaction as they developed. We have not developed or discovered "scientific method" and "applied" it to the physical world. There has been, and continues to be, a dialectical interactive development of knowledge about particular phenomena, of questions, and of methods of research.

Scientific methods, then, are not stable, and they are intricately connected with the kinds of phenomena about which they are used to secure knowledge. There are commonalties in the methods of the physical sciences because there are commonalties in the behavior of the physical phenomena about which the methods have been used to make discoveries—commonalties affected in some degree by the technical means of access we have to the phenomena in question. Most physical phenomena about which knowledge has been sought— to choose some commonalties—have proved amenable to isolation and discrete categorization, and researchers have been able reliably to presuppose continuity, consistency, and regularity in the conditions and behavior of all entities surrounding the variables under study. (Discovery of conditions which suggest even a small threat to these presuppositions leads to major impacts on methodology, as, for example, with the discovery of quantum effects.)

Given the terms in which human behavior has traditionally been conceptualized, the conditions common in the physical world do not seem to hold in the human world. Human behavior does not seem to be made up of discrete units which can be isolated; "behaviors" do not seem to have definable characteristics so much as to have meanings which vary in indeterminable ways depending on contexts made up from things like intentions, history, and other cultural contingencies. In the physical world there is accessible a nature which we can describe and explore. Beneath the shifting particulars there is a set of fairly consistent processes, which we can characterize in ideal terms as laws. In the human world we do not have such obvious access to a level of necessity, a level of nature, underlying the shifting particulars. Such a level, or nature, whose ideal states and processes may be characterized in laws of which particulars may be seen as instances, evades us—or, at least, it is more difficult to describe such a level of necessity in a way that is not clearly affected by the shifting particulars.

Scientific psychology begins with the assumption that the methods of science are the best means of finding out things and making sense of things and, if one wants to find out about human behavior, one should seek ways of applying scientific methods to it. On the face of it, there seem to be some fundamental differences between behaviors of physical entities and human beings, and these apparent differences have presented methodological challenges to psychology, and have been responded to in a variety of ways by different psychologists and schools of psychology.

One response—the most assertively scientific—is represented by radical behaviorism. This program of research has involved abstracting some methods from some of the physical sciences and reconceptualizing human behavior in terms that make it amenable to study by those methods—claiming in the process that the reconceptualization provides a sufficient characterization of human behavior and indeed a more adequate one than has been available in traditional conceptualizations. This program has required treating human behaviors so far as possible like physical entities—isolating subjects for study in such a way that the irregular contingencies which seem to pervade human things are eliminated or controlled so far as possible. A basic presupposition of this program is that fitting human behavior to methods designed to explain physical phenomena will yield theories that will similarly explain human behavior.[5]

What is radical about radical behaviorism is its uncompromising insistence that the phenomena must be made to fit "scientific method." What seems to be occasionally forgotten is that it is an empirical question whether they can be made to do so, and remain the phenomena one set out to explain. Radical behaviorists sometimes claim that they are scientific because their program involves "the use of scientific method in the study of human behavior."[6] But it is not the methods—or singular method, whatever that may be—that are in question; it is the appropriateness of those methods for answering particular questions about human behavior. Science is not a method. Doing science is not a matter of "applying" or "using" a method, but of using the proper methods to answer particular questions about particular phenomena. It is not on the grounds of its failure to apply some kind of "scientific method" that many philosophers and scientists deny that behavioral psychology is a science, but on the grounds that it has yet to discover a scientific method appropriate to questions about its phenomena of interest.[7]

If any element of the interconnecting triad of method, question, or phenomena is at odds with the others then we have something less than a science. If method and phenomena in concert were enough, then we should have to admit alchemy as a science. But there, a refined methodology for dealing with certain phenomena was undercut by inappropriate questions. If method and question were enough we would have to admit parapsychology as a science. At the time of writing, a move is under way to remove parapsychology from its place in the American Academy of Sciences at least until it establishes a single secure fact about its phenomena of interest, or indeed establishes that its phenomena of interest exist. If the use of "scientific method" is enough to make a science, then we have no grounds to exclude alchemy or parapsychology.

Whatever conclusions may be reached about the program of radical behaviorism and its positivistic notion of how to do science, its influence through all branches of scientific psychology and the human sciences generally has been and continues to be very great—to the extent that in some vague sense it must be acknowledged that we are all behaviorists now. This may mean no more, in some cases, than an acknowledgment that one's exploration of the phenomena of the *psyche* must be sought primarily through measurable behaviors, or in the vague acceptance of the vague definition of psychology as the systematic study of human *behavior*—a definition that does not manage to exclude history, poetics, sociology, and so forth. The common acceptance throughout psychology of the very general use of the term "behavior" is an index of radical behaviorism's influence. Along with this general usage comes a more or less subtle implication about the similarities between physical and human behavior: one can, after all, talk about the behavior of atomic particles and human creative behavior. One can suggest further similarities by observing that physical and human behavior are lawful. In acknowledging such things without qualification one is drawn to accept to greater or lesser degree the radical behaviorist program for the discovery of those laws by "the use of scientific method in the study of human behavior."

Given the close relationship in science between methods and particular questions about particular phenomena, we might wisely be wary of any claims about a general methodology—whether a Lullian *ars invenienda veritatem*[8] (method for discovering the truth) or a radical behaviorist's notion of "scientific method." We might char-

acterize one axis of scientific psychology practice as a continuum
representing the degree to which psychologists are willing to accommodate the methodology borrowed from the physical sciences to
their sense of the nature of their phenomena of interest and to what
count as significant and interesting questions about those phenomena—a prominent accommodation being in terms of the degree to
which individual psychologists are willing to recognize mental states
as mediating in whatever degree the results in behavior of external
causal stimuli, or even as having some more or less significant causal
role themselves.

HUMAN BEHAVIOR: CULTURE AND NATURE

The main features of human behaviors that have given rise
to the methodological divisions within psychology are their complexity, apparent inconsistency, irregularity, and seamlessness. In
seeking to tie down any human behavior one is hindered by the
number and complexity of the variables that may be seen to impinge
on it in some way. Complexity, however, is to be distinguished from,
say, irregularity, if one hopes to apply scientific methods to human
behavior. Thus, while admitting considerable methodological problems in trying to deal with some human behaviors, a psychologist
committed to scientific psychology may note: "Our troubles do not
arise because human events are in principle unlawful; man and his
creations *are* part of the natural world."[9]

The trouble with this formulation is that it tends to hide things
that might better be distinguished. Man, is *in a sense* part of the
natural world and human events are *in a sense* lawful. The job scientific methods were designed for, as Cronbach also observes, "is to
ask questions of nature."[10] But, as I have noted above, an integral
part of man's nature is culture. Man, we may say, does not just have
a nature, man has a history, a culture, which in important ways
determine behavior, and determine significantly the meaning of behavior. Scientific methods as we know them were not designed to
ask questions of culture—yet that is what scientific psychology does
if it deals with human behavior. To observe that man is a part of the
natural world, then, is to ignore a sense in which a fuller formulation
would raise larger questions about the program of scientific psychology. Human events are in a sense lawful.[11] So is human history.
Scientific historiography does not accept miracles as explanatory
devices. Scientific poetics studies forms of expression that are in a
sense lawful. To claim that these phenomena are lawful is unexcep-

tionable—our troubles arise from the difficulty of discovering *what kinds of laws* order these phenomena. A related trouble arises from the difficulty of discovering *what kinds of units* the phenomena can be broken into in order to allow fruitful analysis and research. What is an event, or a behavior? We accept history as a lawful, causal process, but the search for laws of history has foundered for good methodological reasons. For not dissimilar reasons—dealing with complexity and seamlessness—some psychologists are forced again to ask "should social science aspire to reduce behavior to laws?"[12]

This distinction between nature and history, or culture—between an image of human behavior as determined by our nature, and so explainable according to physical science paradigms, and of human behavior as determined by our history or culture, and so only understandable within a context of shared meanings—may seem irrelevant to some psychologists. A methodology concerned only with discovering empirical regularities among observable behaviors may be wholly unconcerned with whether their source is in some sense a matter of nature or a matter of culture. But, whatever psychologists make of this distinction, it is a crucial one for education when it comes to seeking implications from psychological theories. *If* indeed we do not have a nature, in the above sense, but rather our behavior is made meaningful and understandable only in the context of our history or culture, this means that psychological regularities discovered are contingent on that history, on the culture in which they occur. This means that psychological theories will be valid only for the range of conditions in which those regularities can be shown to hold. And this has led many psychologists to conclude that psychological theories at best will be of only "local" applicability. We will return to this later on; the point of importance here is that education's concern with prescribing ideals need not be constrained by psychological regularities that are conditioned or determined by historical or cultural contingencies. *Such regularities discovered by psychologists are products of the kinds of forces that it is the educator's job to shape.* Only if the forces are natural, and thus necessary, does the educator have to be constrained by them. This is the argument for the major premise.

This is why my discussion of Piaget's theory focused on showing that it fails to tell us about what is natural in human cognitive development and consequently should not be seen as constraining educational practice. Despite his methodological differences from the mainstream of behaviorally inclined North American psychology, Piaget's commitment to the general program of scientific psychology—"Psychology is a natural science"[13]—leads him into the fundamental problem of trying to distinguish the natural from the cultural in those aspects of human behavior which form the focus of his scientific interests. The apparent successes of Piaget's theory are due to the ingenuity with which he has managed to deal with significant aspects of human development while treating them as nearly as possible like natural phenomena. Crucial to this, as we have seen, is the sharp distinction he has had to etch between the spontaneous and natural part of development, and the culturally contingent part, between "development" and "learning." The former provides the focus of his scientific interest and is seen as a kind of substratum of development on which the culturally contingent learning can take place. It is allowed that cultural contingencies can affect, say, the speed of the natural development, so the matter of speed is thus judged insignificant to the theory—it is excised from what the theory accounts for. The theory's focus is only on what can be considered as natural. The "anti-Piaget" literature raises an array of criticisms about his theory, but I have ignored many of them because my focus turns on the points where the impropriety of his natural/cultural distinction becomes apparent. And these are the points from which I can generalize my argument.

The reasons for finding Piaget's theory lacking implications for educational practice turn at each point on calling into question just what it is that his theory is describing. For an educational theory to be constrained by Piaget's findings, those findings have to tell us something that is true about our nature. To a degree that is very hard to get clear, what Piaget claims as empirical truths—for example, the succession of stages—are in fact logical truths; some aspects of earlier stages have of logical necessity to precede later stages. To a degree equally hard to get clear, some claims are clearly empirical—and it is around these that trouble is gathering. When we put on one side all the claims that seem to be logical truths, we are left with a range of claims that is the subject of dispute in psychology[14] and also forms the basis for many educational recommendations. The crucial question is, what do they describe? Do they describe something natural, something that will happen in any kind of environment that provides the required aliments, something that can be prevented or slowed by lack of these aliments but, to the degree that these aliments are available, will proceed naturally on the regular course described? Given that at least some significant part of that regularity is guaranteed by the logical progression built into the theory (and consequently must be supported by any empirical tests), the empirical evidence about the remaining psychological claims embodied in the theory suggests, at the moment, that the answer is no—no, the psychological claims are not descriptive of something natural and necessary. Those claims that are clearly empirical are about something that is infected by uncontrolled, and, we have some reasons for thinking, uncontrollable cultural contingencies. A significant part of what the theory describes is made up of cultural contingencies. In so far as this is the case, it is foolish for an educational theory to be constrained by them. If we allow them to suggest implications for educational practice we commit the psychological fallacy—allowing a description of something contingent on past forms of cultural initiation to constrain our prescriptions for the future.

(The mixture of the logical and psychological is not something that Piaget does not intend. It is an explicit aim of his genetic epistemology: "Contemporary scientific epistemology reverts to coordinating the results of logic with a certain number of psychological facts,"[15] in order "to reach knowledge mechanisms at their source and development."[16] What is in contention is the status of these "psychological facts," and the nature of the theory which they are used to support.)

My aim in making the above very general points about science and the problems of scientific psychology is not simply to support the minor premise as it stands. I think it is fairly commonly acknowledged that this premise is valid (despite what might seem its odd language):

> Social scientists generally, and psychologists in particular, have modelled their work on physical science, aspiring to amass empirical generalizations, to restructure them into more general laws, and weld scattered laws into coherent theory. That lofty aspiration is far from realization.[17]

Even if one accepts Cronbach's conclusion, nevertheless one might believe that more research and energetic theorizing may well produce the kind of "coherent theory" the program of scientific psychology sets out to generate. My comments, then, are aimed at providing a basis from which to suggest that the minor premise may be made much stronger—that no psychological theory *can* describe or explain constraints on our nature. My argument about the present uses of psychological theory in education does not turn on my establishing this stronger argument—fortunately, because I cannot (especially in the very general terms used here). What I can do, however, is to continue this argument by laying out those reasons which make the stronger claim seem increasingly plausible.

None of this may seem to be making much headway, however, if the major premise is considered the weak point of the syllogism. I have tried to show earlier that the reason Piaget's theory does not have legitimate implications for education is because it does not describe constraints on our nature. Piaget's theory may seem so removed from the day-to-day practice of "applied" research in psychology of education that the major premise may be acknowledged to hold in the case of his theory but not to hold in the case of, say, theories of instruction and the research associated with them. My task now is to show that the major premise does hold in general, even for research which may seem wholly unconcerned with describing "constraints on our nature." My argument is that *only* theories which *can* describe such constraints can have educational implications. So I will be concerned to show that research on, say, teaching effectiveness that draws on, or aims to generate or refine, a psychological theory of instruction, or which seeks to establish even weak laws, generalizations or trends, *in fact has* no implications for education, and has no such implications precisely because the theory does not describe constraints on our nature. (I will persist also in building toward the argument that such theories *cannot* describe constraints on our nature.)

Before going on, however, I need to make a simple distinction, which seems to be rarely observed. An oddity of "educational research" in North America is that almost all empirical research is considered "psychology of education." (Many of the same activities in Britain would be considered "sociology of education.") Psychology is a form of rational inquiry. One of the basic ingredients of any form of rational inquiry may be called, as it was in the previous century, "the numerical method." Thus, if someone claims that bloodletting is physically therapeutic, a rational doctor may—did—count the results of this treatment in comparison with similar cases not so treated, and conclude reasonably that bloodletting is in general therapeutically useless and often harmful. Similarly, if someone claims that psychoanalysis is psychologically therapeutic, a count of the results of such treatment in comparison with similar cases not so treated, may conclude that the claim is unsupported by numbers. If a New York politician seeks to get some political mileage by claiming that New Yorkers in general behave responsibly and intelligently in an "energy crisis" while Californians "panic," the numerical method may be used to show that this claim is unsupported by any relevant data. If someone claims that precocious intellectual ability is followed by early decay—"early ripe, early rot"—the numerical method can be used to suggest that this is not the case.

The numerical method does not yield explanations, but it helps, among other things, to puncture claims that run against or ahead of what evidence there is. The numerical method does not need a theory in order to work. Much of what passes for research in education is simply, occasionally not so simply, the rational application of the numerical method. It is not psychology or sociology or anthropology or whatever. The numerical method becomes an ingredient of psychological research when it is harnessed to a psychological theory; it becomes an ingredient of educational research when harnessed to an educational theory. The numerical method is no less at the service of educational questions than of psychological questions. So I am not arguing that all empirical research in education has no implications for education, nor that all empirical research conducted by psychologists or psychologists of education has no implications for education. I am arguing that all empirical research based on any psychological theory has no implications for education—research that poses questions and uses methods based on the presuppositions of scientific psychology about the nature of its phenomenon of interest—whether "basic" or "applied" research.

Rational inquiry, the numerical method, scientific methods flow into each other imprecisely. A scientific method is composed not just of methods of research, but of methods of research that are appropriate for securely discovering answers to particular kinds of questions about particular kinds of phenomena. One danger within psychology is letting methodology get ahead of sensitivity to questions and phenomena, leading to overconfident "findings" about things more or less subtly unlike the intended phenomena of interest. An alternative danger is letting sensitivity to phenomena get ahead of sensitivity to methodology and questions—leading to claims that run beyond the ability to test them, to "mere opinion" and wild surmise.[18] Both extremes seem equally at fault, the latter usually claiming special insight into things, the former usually overconfident and assertively "scientific." There is a large body of literature condemning the fairly easy target of "mere opinion"; there is rather less aimed at pointing out the practical folly of following overconfident and phenomena-insensitive scientism. My argument is aimed at this latter (hardly with the intention of promoting the former), and I want to identify much of what goes on in psychology of education as an example of phenomena-insensitivity.

Teaching and Instructing: Their Different Objectives

TEACHING EFFECTIVENESS

Physics:engineering::psychology:education—this analogy is prominently used in writings about research on teaching effectiveness and its aim to generate a theory of instruction. Indeed this is seen by many as the prime area where the basic research of psychology is harnessed to applied research in education, yielding a practical pay-off. The methodological sophistication, which the complexity of the phenomena requires in order to answer the question about how to instruct in ways that optimize learning, has led some to note that the distinction between basic and applied research has lost much of its point.[19] In this section I aim to clarify further the impropriety of the above analogy, by indicating some ways in which psychological research on teaching effectiveness is not dealing with the things in which educators are properly interested.

Why is research on teaching effectiveness expected to contribute toward a theory of instruction? Why not toward a theory of teaching? The two words are of course used casually and often interchangeably, but the common preference for the word "instruction" is indicative of a hint of a sense of a distinction between instructing and teaching. It may be suspected by some that instructing is a more precise or value-neutral term than teaching; one that has become yet more precise in the fairly technical meaning it has accumulated operationally in the program of research aimed at generating a theory of instruction. But, I will argue, it is not more precise; it just refers to simpler phenomena than does "teaching." I will try to make a sensible distinction between the two terms and the distinct phenomena they refer to.

Some teaching is better than other teaching. Some teachers are better than others. In what ways? The aim of research on teaching effectiveness is to answer this question, and in answering it, to generate a theory of instruction. Initially such a program of research may seek simple correlations between particular teaching behaviors and learning outcomes. Even casual observation allows us to see things in individual teachers' practice that seem to enhance or inhibit individual students' learning; thus, it is expected, bringing "scientific method" to bear on this relationship should reveal more precise and generalizable principles of good teaching. Unfortunately for the hope of easy success, casual observation also allows one to see that a characteristic we might identify as a cause of one teacher's success may be a characteristic which seems in the case of another teacher to be irrelevant to the quality of teaching, or even a cause of poor teaching. (Mr. Smith's "flare for the dramatic" might be electrifying, whereas Mr. Jones's "flare for the dramatic" might make one want to throw up.)

The usual conclusion of reviews of the considerable body of research on this topic is that it tells us nothing unambiguously; its findings are either insignificant or inconsistent.[20] The steady failure of this program of research to yield a single secure generalization has encouraged some of its proponents to be more modest in their expectations, at least in the short term. But even so, it seems clear to scientific psychologists that the "folk wisdom" and common-sense principles which serve imprecisely in the training of teachers should be replaced at least by "concepts, or variables, and their interrelations in the form of weak laws, generalizations, or trends."[21] Gage, for example, in accepting that there are good reasons to expect that small-scale experiments will continue to yield insignificant or conflicting results, suggests that many of such results will agglomerate into groupings of findings that are regular and consistent.[22] (Even so, he feels it necessary to defend his optimism.)

On the face of it, research aimed at producing even weak laws or generalizations about effective teaching encounters formidable difficulties. The conditions in which scientific methods have worked well seem to be largely absent: one cannot reliably presuppose consistency in teacher and student behaviors, in their understandings and feelings about various subjects and topics, in their shifting distractions, in their changing environments, and so forth *ad infinitum*; one cannot easily see what might count as a unit of teaching or instructing, or a unit of education, or a unit of learning which can be isolated for study. That is, there is the danger—fallen into, I will argue—that in selecting units in this research, these units will not be units of the phenomenon one set out to study. Again, from casual observation, what should count as evidence of effective teaching is problematic. The profoundest effects may not show for a week or a year. Indeed, the most important effects may not be evident until after the particulars through which they have wrought their work are forgotten. Or the particulars may flit virtually unhindered through the students' awareness, but may serve in their passage to restructure some general scheme which profoundly determines their thinking or their way of making sense of things. The researcher might want to discount such things, on the reasonable grounds that one should start by securing knowledge about more straightforward aspects of human teaching and learning. The problem is that there are no more straightforward aspects. These kinds of complexities are central features of human teaching and learning in education. Discounting or ignoring any aspect of the phenomena in favor of what one's methodology can handle may be methodologically permissible so long as one does not forget what one has discounted or ignored. To assert that the reduction of the phenomena forced on one by the present inadequacies of one's methodology is no reduction at all is phenomena insensitivity at its crudest: it is not rational, so it can hardly make claims to being scientific.

CONSTITUENTS OF A THEORY OF INSTRUCTION

What is a theory of instruction supposed to look like? A fairly generally accepted image was set out by Bruner some years ago.[23] Such a theory of instruction should specify how best to predispose children favorably toward learning; should specify how materials should be organized or structured to make them optimally graspable by students; should specify the most effective sequences in which to present the materials; and should specify the nature and pacing of rewards and punishments in the process of learning and teaching. Such a theory must be prescriptive—setting forth rules concerning the most effective ways of teaching and learning, and it must be normative—setting forth criteria and stating the conditions for meeting them. Such a prescriptive and normative theory of instruction, in addition, "must be congruent with these [descriptive] theories of learning and development to which it subscribes."[24]

In light of my earlier argument, there seem to be grounds to question what Bruner means by the theory of instruction being "congruent" with the descriptive theories of learning and development, and to question in what sense it is to "subscribe" to them. He certainly does not seem to mean only that the prescriptive theory will not contravene what they describe. Does it mean that it will attempt to be as coherent as possible with them? Does it mean, for example, that the end-point described by the theory of development provides objectives and criteria for the instructional theory's prescriptions?[25] To consider only development, what does the descriptive theory of development have to describe if it is to serve Bruner's purposes for a theory of instruction? It seems clear from some of his other writings that Bruner thought Piaget's was the kind of theory which would serve his purposes, augmented and corrected by his own work and developmental model and, to choose one other example which he has praised, Margaret Donaldson's.

To begin with, then, the commonly accepted image of what a theory of instruction should look like seems to require psychological theories of a kind we have reason to believe we cannot fashion, and which at the moment we certainly lack. If one accepts the presuppositions on which the program of scientific psychology rests, one does not sit around waiting for adequate theories of development and learning before trying to articulate one's theory of instruction. One goes ahead in the reasonable hope that there will be a dialectical development, whereby work on the theory of instruction may contribute toward refinement of the theories of learning and development. Those presuppositions will also encourage the researcher to disregard or depreciate any apparent distinction between instructing in particulars and teaching; instructing will be seen as a straightforward constituent of education—an educational theory may well prescribe *what* should be learned in order to attain a particular ideal of educational experience, and the theory of instruction may be put to work to ensure the efficient learning of whatever content is required as a constituent of that ideal.

Let us look briefly at the research aimed at discovering empirical generalizations about the relationship between teaching behaviors and learning outcomes, and see what it seems to offer toward the kind of theory of instruction Bruner proposes. The course of a central part of this research has been well described in Cronbach's "two disciplines" papers referred to earlier.

In the first of these papers Cronbach charted the failure of scientific psychology to come adequately to grips with the problems involved in generating a theory of instruction. He recommended, as a move toward a solution to those problems, that experimental psychology should join forces with correlational psychology, combining the rigorous treatments of the former with the latter's greater sophistication in dealing with individual differences. So instead of continuing to seek fruitlessly for the best method of teaching everyone—finding the best instructional "treatment"—psychologists should try to discover what treatments best suit different people's different "aptitudes." Aptitudes, Cronbach pointed out, clearly interact differently with different treatments. Thus, for example, an aggressive extrovert might learn more easily from group discussion than might a shy introvert, and the latter might more easily than the former learn from private study. Scientific research, then, might tell us what kinds of people learn best by what kinds of methods. Thus instead of using a particular method of teaching which suits only a portion of a group of students—and which interacts effectively with only a portion of aptitudes—we might train teachers to use, or make available, say, three or four "treatments" suited to a much wider range of aptitudes. In an ideal world each student would receive the treatment best suited to his or her aptitudes. The finding and securing of such "Aptitude-Treatment Interactions" (ATIs) "will carry us into an educational psychology which measures readiness for different types of teaching and which invents teaching methods to fit different types of readiness."[26]

THE ATI PROGRAM OF RESEARCH

An initial objection to this program, clearer with hindsight, might be to note that no one "has" *an* aptitude; rather each person also "has" an intelligence, a set of personal relationships with teachers and other students, varying distractions and fluctuating abilities to control them, desires, hopes, and the usual changing array of complicated things we imprecisely distinguish and crudely name.

Nearly twenty years later Cronbach reported on the considerable body of research on ATIs.[27] In describing the attempts he made, with Richard Snow, at synthesizing the research reports, he notes: "In attempting to generalize from the literature, Snow and I have been thwarted by the inconsistent findings coming from roughly similar inquiries."[28] And while some ATIs seem somewhat generalizable, one cannot make any secure generalizations because other ATIs seem to interfere with them. Other personality factors, experiences, environments, and so on, prevent one from concluding anything securely about how best to teach anyone. "However far we carry our analysis—to third order or fifth order or any other—untested interactions of a still higher order can be envisioned."[29]

Cronbach's conclusion is rather pessimistic about the program set forth some twenty years earlier, and it may be referred to here to connect my earlier general argument with this particular area of research:

> Our troubles do not arise because human events are in principle unlawful; man and his creations *are* part of the natural world. The trouble, as I see it, is that we cannot store up enough generalizations and constructs for ultimate assembly into a network. It is as if we needed a gross of dry cells to power an engine and could only make one a month. The energy would leak out of the first cells before we had half the battery completed. So it is with the potency of our generalizations.[30]

My argument, which I want to make plausible, is embodied in the fact that the trouble Cronbach finds with the latter part of the foregoing quotation is the result of his inability to acknowledge the trouble in the first sentence: The kinds of "laws" which order human events are not of the same kind, are not expressible in the same way, are not discoverable by the same methods, as those that order the physical world. The kinds of things the psychologist has to deal with when seeking to describe and explain human behavior have a nature which is in some complicated way distinct from the nature of the physical world. The weak argument, which is adequate to my case at the moment, as expressed in the syllogism, is satisfied by noting that we simply do not have any secure generalizations about ATIs, despite the enormous research effort aimed at discovering them.

One problem with the program, Cronbach states as follows: "Too narrow an identification with science, however, has fixed our eyes on an inappropriate goal."[31] Instead of seeking secure generalizations and aiming toward a general theory, however, it may be reasonable to develop small–scale, locally applicable ATIs, that will help teachers in particular schools teach particular things to particular students—thereby using the power amassed in one of the dry cells rather than letting it leak away while trying to amass enough to power an engine. How can one argue that this more modest use of scientific psychological theory cannot have implications for education?

Let us consider Snow's proposal for developing local theories. He begins with the same general observation as Cronbach: "As work on aptitude-treatment interactions (ATIs) has proceeded, it has become clear that interactions, both among individual difference variables and between them and instructional conditions, can be so complex as to push generalizations beyond our grasp, practically speaking."[32] (If our concern is practicality, one may reasonably wonder about the practicality of the kind of large-scale research effort necessary to generate even small-scale ATIs—especially when one recalls that Cronbach and Snow's analysis of the ATI research involved rejecting the greater part of it as so flawed as to be useless.) Snow concludes that while we cannot hope to generate a general theory of instruction we might hope to generate local theories of instruction. "ATI does not make theory impossible; it makes general theory impossible."[33]

A strong argument for not following the path recommended in Snow's proposal has already been made. Gehlbach points out that a crucial reason why the search for more general ATIs and a general theory of instruction has foundered remains to undermine the more modest proposal:

> A major commitment to local theories would be premature . . . [because] it presumes *enough* of the *right kinds* of instructional hypotheses have been subjected to *appropriate* research designs to justify a massive restructuring of the goals for instructional research. . . . A merely realigned focus of attention to local theory construction is not going to solve many problems if the conceptual clarity, methodological rigor and analytic quality of educational research do not improve generally. If, on the other hand, the overall quality of research does improve, then local theories may be unnecessary in our search for generalizable findings.[34]

One purpose in seeking general theories was the establishment of laws; that is, one could explain one's phenomena, and so one could intervene in them confident that one could predict the results caused by particular interventions. What one loses with the reduced ambition to generate only local theories is confidence in explaining causal sequences and consequently confidence that a future intervention will produce results similar to a past intervention.

Gehlbach further points out that the discovery of ATIs may not be best met with the assumption that one must, in instruction, "accommodate" to them—the "psychological fallacy," in educational contexts. Rather, Gehlbach argues, it might be better "to find ways to *eliminate* them (for example, by developing more powerful instructional methods.)"[35] So, if we develop more powerful instructional methods that are effective across the range of normal aptitude differentials, ATI research may become simply a diagnostic tool for detecting weak instructional strategies.

From where, however, are we going to develop more powerful instructional methods? These were supposed to be the promised product of a theory of instruction, which was to have been built with help from ATI research. If ATI research does establish some generalizable ATI findings, how will our theory of instruction know which should be accommodated to, and which eliminated? Gehlbach's suggested aim of eliminating ATIs seems to return us to the program criticized as fruitless in the first of Cronbach's "two disciplines" papers. If we *can* generate more powerful instructional strategies from some source other than a theory of instruction—say, from folk wisdom—we might ask what we need a theory of instruction for. Presumably to systematize and generalize, from empirical study, these products of folk wisdom. But this is what the program of research has failed to do, and what Cronbach and Snow have concluded it cannot do—except in local circumstances. And this local program Gehlbach has given us reasons to believe is impracticable.

Another way of looking at the oddity of the ATI research program is to consider that the more successful it is, the more difficult it becomes to achieve its goals—both the goal of generating a general theory of instruction and the related goal of practical pay-off. If people had two or three distinguishable aptitudes then matters might be relatively straightforward. Discovering by experiment the two or three treatments that interact optimally with these aptitudes would provide some practical guidance to the instructor. But if we find twenty distinguishable aptitudes, for each of which we have discovered the optimal treatment, what do we do? We are faced with insurmountable problems. Aptitude A, let us say, interacts optimally with treatment A^1. That is, if instructed by method A^1 the person with aptitude A will learn better. But learn better than what? Well, learn better than if instructed with treatment B^1. The usual form of ATI research is to pose what seem like binary opposite aptitudes (high/low anxiety, serialist/wholist) and find treatments that best suit the distinct poles. So if we have twenty such clearly established ATIs, how are we to discover whether a person with aptitude A is indeed best instructed by treatment A^1? That is, the person with aptitude A may also have fairly high aptitudes D, J, L, R, V, Z. Do we pretest each individual on each aptitude? And could we design treatments to suit the infinite variety of mixed aptitudes? Perhaps an example might be useful here.

Let us take an ATI more or less at random. If our aim is to improve the effectiveness of our instructional efficiency, Pask and Scott's research[36] suggests we should divide our students into two groups, the one made up of those students who seem to learn better from what Pask and Scott call a "serialist" treatment, and the other made up from those who seem to learn better from a "wholist" treatment. Among the ATIs reported this seems a fairly dramatic, unsuspected, and successful case. The serialist and wholist strategies seem to offer a contribution toward our armament of instructional devices.

In what way does this knowledge contribute toward articulation of a theory of instruction? If we are aiming at a general theory presumably this finding would play a part. Crudely, one might incorporate it as a rule that after pretesting and distinguishing serialists from wholists one should use the appropriate treatment for the appropriate group. This rule, however, would have to be incorporated with a rule recommending different treatments for, say, extroverts and introverts, for high I.Q. and low I.Q., for high creativity and low creativity, for high I.Q./low creativity and low I.Q./high creativity, and so on and on. That is, if the program were successful in discovering twenty clear, generalizable ATIs, they would leave us with a theory of instruction too cumbersome to use. Even if we are satisfied that we will settle for local findings, how do we decide which of the available ATIs we should use? Presumably Pask and Scott's finding applies vividly to the experimental group, and if we wish to instruct them, then that ATI is useful. Treating one group in a serialist way and the other in a wholist way ensures that both groups will learn more than if a neutral treatment is used. But what, in this complex world, is a neutral treatment? Perhaps that particular group divided even more dramatically between high and low anxiety. If they were divided into high and low anxiety groups and the appropriate treatments were used perhaps the learning of the whole group might have been dramatically superior to that achieved by the serialist/wholist division.

These are problems raised for instruction. If our concern is teaching, and thus education, we have additional problems if our hope is to use the results of ATI research for practical improvements. To continue with the particular example above: we have to wonder what is serialism and what is wholism. Are they descriptive of brain differences? Or do they result from different kinds of teaching? Are they independent of I.Q., creativity, anxiety level, and so forth? Are they skills which everyone has but which we use differentially for different tasks? Are they ends of a continuum, or points on some more extensive continuum? If our concern is simple instruction, then we may be able to use this finding in particular cases. But if our concern is teaching, to accept straightforwardly that serialists should be taught serially and wholists wholistically is to commit the psychological fallacy. A description of something which is not a constraint of nature does not imply any educational prescription. Perhaps the teacher should follow Gehlbach's recommendation and find an instructional strategy that will eliminate the ATI—that will teach serialists and wholists equally well, achieving for all students acceptable minimum performance. Perhaps the teacher should teach serialists in a wholistic way and wholists in a serial way, in order better to develop greater flexibility in the thinking of the two groups—in such a case, of course, the teaching of the particular content would be subordinate to teaching greater flexibility of thinking. Perhaps serialism is an inferior form of thinking, which should be extirpated, and serialists should be taught to become wholists. That is, the datum provided by Pask's and Scott's study leads to no particular educational implication—unless it describes a constraint of nature. But, it might be argued, while it has no *particular* educational implication, it would seem to have some kind of implication for education—an educational theory would surely not ignore it. I will return to this point in the section "Educational Theories and Facts" in the Conclusion.

As nothing in particular is implied for educational practice by Piaget's descriptive theory because we cannot be sure that he is describing a constraint of our nature, so a vast bank of ATIs would leave us in the same predicament—with the additional difficulty of utilizing a bank of ATIs when we see how the ATIs interact with each other. Even if we look no further than the observation that, on frequent replication in varying conditions (something we still lack), certain ATIs represent empirical regularities, their incorporation into a theory of instruction remains problematic at best.

So far, then, we have reason to doubt our ability to generate the kind of theory of development which is to serve, in some way not elaborated by Bruner, as a support to a theory of instruction. (A similar argument could be made about the theory of learning.) That neither theory presently exists seems generally accepted. One of the central thrusts of research toward a theory of instruction seems to have foundered, and there seems no persuasive reason to think it can get out of its present impasse.

BEHAVIORAL OBJECTIVES FOR INSTRUCTION

Elaborations of Bruner's model for a theory of instruction usually require that a part of any instructional strategy must include the specification of instructional objectives. What contribution does this make toward a theory of instruction and what implications might it have for education? Or, rather, not to be coy about it, on what grounds can I claim that this area of research has no implications for education? I will try to clarify a distinction between psychology's "instructing" and education's "teaching" in this discussion; and try to show that because this research is dominated by the presuppositions of scientific psychology, with its aim of generating a psychological theory, the phenomena on which it focuses are not those which properly interest educators.

It is commonly assumed by researchers in the tradition of scientific psychology that education's folk-wisdom principle that it is usually helpful for the teacher to sketch out the aims of any particular unit in advance, and it is usually helpful to let students know in advance what is to be learned, can be turned, by the use of a "scientific method," into a precise principle that can enormously improve instructional efficiency. There has been a huge body of writing about such precise principles, under the heading of "behavioral objectives." These are key tools in developing instructional strategies that will control students' behavior in the direction of more efficient learning:

> It is clear that a model or theory of instruction is in fact a special case of what has come to be known in the mathematical and engineering literature as *optimal control theory*, or, more simply, control theory. The development of control theory has progressed at a rapid rate both in the United States and abroad, but most of the applications involve engineering or economic systems of one type or another. Precisely the same problems are posed in the area of instruction except that the system to be controlled is the human learner, rather than a machine or group of industries.[37]

When Atkinson notes that precisely the same problems are posed, we must agree that one can pose the problem about controling human learning in a form that is exactly analogous to the way the problem of the control of an engineering function may be posed. Whether posing it this way will enable one to answer it adequately is another question. In order to study this question it is necessary to be precise about what effective instruction is being effective at, and so we need to know precisely how we can tell whether or not any particular instructional act has been effective. Thus, for any instructional unit, objectives need to be spelled out in precise terms, and there must be some means of measuring precisely whether or not those objectives have been achieved. So a statement of objectives should be a mirror image of what is to be evaluated at the end of the instructional act. What is to be evaluated must then be measurable in terms of some observable behavioral change, and so the objectives need to be stated in terms of the behavioral changes that the instructional act will bring about.

A point in passing: These procedures are designed in order to study instruction; to find out what kind of instructional strategies work in which kinds of circumstances with what kinds of people. One may note the unthinking ease with which experimental procedures are converted directly into recommended procedures for practice within education. Conditions made necessary in order *to study* instruction are asserted to be the best for *the practice* of teaching, even before the study has yielded any clear results. This observation is apparently either not noted or not thought at all odd by proponents of the use of behavioral objectives. It is, however, undeniably odd.

Much of the contention about behavioral objectives in education has turned on some teachers' claims that their aim is, say, to teach "an appreciation of the beauty of Shakespeare's sonnets," or to teach toward "the development of an historical consciousness." These teachers claim that these things cannot be expressed in behavioral terms. Proponents of the use of behavioral objectives tend to respond that while indeed such a general aim must remain ineffable in some sense, constituents of this general aim are not. That is, the teachers who claim to have these general aims nevertheless have to do something on Monday morning, and that something will be a constituent of the general aim; and if the teachers can express what is to be taught on Monday morning and how they will recognize whether or not it has been learned, then the technology of behavioral objectives may help in making the learning of this constituent of the general aim more effective. So from general educational aims may be derived particular instructional objectives. The achievement of these objectives is the job that the developing technology of instruction can make clear and efficient, and in the accumulation of such achieved objectives the educational aim may also be achieved (in so far as it can be stated in terms that allow one to perceive whether or not it has been achieved).

(In the writings about behavioral objectives a fairly simple distinction tends to be accepted: "aims" are vague and long-term; "objectives" are precise and relatively short-term, and their achievement can be precisely measured if they are properly stated. There are, though, some distinctions made among objectives—for example, "expressive," "experiential."[38] It is assumed that objectives may be fairly straightforwardly "derived" from aims. Both the distinction between "aims" and "objectives," and the assumption about deriving one from the other involve problems that are largely ignored in these writings,[39] but I want to pass over them, at least as they are posed in those terms, since they are peripheral to my argument.)

I want to make only two points about behavioral objectives in education; the first is a simple empirical matter, the second I think crystallizes why many good teachers, and no doubt bad ones, and many sensible educators, and no doubt senseless ones, oppose them.

Proponents of behavioral objectives adopt in their writings the authority of science. They treat opponents as might the medical scientist bringing to witless peasants a cure for the disease from which they suffer, but which they resist on grounds of primitive superstition. (The case is not, I think, this bad. Indeed, the balance of superstition seems to reside with the "scientists.") The excessive self-confidence with which proponents of behavioral objectives insist that their technology will improve educational practice is such that one assumes their prescriptions must have the backing of overwhelming empirical support. On no other grounds could they so confidently turn their experimental procedures into educational prescriptions. This program involves a simple empirical claim: instruction (and teaching) that uses behavioral objectives in the prescribed form will be more effective than instruction (and teaching) which does not, other things being equal. (The final phrase, of course, provides reasons for expecting some ambiguity in any results from comparative experiments.) Such an empirical claim is embedded in assertions like:

> the more explicit the instructor can be regarding the statement of instructional objectives, the better. The only kind of specificity that really helps in improving teacher behavior empirically is the specification of goals in terms of student behavior changes.[40]

Or: "A statement of an objective is useful to the extent that it specifies what the learner must be able to *do* or perform when he is demonstrating his mastery of the objective."[41]

Proponents of such a program are not claiming that it will merely make instruction a little more efficient: "In our view this development is one of the most important educational advances of the 1900s and signals a very significant attack upon the problems of education."[42] The somewhat bizarre feature of all this is that there is no convincing empirical support to show that even simple instructional tasks are improved in efficacy by the use of these procedures.[43] There is no support, that is, for these strong claims when applied to instruction, and their easy application to education—which we have yet to come to—is, one might say, a scientistic fantasy.

It is perhaps worth stressing this simple point. It is not that teachers who resist using behavioral objectives need to make a strong case to excuse their ignorant boldness, their flying in the face of science. There is not as yet, and I will try to show that there never will be, a case to answer. Asserting that one *ought* to use these procedures in education, when there is no convincing empirical support that they are effective in improving even simple instruction, contravenes the first principle of rational empiricism. This kind of behavior is not rational, thus it can hardly make claims to being scientific. One would think that the consistent empirical disconfirmation of the dramatic claims made for the huge improvements we would see if we applied scientific principles to the control of the learning process—a disconfirmation that has been continuing routinely for over half a century to the various "scientific" proposals of Dewey, Thorndike, Skinner, and now to the proposals of criterion-referenced instruction—would make their proposers reflect on their presuppositions. Opponents of these "scientific" proposals are branded as "romantics," and much worse, but it needs to be stressed that the opponents of these procedures stand on firm empirical grounds. The rational empiricist opposes these supposedly scientific proposals on the grounds that they exemplify phenomena-insensitivity, of a rather gross order, and that they seem to result from a romantic intoxication with a simplistic association with "science." Intoxication seems not too strong a word for the odd behavior displayed in claiming the authority of science in recommending procedures that lack empirical support. The proposers apparently have not noticed that their claims for their recommended practices lack such support or perhaps they think their association with science is so compelling that they do not need it. Whatever the case, it is very odd.

The second point I want to make is that one cannot put a unit of education into the form of a behavioral objective. It is assumed without question in the writings of proponents of these procedures that while vague aims like "appreciating the beauty of Shakespeare's sonnets," or "developing an historical consciousness" cannot be put into behavioral terms, constituents of these can be put into the form of precise objectives. A simple preliminary point: "appreciating the beauty of Shakespeare's sonnets" or "developing an historical consciousness" are no more *vague* than the most rigorous behavioral objective. They are precise referents to complex phenomena. "Appreciating the beauty of Shakespeare's sonnets" refers to an experience, a rather refined one, based on a range of knowledge and experiences, and one which will be in some ways different for different people. None of this makes it imprecise or "ineffable." It may make it immeasurable by the gauges educational psychologists have available, or know how to "read," but this is different from the aim being imprecise. We cannot measure—something rather different— the pain of a toothache, but that hardly makes one's toothache vague and imprecise. If we dismiss what we cannot measure precisely we have no incentive to increase the sophistication of our measuring tools.

If one wants to break up an educational aim into constituent units one must be sure that the units are indeed units of the thing one is aiming to compose from them. It is taken for granted by proponents of educational objectives, and, so far as I can see, by virtually all educational psychologists, that educational units are fairly straightforward; or, rather, while accepting the theoretical difficulty they commonly proceed in experimental practice as though the theoretical difficulty did not *really* matter. Teachers teach history by means of facts and concepts. If one opens a history book, therefore, one has on the page constituent units of education. If a teacher wants to object and say, no, these bits and pieces are only the means to help students "develop an historical consciousness," the educational psychologist considers this "vague" general aim as irrelevant to the area where the technology of behavioral objectives may help make the teaching task more efficient.

Let me use a metaphor to indicate roughly the distinction I want to make. The technology of behavioral objectives works by dividing a teaching topic into units. It is assumed that in doing this the instructional technologist is doing nothing different from what the teacher does in breaking down a topic into units and lessons, except that the technologist is being more precise and efficient. There is, however, a crucial difference. Let us consider the general educational aim as an image or picture. The instructional technologist assumes that the picture can be broken into constituent bits and pieces, and when these bits and pieces are put together one has reconstituted the picture. If, that is, the general educational aim can be stated precisely enough, it can be broken into constituent objectives which, using the recommended procedures, may be efficiently learned by the student, thereby achieving the general educational aim. My point is that this notion is false because in education the images or pictures of our general aims are not of a kind amenable to this treatment: to continue the metaphor, there are no such two-dimensional pictures; educational aims, rather, are like holograms.

If the photographic plate containing the interference pattern of the holographic image is broken into bits and pieces, each piece contains, in however blurred a form, the image of the whole. The ear of the Mona Lisa tells nothing of the lady's smile. A small section of the holographic image of a modern enigmatic lady would, with the laser's light, reveal, however vaguely, the bewitching smile and ear and chin and whatever else. An educational objective, I am suggesting by this metaphor, is like a piece of a hologram rather than a piece of a two-dimensional picture. This suggests why one cannot specify an *educational* objective, or teaching objective in education, in behavioral terms unless one can also specify the general educational aim in behavioral terms; one cannot specify behavioral objectives for a lesson on the causes of the French Revolution unless one can also specify in behavioral terms what it means to possess an historical consciousness. There are no instructional constituents which do not entail the image of the whole.

This may appear a bit arcane. Am I denying that instructing students efficiently about the main facts, concepts, and causes of the French Revolution is of no educational value? I think everyone recognizes a sense in which such knowledge may be worthless, remain inert, for some people, but may be used in educational development, provide an aliment, for others. Whitehead's observation that the merely well-informed man is the greatest bore on God's earth catches the sense in which education requires something additional to facts, concepts, causes, and so on. What is it that in some cases makes a set of facts and concepts of no educational value and in others makes the same facts and concepts of the greatest value? What is it that in some cases makes a set of facts and concepts not educational units, but in other cases does make the same set of facts and concepts educational units? My metaphor is intended to point toward the answer that what makes a set of facts and concepts educational units is that they contain in their organization an image of the whole of which they are units. What makes the same set of facts and concepts educationally inert in some cases is that they are not units of an educational whole. The technology of behavioral objectives guarantees that its units will be of the latter kind—educationally inert.

Still arcane perhaps. The proponents of behavioral objectives may respond—after no doubt sighing about my obscurantism—that all they are recommending is that we do efficiently something that is normally done inefficiently. While I agree that teaching is often done inefficiently, I want to continue my argument that the efficiency which the use of behavioral objectives purports to offer is—if successful—even less efficient than poor teaching if its goal is an educational one. But if learning about the French Revolution serves an educational aim, how can instructing students in the main facts and concepts about the French Revolution not contribute toward that aim? Surely knowing such facts and concepts is a necessary condition for "understanding" or "appreciating"—or whatever obscure term I may want to insist on—the French Revolution. So even if I want to insist that knowing such facts and concepts is not a *sufficient* condition for "understanding" the French Revolution why can I not use the technology of behavioral objectives in teaching the *necessary* knowledge and do whatever else I think is necessary to make "understanding" possible by whatever arcane means I wish? Because this procedure presupposes a distinction which in education does not exist. There is no such thing in education as an objective, a piece, that does not entail at the same time the general aim. The general aim to develop an historical consciousness and, as a part of that, to teach an understanding of the French Revolution and, as a part of that, to teach the ten main facts, seven main concepts, and four main causes of the French Revolution, yields a situation where one cannot properly teach the ten main facts, seven main concepts, and four main causes of the French Revolution without at the same time teaching the development of an historical consciousness. That one can instruct in the facts, concepts, and causes independently of the general aim is obviously the case—and one can use behavioral objectives in the process—but the case is no longer an educational one. The particulars in such a case are not like parts of a hologram—the laser's light leaves us only with an ear or a bit of hair. The more general image has to be ever present in each particular to make it an educational aliment.

(I may seem to be condemning the use of behavioral objectives by comparing them with an impossible ideal. In fact a great deal of teaching is of disjointed bits and pieces. While this is regrettably true, and no doubt always has been,[44] I would prefer to call such disjointed behavior merely instructing. One does not, however, improve an enterprise by taking an obvious abuse and trying to make it more efficient.)

My second point, then, is that the kind of unit one can put into the form of an instructional objective cannot be an educational unit. Certainly one can assert that these behavioral objectives, when achieved, accumulate into a picture which may indeed look like one of education's holograms—or, at least, they may look like holograms if one persuades the looker to stand dead still and close one eye. And no doubt in the land of the blind such one-eyed observers will seem like kings. If we open both eyes and move about, however, the difference between a hologram and a two-dimensional picture is vivid and fundamental. The sense of strain in making this distinction with regard to the reality of educational phenomena is that it is so obvious, everyone recognizes it, but if someone suddenly insists on standing dead still with one eye closed it is not easy to point out how the image of the picture is fundamentally different from that of the hologram. If one claims that words like "appreciate" and "understand" cannot be used then it is indeed rather difficult to point out the difference between being able to repeat a set of inert facts and concepts and being able to understand and appreciate what those facts and concepts refer to. The point is that there is no reason at all to forbid use of the words; they are perfectly clear; they refer to things we all recognize; they serve to help us make crucial distinctions between clearly distinguishable things; and they are frequently extremely precise referents to complex phenomena which exist and cannot be adequately referred to by using any other terms. Which is to say that the linguistic constraints insisted on by proponents of behavioral objectives are entirely arbitrary and serve—like standing dead still with one eye closed—only to block out from one's range of vision absolutely crucial aspects of the phenomena which one is supposed to be looking at and studying. Ignoring parts of one's phenomena of interest is not rational, so it can hardly be properly recommended as scientific.

But what is it that makes some facts and concepts educational units? And if that can be answered precisely do we not provide things on which the technology of behavioral objectives may work? And surely all those teachers who have been forced by their school boards to write their objectives in behavioral terms are not thereby made into mere instructional technologists unable to contribute to their students' education? Firstly, and fortunately, the complexity of practice will ensure that teachers will not merely instruct toward the achievement of their stated behavioral objectives; they will also teach by imbuing the particulars with more general and diffuse aims. Indeed in most cases the writing of behavioral objectives will have very little influence on actual teaching—a fact already noted and bewailed by their proponents.

An oddity of educational, as distinct from instructional, objectives is that their achievement in each individual case may be different. The sophisticated historical consciousness of A.J.P. Taylor is different from that of J.H. Hexter, which in turn is different from that of F. Braudel, and on and on. Similarly, each individual child will develop an historical consciousness—when it is achieved at all— by different means, using different facts and concepts in different combinations. Yet "historical consciousness" is the precise term to use for the educational objective toward which the good teacher steers each child; it is the criterion by reference to which one tries to decide in each individual case whether a particular form of knowledge is an educational unit or not.

Why is not "the fact" a proper unit of education? Well, clearly because accumulating lots of facts does not add up to being educated. Learning or remembering the name of the horse of the Lone Ranger's faithful Indian companion may be "entertaining" but it is not a necessary contributor toward someone's educational development. But, then, neither is any particular piece of knowledge *necessary*. If "the fact," or, for the same reason, "the concept," is not a proper unit, what is? I have begun to answer this question elsewhere, and aim to finish answering it somewhere else;[45] my task here is to move from the truism that education accumulates by the accumulation of educational units, to pointing out that the units expressible in terms of behavioral objectives are not educational units. For a unit expressed in terms of a behavioral objective to be an educational unit, it must be a necessary component of a student's educational development. This, I am claiming, is impossible because for a unit to be an educational unit it must embody in however blurred a form an image of the whole of which it is a unit, and this can be achieved only if the complex educational aim can be incorporated in the description of the behavioral objectives of the unit—and this, it is acknowledged, is impossible. (Because such aims are too vague and imprecise, say the proponents of behavioral objectives; because the behavioral objectives are inadequate to expressing units of the aim, say I.)

I may seem to be running on rather repetitiously, but I do so from a perhaps excessive sensitivity that my argument will remain opaque to proponents of behavioral objectives. To someone who has never questioned that facts and concepts may not be educational units, it may be difficult to see what image of education—and teaching as distinct from instructing—is involved in my distinction between educational units and noneducational bits and pieces of facts, concepts, or whatever—especially as they may, to a superficial glance, seem alike.[46] And even if they recognize this distinction it may seem far from clear that one cannot simply leave the fact and the concept teaching to the procedures they propose and deal with the additional educational bit separately: that is, leave the plain job of shaping observable behaviors to the scientists and let others delve in the mystical stuff, if they insist on it. What I am trying to make clear is that my argument is not promoting but opposing obscurantism. We all recognize that mere information does not make a person educated, and that what marks the distinction between the well-informed and the well-educated person is complex. The argument I am presenting about the necessity of identifying what one does as a proper unit of education is central to the search for clarity and precision in dealing with educational phenomena. Obscurantism results from ignoring such complexities, and thus making truly obscure the nature of the very phenomena one is supposed to be dealing precisely with.

The previous paragraph was intended, when begun, to restate my distinction between an educational unit and any noneducational set of facts or concepts in a different way; a way more accessible to people who are inclined to ignore it, or claim it is irrelevant to their arguments about the educational value of using behavioral objectives. As the paragraph turned rather toward a further rhetorical assertion I suspect I have made the argument as clearly as I can at present, so let me sum up this section and move on.

I have considered some aspects of that research aimed toward establishing a theory of instruction which is governed by the presuppositions of scientific psychology, because this research seems the central area where one should find implications for education. We have seen that the kinds of "basic" psychological theories that are required to support a theory of instruction are lacking, and that we have some reason to expect that such theories cannot be formulated. We have seen that a central part of the "applied" research—establishing regularities between instructional "treatments" and particular "aptitudes"—runs into intractable practical problems, and, again, we have, on conceptual grounds, some basis to believe that these problems are not resolvable within the current program, based on the prevailing presuppositions, of scientific psychology. We have looked also at the strange case of the behavioral-objectives movement. Here we have seen that procedures that were made necessary to study the phenomena in question, given the prevailing presuppositions of scientific psychology, have been directly converted into recommendations for educational practice despite the lack of empirical support for the millennial claims made for them. In addition we have reason to believe that such objectives do not in fact make any part of the educational process more precise; rather, they obscure, deform, and trivialize education—not just in contingent practice, but of necessity. Wherever we look we have grounds for thinking that this research has not yet yielded legitimate implications for education—it clearly has not—but that it is foundering rather than making progress. It shows no signs of even approaching educational phenomena.

There are, however, large numbers of psychologists and psychologists of education who would be wholly undisturbed by an argument concluding that research aimed at developing a theory of instruction is ill-founded. They too would criticize such research, reeking as it does with cognitivism. Many psychologists would argue that the way to affect education is not through such "applied" research, where the methods of science cannot work properly in the confusing mess of the everyday world, but rather must be achieved through "basic" research, whose secured knowledge will filter down into educational practice.

In an exchange about the relative values for educational practice of "basic" and "applied" research, Kerlinger states that "educational research does not lead directly to improvements in educational practice."[47] This might seem a curious state of affairs. What would we think if an engineer noted that engineering research did not lead directly to improvements in engineering practice? We might think there was something seriously amiss with our researchers. Perhaps they do not know what the engineers are trying to do? Perhaps they are dealing with the wrong concepts—with, say, cell reproduction rather than force and stress. Kerlinger's odd claim becomes clearer as one realizes that about half the time he uses the word educational he means psychological and the rest of the time he seems to mean educational. Slavin's reply, which notes this confusion, seems in some ways even stranger. His perception of the central question is: "Should education be philosophy or should it be science?"[48] Slavin's response to this question is worth noting because it seems to point to an area of research that might undermine the minor premise of my syllogism. Slavin claims that "one area of education *is* a science";[49] that there is an area where psychological theory has led to applied research which has direct implications for the improvement of educational practice. The area Slavin identifies is "special" education, and the body of theory is that associated with behavior modification.

The area of behavior modification is of interest to my argument because it may seem to challenge it, and in showing why it does not I should further clarify my argument, or my confusion. I am particularly concerned with a range of supposedly firmly established psychological theory that is often assumed to have implications for education. First, however, it may be noted in passing why Slavin's chosen area leaves my syllogism undisturbed. "Calling infinity a number," as Auden once observed, "doesn't make it one." Calling something education doesn't necessarily make it education. This is the bewitchment of words, on an unsubtle scale. Slavin is not refer-ring to education at all, but rather, at best, to establishing preconditions for education. In the diagnosis and treatment of certain "special cases," or pathologies, the norms that serve as objectives and gauges of measurement are relatively value-innocent. They are norms which ordinarily present no problems; they do not involve contentions over the ends of such education—the ends are largely given in what is counted normal behavior. "Education," used for this kind of training, is an honorific extension of the term's proper meaning. Such training is of course of the greatest humanitarian importance, and we have cause to applaud its every advance. But it is simply a primitive confusion to assume that because we call it education, principles which are found operative within it may be legitimately claimed as having general *educational* implications.[50] Whether or not such prin-ciples may be generalized to education proper we will consider now.

The Analytic and the Empirical

THE EMPIRICAL AND THE PSEUDO-EMPIRICAL

Empirical hypotheses within psychology seek to establish regular relationships between two distinct things—say, "motiva-tion" and "learning," or rate of bar pushing and schedule of rein-forcements. The relationship is assumed to be a contingent one and experiment is required to find out what it really is. The aim of sci-entific psychology has been to establish sets of such empirical re-lationships securely and so fashion reliable laws and theories. A large body of theory within psychology, which is often pointed to as among the successes of scientific psychology, seems not to estab-lish empirical regularities but rather to articulate analytic truths—things that are true not as a matter of experiment but of necessity or by definition once one has analyzed the language in which they are stated. I want to argue here that a range of psychological theories which are often assumed to have implications for education are sim-ply not psychological theories.

An example of such a pseudo-empirical theory which is in fact an analytic truth is Thorndike's formulation of the "law of effect." It has often been pointed out that this "law"—that people tend to repeat behaviors which have pleasurable consequences—is true in-dependently of, say, Thorndike's line–drawing experiments with blindfold subjects that are assumed to support it. It is true because choosing to repeat a behavior, if one can, and expecting pleasurable consequences from so choosing are not independent things; they are conceptually tied together. Choosing to repeat a behavior is tied up in the expectation of pleasurable consequences. Is it conceivable that experiments could disconfirm the hypothesis? If our experiments routinely turned up cases of people who did not choose to repeat behaviors they expected to be pleasurable, we would surely conclude that there was something wrong with the way we were identifying what was pleasurable for them.

In the days of my theological discussions mentioned in chapter 1, the precocious atheists among us would goad us under the street lamps on autumn evenings with the assertion that notions of goodness and sin were nonsense because everyone always did what gave them most pleasure, and those who ran the church simply defined as "good" what gave them pleasure and "sin" what did not. We defenders of the ancient ways would counter with the case of the martyrs—in my memory it seems always to have reverted to the case of St. Peter not running away from martyrdom and choosing to be crucified upside down. Ah, they would respond, it was easier for him to accept martyrdom than to run away and deny Christ again. He'd made the other choice earlier, thinking it was easier, but he had suffered unbearable remorse—his tears, we had learned in Sunday School, had worn deep grooves in his cheeks. Accepting the same form of crucifixion as Christ seemed sacrilegious to him, so, again, it was easier to choose to be crucified upside down. In general, the expectation of heaven made all these choices easier, especially as hell was the alternative. This and many other cases were hammered out between games of kick-the-can, and we traditionalists knew there was something fishy about the whole argument, and, as I recall, we came up with the observation that "what was easiest, or more pleasurable" was implied in the notion of "choosing to do." They were not separate things whose connection could be established or refuted in light of empirical cases. One simply interpreted whatever someone chose to do as that which was easiest or gave most pleasure—or, rather, that is what we *mean* by "choosing to do" something. The law of effect in Thorndike's formulation and in that of the under-ten-year-olds in Manchester's back streets tells us nothing about the world; it simply states relationships among the concepts we use in describing the world. This latter is far from a trivial task; it is, however, the task traditionally accepted as the philosopher's domain.

If we consider the list of propositions which Hilgard claimed psychologists have established with some degree of security, we find that the bulk of them are of the same logical kind as the law of effect, or the proposition that all bachelors in the city of Vancouver are unmarried. We could conduct an empirical inquiry into the latter, but we would be making a simple mistake if we announced that our empirical research established the truth of the proposition. Our empirical research is irrelevant to the truth or otherwise of the proposition, and indeed if we found that our research indicated that a small percentage of the bachelors in Vancouver were married we would conclude there was something wrong with our methodology or definitions.[51]

Hilgard's first proposition is that "brighter people can learn things less bright ones cannot learn."[52] As a product of empirical inquiry it is assumed that careful experimental work has securely established an empirical relationship between brightness and ability to learn. But what we mean by brightness is tied up in what is meant by being able to learn more. How could one measure brightness independently of ability to learn more, and if some criteria were articulated for doing so, would we not object that "ability to learn more" should be included centrally in a proper profile of what is meant by being bright? Hilgard's second proposition, that "a motivated learner acquires what he learns more readily than one who is not motivated," presents a similar problem of identifying what it means to be motivated independently from more readily acquiring learning. One identifies the motivated learner by behaviors which exemplify more ready acquiring of learning. The proposition does not establish an empirical relationship between two distinct things but rather articulates a partial definition of the former—that is, a motivated learner is one who acquires what he learns more readily.

The point is *not*, as it sometimes seems to be taken by psychologists, that the layman is claiming that such findings are obvious, or common sense, or trivial. A proper response to such a claim is that science is often concerned with fashioning hypotheses about what may seem like common sense. Making common-sense observations secure in a scientific context may be a crucial step to developing sophisticated laws and theories with great explanatory power. But this response is not appropriate to the point being made here. I am not arguing that the search for general psychological theories is producing trivia or articulating common-sense observations in technical language, but, rather, I am arguing that it is, more frequently than many psychologists seem to recognize, presenting as results of empirical research conclusions that are conceptual truths, that are matters of logical necessity.

PHYSICS OR GEOMETRY AS A MODEL FOR PSYCHOLOGY?

Scientific psychologists when being most assertively scientific often have recourse to analogy. Thus we have frequently been told that physics could not emerge as a scientific inquiry while stones were conceptualized as having consciousness and intentions; similarly, the study of human behavior can become scientific only when it is conceptualized in a manner which removes consciousness and intentions as inevitable causal agents. An alternative analogy for the science of human behavior might be with geometry rather than physics.[53] Originally geometry was an empirical matter; one measured things and discovered relationships among lines and angles and circles. After a while, however, it became clear that these relationships were not merely empirical matters. Euclid could, thus, sit down and work out what such relationships *had* to be. People might still revert to empirical measurements as heuristic props when things became complicated conceptually. Such measuring did not make the relationships established empirical regularities. Of course they were empirical regularities, but of necessity. As with our research about unmarried bachelors in Vancouver, so if empirical measurements were at variance with geometrical theorems, one concluded that there was obviously some error in the measuring device or the way its readings were interpreted. General theory in psychology, to continue the analogy, has been working through its empirical phase, assuming that the regularities it has uncovered are empirical relationships between independent entities. But, in fact, they are no more empirical regularities than are the theorems of geometry. One may then see the attempt to generate theories along the model of the physical sciences as a false start for psychology, and as preliminary to the proper task of a new formal discipline of psychology which seeks to chart a set of necessarily true theorems about aspects of human behavior. The program of scientific psychology, according to this analogy, has now reached the point where its Euclid (rather than its Newton) will set out clearly how it should generate the formal logical geometry of the terms embedded in ordinary language about things psychological.

Enough of analogies. I am trying to move in a slow, sideway sort of shuffle to confronting radical behaviorism and showing that my syllogism equally applies to it as to the various brands of psychology so far addressed. Let me continue to shuffle forward a little by considering briefly what is the present status of attempts to apply behavior modification principles in classrooms.

But, first, what is behavior modification about? We may accept a brief definition from the source: "By 'behavior modification' I mean what the term was introduced to mean—changing behavior through positive reinforcement."[54] This seems to be generally accepted in books for teachers that purport to show how the principles of behavior modification can be applied in classrooms: "A positive reinforcer . . . must be given immediately after the response occurs. This probably is the single most important principle of operant conditioning . . . and consequently of behavior modification."[55]

What, then, is a reinforcer? A reinforcer is defined as any stimulus which increases the rate or intensity of any behavior. Thus praise following immediately on successful learning, may be a reinforcer of such learning if the rate of learning thereafter increases. The apparent circularity here is irrelevant to the behaviorist because which stimulus serves to reinforce which behavior is clearly an empirical matter. Establishing empirical relationships between particular stimuli and particular behaviors is what behavior modification is about. Having established empirically what reinforces what behavior, one may then control or shape or modify behavior into desirable patterns. The possibility of establishing such empirical relationships between reinforcers and behaviors is, it is claimed, what makes psychology an empirical science.

Some of the objections to drawing implications from psychological theories and research that were dealt with in earlier sections seem to have some weight when applied to the claims made for behavior modification in education. As even the most enthusiastic proponents of behavior modification admit: "what may be a positive reinforcer for one student may be a negative reinforcer for another"[56] and "what might serve as a reinforcer one day might not serve as a reinforcer the next day or the next week."[57] It is an empirical matter what is, in fact, the appropriate reinforcer of the desired behavior in any particular individual at any particular time. At one moment it may be candy, but when feeling sick from overeating, it may be a carbonated soft drink. Unless the teacher knows what is the particular reinforcer at a particular time for each student, and unless the teacher can deliver the appropriate reinforcer to each student immediately after the accomplishment of the desired behavior, then the power of the main principle of behavior modification is reduced.

Nor can it be clear when a student may be having a wonderful idea, and so we cannot know when to reinforce such educationally important "behaviors." This returns us to the central criticism of so much of psychology's attempts to deal with educational phenomena—and the reason for its consistent failure to improve education; that is, it does not deal with educational units.

If one places a child in a white room that has only a bar-press in it, then the child will sooner or later press the bar. If the bar being pressed delivers a candy into the chute below it, the behavioral scientist can provide a probabalistic prediction of the curve of frequency of bar-pressing. It will be comparable to that for a rat which gets a pellet of food from a similar operation in a similar environment, except that the child will probably catch on more quickly and the frequency of the behavior will increase more rapidly than will that of a rat. If the child hates candy, however, the prediction will be confounded. That is simply because candy will not serve for that child as a reinforcer of the bar-pressing behavior. If the child likes candy but has just eaten tons of the stuff, the prediction will also be confounded. In that case, candy has ceased to be a reinforcer of the bar-pressing behavior at that time. If we can determine whatever serves as a reinforcer of the behavior, however, we can get the child to press the bar in the predicted way. The empirical relationship between food and bar-pressing, however, allows us to tell more about the environment in which it occurs than it does about the organism which is "behaving" within that environment. Even in the simplest environment the variability among human beings makes prediction of specific behavior difficult. This is not to claim that radical behaviorism is aiming to predict behavior in the way these illustrations suggest; but that if our concern is to apply the principles in classrooms, variability and complexity seem to make the problem of establishing the appropriate reinforcers for particular behaviors similar in kind to that which has undone ATI research. (That is, disregarding entirely the question of the scientific status of such psychological knowledge, it is far from clear that the teacher armed with knowledge of this scientific basis of the art of teaching is in practice any better off than the teacher who relies on folk wisdom. When we consider the question of the scientific status of such knowledge, and its appropriateness in educational contexts, we may conclude that the teacher so armed is being diverted from proper educational activities, and consequently is worse off.)

The point about the appropriateness of this kind of knowledge in educational contexts may usefully be stressed here. One may discover by experiment the contingencies of reinforcement that will most effectively ensure the learning and memorization of something. One might be able to graph what is sometimes called a "memorization curve," which shows at what intervals repeating a stimulus and rehearsing the relevant response optimize long-term memorization of whatever was learned. This curve may be equally applicable to pigeons and humans. It might then be argued that this knowledge has clear implications for education. All teachers should be taught this as a part of their training. Even if they cannot apply the knowledge exactly in practice, their acquaintance with this part of the scientific basis of teaching can make their art more effective; by approximating the "memorization curve" they will make learning and memorization of any content more likely. The "memorization curve" is merely an empirical regularity of human behavior.

If I learn that I have just won a huge amount of money in a lottery and that I may collect the money at my bank two weeks hence, I will not need reminding that I won the lottery at the appropriate intervals suggested by the "memorization curve." The aim of psychology in such cases is not to account for divergences from the rule, but simply to establish the rule. (The divergences might become data for establishing additional rules.) To do this in the first instance, infections from contingencies that interfere with the underlying mechanisms of learning and memorization have to be blocked out as far as possible. Thus, much of the research aimed at establishing the underlying psychological mechanism uses random words, nonsense phrases, isolated sentences. The law so established is in one respect exactly similar to the laws established in the physical sciences. They too refer not to particular quotidian events, but rather to underlying ideal mechanisms. Bodies falling in a perfect vacuum are as ideal and abstracted from particular events as is the law embodied in this "memorization curve." As a formal finding such a psychological law is fine and interesting. The analogy with physical science laws breaks down, however, when we consider how to apply such laws in the everyday world. Because we can presuppose regularity and consistency in so much of the working of the physical world, we are able to calculate differences between predictions implied by our ideal–condition physical laws and the practical reality to be dealt with. In human events it is far less clear how we can use the formal finding expressed in the psychological law. The utility of the psychological finding seems to hold only for the stark conditions in terms of which it is articulated. The variety and degree of infections which intrude once we remove the finding from its stark formal environment to the world of everyday learning are so great and complex that we cannot calculate them as simple infectors of the law; very quickly—indeed, as soon as the ideal conditions no longer hold—the applicability of the law is destroyed. But this is only a part of the problem for the educational psychologist.

It is far from trite to point out that in education we are never concerned to get children to learn and remember nonsense phrases or random words. If we are doing our educational job properly the things we want to teach children—the educational units—should be organized in such a way that the child immediately grasps them and remembers them because of the context of meanings into which they fit and which they extend.[58] That is, the job of the educator is not to accommodate to the knowledge of this memorization curve, but to obliterate its relevance.

What the educational psychologist does in persuading teachers to accommodate to psychological laws, such as that represented by this "memorization curve"—persuading them that such things form the scientific basis of their art—is to focus their attention *away from* the proper educational task of obliterating their relevance to the teaching act. Nor does one have to know about such laws to obliterate them; their obliteration is an incidental part of learning how to engage children and how to organize knowledge into proper educational units corresponding to children's paradigmatic forms of understanding.

This is to argue that even if radical behaviorism can establish empirical laws of human behavior, the application of these laws in educational settings—in order to modify children's behavior toward educational ends—remains problematic. Furthermore, there is no reliable evidence that the use of behavior–modification principles improves even crude instruction, and none that it can improve education.

The weak form of my syllogism, then, seems to hold against these attempts to apply the findings of radical behaviorism to education. The assertive claims to being scientific tend to be loudest in this branch of psychology, and, in proportion, its claims to offer enormous benefits to education are extreme. All such claims, however, lack reliable empirical support. In the supposedly clear case of translating some aspects of a radical behaviorist learning theory into an instructional technique—Skinner's form of programmed learning—there is, after a quarter of a century, no evidence that this technique instructs more efficiently than any technique that takes an equivalent amount of instructor time in its preparation and is reasonably coherently organized. Indeed, the inability of Skinnerian programs to perform better than some branching programs which lack what are supposed to be vital features of an effective instructional technique must put into doubt either Skinner's translation of his learning theory into a technique or the learning theory itself. Or, at least for those who respect empirical results above theoretical assertions, the consistent failure of linear programed instruction to achieve the great promises made on its behalf give grounds for reassessment somewhere along the line. And this is to discuss only its use in "two-dimensional" instructional tasks; again this technologizing of a learning theory is vulnerable to my earlier argument that it cannot encompass a "three-dimensional, holographic" educational unit.

But there is another attempt to apply behavior–modification principles in education that should be looked at.

SOCIAL LEARNING THEORY AND
COMMON-SENSE THEOREMS

Everyone knows that we can persuade or force or condition people to do certain things in certain circumstances by means of making clear what consequences will follow on their behavior. This informal sense of the law of effect has been applied by Genghis Khan in one way and by, say, IBM in another. We can also sketch certain relationships between key terms used to describe behaviors and the conditions in which they occur. For example, we can say things like the following:

1. If a person performs an act, he both can do it and tries to do it. Conversely, if he does not perform an act, he either cannot do it, but tries; or can do it, but does not try; or neither can do it nor tries to do it.
2. If a person wants x and gets x, he will get some satisfaction from this. If a person gets no satisfaction from getting x then it is not x that he wants.
3. If a person wants x and knows that act A will lead to his getting x and he can do A and no other want or knowledge interferes, then the person will do A.
4. If a person wants x and does A and gets x and believes that A always leads to x, then the next time he wants x he will again do A.[59]

These sentences seem to be universally valid. Perhaps they could be tightened up a bit, but as they stand they describe relationships which *must* hold among things like "wanting," "acting," "satisfaction," and so on. One might compose an indefinite set of such sentences which describe similar relationships among other terms. They are relationships which would always be supported by empirical tests; but the empirical tests would not establish their truth. They are analytic truths, and it would be a conceptual confusion to try to establish them empirically, just as it would be to establish a geometrical theorem empirically. They are sketches of some of the simpler logical relationships which exist in our natural language among certain terms common in some branches of psychology. Smedslund calls them "common-sense theorems"—they may serve as axioms for psychological inquiry.

I may seem to be shuffling away from radical behaviorism again by introducing all these mentalistic terms. But I want to shuffle sideways and then forward a little by considering some other attempts to use principles of behavior modification in education. Some proponents of the use of behavior modification in education point out that the proper aim of their program is not to keep doling out candy to reinforce desirable behaviors. This may be merely the crude beginning of a process which is to move from "reinforcement from concrete tangibles to social reinforcement and ultimately to self–reinforcement."[60]

This program takes us into the domain in which Albert Bandura's social–learning theory and his notions of self–efficacy hold sway. These are now being promoted as having major implications for education. There are a number of grounds on which one might be critical of Bandura's work. One may note B.F. Skinner's objection, namely, that if one accepts the basic principles of behavior modification and reinforcement, the notion of self–reinforcement is an empty redundancy. Behaviors are reinforced by contingencies of environmental responses: to claim that the self may arrange contingencies of reinforcement for desired behaviors in the environment, ignores the fact that prior—in a logical sense—environmental contingencies determine whether and how the self arranges those contingencies. Bandura has, on this account, merely erected another of those redundant "mental way–stations": he has introduced what may appear to some as a richer and more attractive language, but at a disabling cost.

One may, connectedly, be concerned with whether Bandura's formulations and procedures in fact discriminate anything tangible between self-reinforcement and external reinforcement. Martin's review of the results of a set of comparative experiments, and his analysis of methodological and theoretical issues raised by them, provide scant support for Bandura's claims.[61]

Despite this, the growing influence of Bandura's work within education makes it worth considering here; especially as it allows me to set in place a further prop to my argument against certain kinds of psychological research and theory having implications for education.

Consider the following claim of Bandura's: "The strength of people's convictions in their own effectiveness is likely to affect whether they will even try to cope with given situations."[62]

This is presented as a regularity, discovered as a product of empirical research. Smedslund's reply is to derive this finding from a set of common-sense theorems which are necessarily true. It is worth quoting these at length:

> Three common-sense theorems correspond to this formulation. They are more explicit than Bandura's formulation and go beyond it in their scope.

> Theorem 1. *If P wants to do T in S and P believes with complete certainty that he can do T in S, and no other circumstances intervene, then P will try to do T in S.*

> Proof: The alternative to P trying to do T in S is P not trying to do T in S. But P *not* trying to do T in S is not acceptably explained by P's wanting to do T in S and P's certainty that he can do T in S. Hence, some additional circumstances must be invoked to make the explanation acceptable. However, this is impossible, since no other circumstances intervene. Therefore, P cannot under the given circumstances be assumed not to try to do T in S, so he must be assumed to try to do T in S. The theorem represents an acceptable explanation of why P will try to do T in S. Hence Theorem 1 is proved.

> Theorem 2. *If P wants to do T in S and if P believes with complete certainty that he cannot do T in S, and no other circumstances intervene, then P will not try to do T in S.*

> Proof: The alternative to P not trying to do T in S is P trying to do T in S. But P trying to do T in S is not acceptably explained by P's wanting to do T in S and P's certainty that he cannot do T in S. Hence, some additional circumstances must be invoked to make the explanation acceptable. However, this is impossible, since no other circumstances intervene. Therefore, P cannot under the given circumstances be assumed to try to do T in S, so he must be assumed not to try to do T in

S. The theorem represents an acceptable explanation of why P will not try to do T in S. Hence Theorem 2 is proved.

The next theorem deals with likelihood of occurrence and hence presupposes some random intervention of other circumstances. Therefore, the expression "no other circumstances intervene systematically" is used.

Theorem 3. *If P wants to do T in S and if no other circumstances intervene systematically, then, the stronger P's belief that he can do T in S, the more likely it is that he will try to do T in S, and the stronger P's belief that he cannot do T in S, the more likely it is that he will not try to do T in S.*

Proof: The alternatives to the assumed direct relationship between strength of belief and likelihood of trying and of not trying, would be an inverse relationship, no definite relationship at all, or some complex relationship. But assuming an inverse relationship, i.e., the stronger the belief, the less the likelihood of trying or of not trying, would be inconsistent with Theorems 1 and 2, since it implies that belief with positive certainty corresponds to not trying, and that belief with negative certainty corresponds to trying. An assumption of no definite relationship would also be inconsistent with Theorems 1 and 2, which both assume a definite relationship. An assumption of a complex relationship would involve assumptions about changes in likelihood of trying not explainable by corresponding changes in strength of belief. These changes would, therefore, have to be explained by some additionally systematically intervening circumstances. But this is impossible, since no other circumstances intervene systematically. Therefore, only a direct relationship is consistent with the given assumptions and hence Theorem 3 is proved.[63]

These theorems may appear a little inelegant in their formulation, and some of the qualifiers—like "other circumstances intervening systematically"—may seem a little bit shaky. (Smedslund defends this adequately I think.[64]) What Smedslund succeeds in showing by means of these theorems is that a wide range of questions dealt with in psychology are not in fact empirical questions at all. Smedslund takes *all* the supposedly empirical findings in Bandura's well-known article and *derives* them from thirty-six common-sense theorems.[65]

The program of radical behaviorism may not seem vulnerable to an extension of Smedslund's critique because the program excludes from its language precisely those terms in whose complexities and ambiguities much cognitivist and social psychology becomes entrammeled. I am not convinced of this invulnerability, but establishing that some radical behaviorist findings can be derived from an extended body of such theorems is obviously a task beyond me here (or, likely, anywhere).

There are two observations to be made about the kinds of analyses Smedslund is performing. First, if such a program and its presuppositions replaced the kind of research currently dominant within scientific psychology then the minor premise of my syllogism would no longer hold. This kind of psychology could indeed describe constraints on our nature which would have to be acknowledged, in the sense of not transgressed, by an educational theory.

Second, and much more important for upholding the syllogism against much of present psychological research in education, the confusion of the analytic and the arbitrary seems very common in what are taken as significant findings in educational research. As with Piaget's theory, the invariant sequence of stages involves both an analytic element—it is a matter of logical necessity that the general sequence is as it is—and an arbitrary element—particular cultural contingencies affect the particular variations within the overall sequence. By confusing the two, and considering the general question wholly empirical, it looks very much as though one can establish empirically a general sequence with some variability, accounted for by *ad hoc* metatheoretical glosses.

To consider perhaps a simpler example. If one asks for a securely established finding from psychological research one may be told that people recognize, learn, and remember patterned forms or sequences better than random ones. An educational implication of this finding might be that if one wants children to learn, say, lists of names, then one should organize them into some kind of pattern. It is assumed in the research that establishes this finding that an empirical relationship has been established between distinct things: "recognize" or "learn" and "patterned" or "ordered." Here again, however, we may see a confusion of the analytic and the arbitrary, yielding a general pseudo-empirical finding. The analytic part is due to the fact that what is meant by recognize or learn is not separated and distinct from what is meant by patterned or ordered. If as a result of our experiment we discovered that the random list was learned more readily and remembered longer, we would not happily record such a finding, we would be astonished. We would be astonished not because this would be a counterintuitive empirical finding, but because it would not make sense. Again, this is not a matter of criticizing the obviousness of the finding, it is a matter of pointing out that there is a conceptual tie between the concepts of orderedness and pattern and what it means to recognize and learn things. The arbitrary element is the truly empirical finding: that different people will recognize or learn an ordered pattern or list somewhat differently. To some people it will be an arbitrary matter that because of their history, culture, experience some kinds of patterns will be more readily recognized than others and some lists will be better learned than others. These can be gross differences explainable by gross differences in cultural backgrounds or they can be small differences in the scores of individual children in the same class, explainable by particular past experiences or learning. What is *not* established empirically here is the general relationship between "patterned" and "recognition" or "ordered" and "learning." That is an analytic matter. What is established empirically are the arbitrary differences between particular children or groups—and these are arbitrary in the sense that their causes are tied up in matters of past experience and learning which are not at all the focus of the experiments. That is, even apparently secure findings are commonly not empirically established constraints on our nature. The constraints are more like those Smedslund characterizes, or even more like the bachelors-unmarried-men-in-Vancouver example. What *is* empirically established are matters that are local and arbitrary. Psychology can indeed establish, say, what particular patterns are more readily recognized by what subgroups under what conditions. What it cannot establish empirically is that people recognize patterns more readily than randomness. That is an analytic truth.

In describing local examples of this truth, however, psychologists are describing things which educators may properly consider as their job to shape. Educators cannot, of course, aim to teach people to learn random lists more readily than patterned ones—not because it is empirically impossible but because it is a logical contradiction. (If what was assumed to be a random list was learned more readily, we would examine it closely to discover what hitherto unsuspected pattern lay within it.) Educators may, however, decide that certain local patterns are less appropriate than others and so teach sensitivity to the more educationally desirable ones.

Conclusion

THE INTUITIVELY obvious observation which has fueled the industry of educational psychology is that because it aims to study scientifically those things in which educators are interested, it will produce knowledge that can lead to better educational practice. I have argued that this observation is based on a too crude assumption that when psychologists study things like learning, motivation, development, and so on, they are studying what educators mean by those terms, and that consequently they are asking educationally relevant questions and concluding with answers that have implications for education. I have argued that this is not the case. I have argued also that it has been, and continues to be, insidiously and persistently damaging to education not to have clarified—in educational theories—the distinction between education's interests and those of psychology. The lack of such theories has led to the creeping destruction involved in educators too frequently accepting that, when it has become clear that there is a distinction between the ordinary sense of, say, "learning" and psychology's meaning, that this difference is due to educators' use of the term being too vague and sloppy. This situation is then "rectified" in the direction of education accepting psychology's use with the deceptive comfort that this makes the study of education more precise and scientific.

I have argued that a considerable amount of supposedly empirical research in education is in fact pseudo-empirical; it is doing epistemology the hard way. It merely articulates in confused terms what are analytic truths. I have argued also that much research that does deal with clearly empirical questions, such as that which aims to support a theory of instruction, allows its methodological procedures to obliterate the very educational phenomena it ostensibly claims to deal with.

Put at its simplest, I have argued that my opening syllogism survives unscathed because that research which establishes merely local regularities describes the results of forces which it is the educator's job to shape, thus, obviously, such findings should not constrain educational prescriptions; and that research which aims at establishing general theory that would describe constraints of our nature has so far simply failed to achieve this aim. Additional support for the syllogism is found in the crude lack of empirical support for the claim of any branch of educational psychology of showing reliably that any of its findings yield implications that improve educational practice. The syllogism is strengthened further in demonstrating that most of this research is only peripherally related to education, and its methodological procedures prevent it from dealing with educational units.

My central argument throughout is that attempts to apply psychological theory to education have seemed to have success only at the cost of improperly transforming educational phenomena. We do not simply apply theory to practice; the theory provides, as it were, the lens through which we see the phenomena; it is the syntax by means of which we make the phonemes into meaningful sentences. "We do not apply theory to practice, but rather structure experience in terms of theory."[66] What has been happening so commonly in educational research is that the researchers have been structuring educational experience in terms of psychological theory. Only educational theory can provide a proper structuring of educational experience to allow educationally fruitful research. The disabling gap in educational psychology is "not between theory and research; but *between theory and the object of research.*"[67]

In one of the more sensible books that seeks clues to better educational practice in psychological research, McFarland, in conclusion, notes that his practical recommendations "do not 'just follow' from the psychological analysis. One can claim only that they seem to correspond more closely to what is psychologically the case"; and that he has attempted throughout his book "to suggest fairly definite policies that might be considered consistent with the accompanying psychological analysis."[68] After such cautious language, he justifies his search on the grounds that "Both psychology and sociology are educationally useful in suggesting some of the limits of modifiable behavior."[69] Even allowing for that "suggesting," my argument is that psychology and sociology would be educationally useful only if they could securely describe constraints of modifiable behavior; anything less means that they are describing the symptoms of forces which educational prescriptions may legitimately seek to shape. And accepting suggestions from such insecure descriptions means accepting unnecessary and possibly improper constraints on what may be prescribed in an educational theory; it constantly seems perilously close to committing the naturalistic fallacy.

I am not at all against experiment in education. I am far from an anti-empiricist. Indeed, it is largely on empirical grounds that I question almost the whole of what passes for educational psychology. I am in favor of counting things and getting as objective a view as possible. I am against becoming so caught up with the techniques of counting and getting an objective view that we forget or become careless about the very things we set out to count or see objectively. If we are to apply educationally sensible empirical tests and use refinements of the numerical method in education then we need to be guided by an educational theory. If we accept the guidance of psychological theories we may well learn something of interest to psychology, but not to education.

I tried to show in chapter 4 that doing significant educational research may be difficult, given the complexity of educational units. But we must also be wary of the simple-minded confusion of equating complexity with vagueness and simplicity with precision.

Throughout this chapter, I have been trying to support the opening syllogism in both a weak and a strong sense. I would not like the weak sense—which is strong enough—to be ignored because the strong sense is not sustained. Supporting the strong sense would require a critique of programs of the various branches of psychology. What I have tried to do above (using a few cases) is to suggest that the strong sense of my argument is not some wild absurdity. It is a perfectly sensible position to believe that the minor premise of the syllogism remains valid if the wording is changed to argue that given the present presuppositions of the program of scientific psychology, no psychological theory *can* describe constraints of our nature. Although I have in no case presented the argument sufficiently to establish the strong sense, I have, in a number of cases, given reasons that support it as a sensible position to hold.

The most general reason I have given for not seeking educational implications from psychological theories is that psychological theories do not deal with units of educational phenomena. Much of the argument of this chapter seeks to support Wittgenstein's observation:

> The confusion and barrenness of psychology is not to be explained by calling it a "young science"; its state is not comparable with that of physics, for instance, in its beginnings. (Rather with that of certain branches of mathematics. Set theory.) For in psychology there are experimental methods and *conceptual confusion.* . . . The existence of the experimental method makes us think we have the means of solving the problems which trouble us; though problem and method pass one another by.[70]

Conclusion

Educational Theories and Facts

AM I ARGUING that the study of education cannot be scientific, in the soft sense of "scientific" proper to psychology? Am I suggesting we should give up on the aim of making educational research more rigorous, more scientific? Of course not. I am arguing that we will not achieve this desirable end if we persist in using psychological theories in what is supposed to be educational research. What I am arguing in favor of, in order to make educational research more scientific, is that the educational researcher should use educational theories. Educational theories should determine the appropriateness of educational questions and should provide the criteria for recognizing adequate answers. If one uses a psychological theory, one will be able to ask only psychological questions and provide only psychological criteria for recognizing adequate answers to those questions.

That seems fairly simple and straightforward. But it requires that our researchers are able to distinguish an educational from a psychological theory, which in turn requires their ability to distinguish educational from psychological phenomena, which in turn requires their ability to distinguish differences between education's use and psychology's use of "learning," or between teaching and instructing. If our researchers are trained to see education through the eyes of psychology, they may persist in seeing, say, the differences between

178

education's proper use and psychology's proper use of "learning" as degrees of vagueness and imprecision in the former which are corrected in the more "scientific" use of the latter. So even if my argument is correct, it has in practice a hard row to hoe.

But how are these educational theories to be composed? Surely, facts established in psychology will be relevant to constructing such theories, and, if so, whatever research secured those facts has implications for education? Am I not involved in a contradiction here? I have taken a great deal of trouble to try to show that no psychological theory or research has any implications for education, and now I am saying that an educational theory may well incorporate findings from psychological research. How can I support both claims?

In a trivial sense, facts may have implications for educational theories in that the prescriptions of any educational theory cannot contravene them. In this sense, the law of gravity has implications for any educational theory. The educational theory may ignore as wholly irrelevant a vast range of facts which nevertheless it will not contravene. Facts represent the constraints within which a theory of any kind must be constructed. A theory which contravenes something that we know securely about the world or human behavior will simply fail to engage our scientific interest.

Facts represent the universe of particulars that we may organize into more general meaningful claims about the world. Making facts articulate requires their organization within theories. A distinguishing feature of any field of study or activity is the kind of theories it generates in order to organize in the best way appropriate facts into appropriate claims. In short, the theory is the thing that makes facts articulate, that puts them into meaningful structures, that determines the kind of meaning they make. My argument is that facts generated in, say, psychology are certainly available for application to the practice of education; but by themselves they are mute, having no implications for educational practice; when organized within a psychological theory that theory has no implications for educational practice. To carry implications for educational practice, facts have to be organized within an educational theory. That is, the only route to dealing sensibly with educational practice is through an educational theory.

The problem for generating educational theories that draw significantly on facts established in psychology is not that psychology lacks such facts. Indeed, it has accumulated mountains of them. The problem for psychology is that it seems unable to generate laws and theories that can reduce the mountains into an orderly landscape of the *psyche* or human behavior; the related problem for education is the conditional nature of the mountains of facts. They are conditional on specific environments and circumstances, and we cannot rely on their holding outside those particular environments and circumstances. We have mountains of facts, such as Pask and Scott's ATI, or in a, b, c circumstances a group of students with x, y, z characteristics achieved p and q in percentages ranging from n to m. Some of these may be suggestive of things that are educationally desirable and the educational theorist may then include them as prescriptions within an educational theory. But by "implications" I mean something less trivial than this, and so I think does everyone who claims that some psychological research or theory has implications for education. The kinds of facts so commonly available in psychology are not of the kind that allow the construction of secure theories which are descriptive of constraints on our nature: the kind which, I have argued, *can* have implications for education. The stronger sense of implication involves the notion that the psychological facts or theories constrain, to some degree, what an educational theory may sensibly prescribe; in the sense that Piagetian programs embody the belief that Piaget's description of the various stages imply constraints on what can be taught meaningfully at each stage, or what ought to be included in the curriculum.

But again, the conclusion that the only proper route to educational practice is through educational theory may appear unexceptionable; a rather limp justification for our journeying through Plato's and Piaget's theories, and through some areas of educational psychology. If, however, the need for educational theories was generally acknowledged, the study of education would be very different from its present state. At present, education commonly borrows a range of psychological theories, and, it seems to me, educators typically are insufficiently sensitive to the fact that in so doing they borrow also psychology's focus of interest, its semantic colorings, subject matter, methodologies, and the nature of the claims it makes. If there is such a thing as education and we want to talk sensibly about it, the theories of psychology are of no more use to us than the theories of physics. Because psychology deals with, and generates, facts more likely to be of interest to education than does physics means that we will incidentally be more likely to be familiar with psychological theories. But this should not result in seeking in them implications for education. This is to see education as something so arcane and alien that one can only hope to approach it obliquely.

Obviously, I am simplifying the nature, and relationships, of facts and theories, but not, I think, to a degree that invalidates my argument. My concern is to stress that the first need of an educator is an educational theory. Education, however, is characterized at present by its theoretical poverty—one symptom of which is the ease whereby "outside" theories invade it, and persuade educators that their interests are identical with those of the invaders. Even if psychological theories gave us descriptions of constraints of nature in secure theories of learning, motivation, and development, such theories and their supporting data would provide only slender constraints on what an educational theory might prescribe. What seems foolhardy at present is the borrowing of insecure psychological theories which are about phenomena of peripheral interest to education, permitting them to usurp the proper place of educational theory, and allowing their insecure claims to serve as constraints on educational practice. The entailed distortions of focus and diversions of educators' interests seem to justify the rather polemical observation made by Hobsbawm:

> What purport to be the human and social sciences may actually diminish our knowledge, in so far as they substitute their confident inadequacy for the actual knowledge and praxis of man's social experience.[1]

If we substitute "educational experience" for "social experience," we have an assertion that is perhaps rather more extreme than one would like to make but which points out a very real danger so far as the study and practice of education are concerned.

Why So Few Educational Theories?

AS AN EXPLANATION of why educational research, in the tradition of scientific psychology, has contributed so little to educational practice the argument of this book has a certain elegant simplicity. It is not a matter, as some argue, of complex methodological issues: simply that so-called educational research is not about education. If what will enable educational psychologists to do genuine educational research is an educational theory, we must ask why are there so few of them around? Educators do not turn to psychology out of perversity for their theories.

Education is a complex business. It is about how best to live. Most of us are satisfied with trying to answer less overwhelming

questions. But if our concern is education we must not let our eyes
be drawn away from the Platonic sun toward the shadows in the
cave. Crucial to the task is the bearing constantly in mind the very
stuff of education—the stuff that accumulates as the process proceeds. Some things accumulate; there are elaboration, refinement,
sophistication, discrimination in the ways we make sense of the
world and experience. And if nothing much seems to remain the
same during this process, there is a stable something which can
benefit from this growth. "The oldest soul that is inside each of us
is the youngest—the soul we had when we were boys."[2] The souls
we had when we were children are still there, enriched and encum-
bered with the gifts and burdens of experience and knowledge. Becoming educated is learning how to use experience and knowledge
as gifts that enrich the soul we started with. If we hope to talk sensibly
about education, or inquire into it, or do research about it, then we
need to be able to identify what accumulates in the process of becoming educated. If we cannot clearly recognize and characterize
this very stuff of education, we cannot hope to discuss, inquire, or
research sensibly.

There are so few educational theories because to do all this, and
the other things indicated in chapter 4, is very hard. It seems much
easier to work within a "paradigm" of research or seek implications
from that research for education. And it *would* be easier if it were
possible to benefit education that way. My argument is that we have
a choice between a hard way to benefit education and an impossible
way. We have been trying the impossible way long enough: it is time
we reverted to trying the hard way.

NOTES
INDEX

Notes

Chapter 1: Education and Psychology:
A Sense of Differences

1. Use of this industrial metaphor is not to be seen as implying a crude means-end view of education. I use it here innocently, for the sake of brevity. The means in education, of course, become constituents of the end—if the curriculum, for example, is the means to making someone educated, the educated person who results from following such a curriculum is in part constituted of the content of that curriculum. The means are not discarded in the process of education, they are parts of the accumulating product. See R.S. Peters, "Education and the Educated Man," *Proceedings of the Philosophy of Education Society of Great Britain*, vol. 4 (January, 1970), pp. 5–20.
2. See Deanna Kuhn, "The Application of Piaget's Theory of Cognitive Development to Education," *The Harvard Educational Review*, vol. 49, no. 3 (1979), pp. 340–60.
3. Jean Piaget, "What Is Psychology?" *American Psychologist*, vol. 3, no. 7 (1978), pp. 648–49.
4. David Elkind, *Child Development and Education: A Piagetian Perspective* (New York: Oxford University Press, 1976), p. 196.
5. J.H. Flavell and J.F. Wohlwill, "Formal and Functional Aspects of Cognitive Development," in D. Elkind and J.H. Flavell (eds.), *Studies in Cognitive Development: Essays in Honor of Jean Piaget* (Toronto: Oxford University Press, 1969), pp. 81–82.
6. Stephen Toulmin, "The Concept of 'Stages' in Psychological Development," in Theodore Mischel (ed.), *Cognitive Development and Epistemology* (New York: Academic Press, 1971), p. 53. We need not, of

course, accept Toulmin's distinction uncritically to accept that psychology initially faces greater methodological problems with normative matters than does physiology.

7. Elkind, *Child Development and Education*, p. 212.

8. See, for example, Roy Hallam, "Piaget and the Teaching of History," *Educational Research*, vol. 12 (1969), pp. 3–12.

9. For help with such a task see Karl Bühler, *The Mental Development of the Child*, trans. Oscar Oeser (Vienna, 1919; London: Routledge & Kegan Paul, 1930); and Arthur N. Applebee, *The Child's Concept of Story* (Chicago: University of Chicago Press, 1978).

10. See D.W. Hamlyn, "The Logical and Psychological Aspects of Learning," in R.S. Peters (ed.), *The Concept of Education* (London: Routledge and Kegan Paul, 1967), pp. 24–43.

11. For Piaget's neo–Lamarkian ideas on the way individuals recapitulate the species' attainment of knowledge see Jean Piaget, *Biology and Knowledge* (Chicago: University of Chicago Press, 1971), and the extension of this argument in "Phenocopy in Biology and the Psychological Development of Knowledge," in Howard E. Gruber and J. Jacques Voneche (eds.), *The Essential Piaget* (London: Routledge and Kegan Paul, 1978).

12. Jean Piaget, "How Children Form Mathematical Concepts," *Scientific American* (November, 1953).

13. For similar developmental schemes see Kieran Egan, "Teaching the Varieties of History," *Teaching History* no. 21 (Summer, 1978); and Kieran Egan, "Progress in Historiography," *Clio*, vol. 8, no. 2 (1979).

14. Thomas S. Kuhn, *The Structure of Scientific Revolutions* (Chicago: University of Chicago Press, 1962).

15. If one seeks for some general reason to suppose that there *might* be a similarity in the development of scientific understanding in child and culture, one may convert (and abuse) Kuhn's thesis something like this: The relatively innocent eye of the child and the theory-free ancient may respond "naturally" to certain physical phenomena by composing similar kinds of hypotheses—which we will associate with a loosened sense of "paradigm." Any paradigm leaves a particular, limited range of phenomena unexplained, and they appear as anomalies. The anomalies lead to revision of the paradigm, and the limited range of what is seen as anomalous restricts the limits within which a revised paradigm is constructed in order to account for them. What we have, then, is a process of changing paradigms determined in general sequence because there is a limited range of revisions of any paradigm which will account for the anomalies. The same process may well apply to individual and historical development. So there may be in the sequence of paradigms evident—or discoverable—in any subject's development a *logical* progression which may prove the most effective underlying structure on which we can build our curriculum.

16. Jerome S. Bruner, *The Process of Education* (Cambridge, Mass.: Harvard University Press, 1960), p. 33.
17. *Ibid.*, p. 54.
18. Elkind, *Child Development and Education*, p. 196.
19. *Ibid.*

Chapter 2: *Plato's Developmental Theory*

1. Gregory Vlastos (ed.), *Plato: A Collection of Critical Essays* (New York: Anchor Press, 1971), p. 1.
2. Plato, *Laws* VII. 803 (trans. B. Jowett). References for further quotations from Plato will be given in the text, using the following form: R. VII.517 = *The Republic*, VII.517; L VII.810 = *Laws*, VII.810. I use Jowett's translations of *Laws* (New York: Random House, 1937), and F.M. Cornford's translation in his *The Republic of Plato* (New York: Oxford University Press, 1941).
3. Cornford, *The Republic of Plato*, p. 222.
4. Jean Piaget, "Children's Philosophies," in C. Murchison (ed.), *Handbook of Child Psychology* (Worcester, Mass.: Clark University Press, 1931), pp. 377–91.
5. Cf. Plato, *Timaeus*, 52. And, "True opinions are a fine thing and do all sorts of good so long as they stay in their place; but they will not stay long. They run away from man's mind, so they are not worth much until you tether them by working out the reason. Once they are tied down, they become knowledge, and are stable. That is why knowledge is something more valuable than right opinion. What distinguishes one from the other is the tether." Plato, *Meno*, 98A.
6. I realize this is tendentious, and that this characterization may seem to ignore much of the huge body of literature on Plato's Forms/Ideas. I read the "parable of the line" as a metaphor which is intended to be suggestive rather than precisely descriptive. Plato is deliberately vague about these characterizations of his ideal of knowledge—"much must be left unspoken" (R.VI.508)—and seems more intent on *suggesting* what seemed to him the direction toward the securest kind of knowledge. Given the advantage of being able to see the development of the natural sciences, and the establishment of a method for finding knowledge of a security unguessed in the ancient world, it seems reasonable to translate Plato's metaphor into modern terms.
7. Cornford, *The Republic of Plato*, p. 176.
8. I will ignore questions of what classes were to get what kind of education, and I will impose our modern democratic ideal whereby the best education should be accessible to all.
9. R.L. Nettleship, *The Theory of Education in Plato's Republic* (London:

Oxford University Press, 1935), p. 215. This was first published as an essay in *Hellenica* in 1880.

10. Bruno Bettelheim, *The Uses of Enchantment* (New York: Knopf, 1976).

11. Nettleship, *The Theory of Education in Plato's Republic*, p. 52.

12. Ibid., 92–93.

13. For a useful move in this direction see Cornel Hamm, "The Content of Moral Education," *School Review*, vol. 85, no. 2 (February, 1977), pp. 218–28.

14. Plato's use of mathematics in this context remains somewhat confusing to a number of scholars. See Anders Wedberg, *Plato's Philosophy of Mathematics* (Stockholm: Almquist and Wiksell, 1955).

15. It may be worth noting that "temperance" refers not to the meanings that have become common in North America, but to the notions of balance or harmony. Plato saw that one of the most difficult things to achieve in education was a harmonious development of the various aspects of character. He notes that "keen wits are apt to lose all steadiness and veer about in every direction. On the other hand, the steady reliable characters, whose impassivity is proof against the perils of war, are equally proof against instruction. Confronted with intellectual work, they become comatose and do nothing but yawn." (R.VI.503)

16. The image of Plato as the father of totalitarianism has been most vehemently argued by Karl Popper in *The Open Society and Its Enemies* (London: Routledge and Kegan Paul, 1945).

17. The propriety, or otherwise, of this cavalier enthusiasm for interpretation will be discussed in the conclusion to this chapter.

18. See Robin Barrow, *Plato, Utilitarianism and Education* (London: Routledge and Kegan Paul, 1975); *Plato and Education* (London: Routledge and Kegan Paul, 1976); and "Plato and Politics," *Didaskalos*, vol. 5, no. 3 (1977), pp. 410–21.

19. The problem of initiating children into abstract thinking is one of the most important and neglected educational tasks. Among the considerable contributions made by Margaret Donaldson's *Children's Minds* (London: Croom Helm, 1978) is to make the educational meaning of "abstraction" more precise and to point up the educational problems that follow from its nondevelopment.

20. Plato says that one necessary precaution is to prohibit students from joining in dialectical arguments before mastering the *dianoia* curriculum. "You must have seen how youngsters, when they get their first taste of it, treat argument as a form of sport solely for purposes of contradiction. When someone has proved them wrong, they copy his methods to confute others, delighting like puppies in tugging and tearing anyone who comes near them. And so, after a long course of proving others wrong and being proved wrong themselves, they rush to the conclusion that all they once believed is false; and the result is that in the eyes of the world they discredit, not themselves only, but the whole

business of philosophy. An older man will not share this craze for making a sport of contradiction. He will prefer to take for his model the conversation of one who is bent on seeking truth, and his own reasonableness will bring credit on the pursuit. We meant to ensure this result by all that we said earlier against the present practice of admitting anybody, however unfit, to philosophic discussions, and about the need for disciplined and steadfast character." (R.VII.539)

21. This use of the story form and game form in teaching is dealt with in some detail in Kieran Egan, *Educational Development* (New York: Oxford University Press, 1979), ch. 1, 2.

22. Marcel Proust, *Remembrance of Things Past*, trans. C.K. Scott Moncrieff (London: Chatto and Windus, 1964), vol. 1, p. 200.

23. R.M. Hare, "Plato and the Mathematicians," in Renford Bambrough (ed.), *New Essays on Plato and Aristotle* (London: Routledge and Kegan Paul, 1965), p. 38.

Chapter 3: Piaget's Developmental Theory

1. Brian Rotman, "A Hymn to Equilibrium," *Times Literary Supplement* (April 7, 1978), p. 373.

2. Jean Piaget, "Autobiography," in E.G. Boring et al. (eds.), *History of Psychology in Autobiography* (Worchester, Mass.: Clark University Press, 1952), pp. 237–56.

3. J. McV. Hunt, "The Impact and Limitations of the Giant of Developmental Psychology," in David Elkind and John H. Flavell (eds.), *Studies in Cognitive Development* (New York: Oxford University Press, 1969), pp. 3–66.

4. See the various interpretations given by the philosopher-contributors to Theodore Mischel (ed.), *Cognitive Development and Epistemology* (New York: Academic Press, 1971).

5. See, for example, Jean Piaget, *The Child and Reality*, trans. Arnold Rosin (New York: Grossman, 1973), p. 8.

6. Jean Piaget, *The Child's Conception of the World* (1929), trans. Joan and Andrew Tomlinson (1929; New Jersey: Littlefield, Adams and Co., reprint, 1967), p. 1.

7. Jean Piaget, "Development and Learning," in Richard E. Ripple and Verne N. Rockcastle (eds.), *Piaget Rediscovered* (Ithaca, New York: School of Education, Cornell University, 1964), p. 9.

8. Jean Piaget, *Biology and Knowledge*, trans. Beatrix Walsh (Chicago: University of Chicago Press, 1971), p. 3.

9. Jean Piaget, *Comments on Vygotsky's Critical Remarks* (Cambridge, Mass.: MIT Press, 1962), p. 11.

10. Introduction to *Goals for School Mathematics*, report of the Cambridge (Mass.) Conference on School Mathematics, quoted in Jeremy Kilpa-

trick, "Cognitive Theory and the SMSE Program," in Richard E. Ripple and Verne N. Rockcastle (eds.), *Piaget Rediscovered* (Ithaca, N.Y.: School of Education, Cornell University, 1964), pp. 129–30.

11. For an example of this case see J. Berko and R. Brown, "Psycholinguistic Research Methods," in P.H. Mussen (ed.), *Handbook of Research Methods in Child Development* (New York: Wiley, 1960), pp. 517–57. *See also* A.R. Luria and F. la Indovich, *Speech and the Development of Mental Process in the Child* (Harmondsworth, Middlesex: Penguin, 1971); Susan Isaacs, *Intellectual Growth in Young Children* (London: Routledge and Kegan Paul, 1930); Margaret Donaldson, *Children's Minds* (London: Croom Helm, 1978), ch. 6.

12. Piaget, *The Child and Reality*, p. 2.

13. Jean Piaget, "Piaget's Theory," in P.H. Mussen (ed.), *Carmichael's Manual of Child Psychology*, vol. 1 (New York: Wiley, 1970), p. 716.

14. Jean Piaget, *Biology and Knowledge*, trans. Beatrix Walsh (Chicago: University of Chicago Press, 1971), pp. 312–13.

15. Jean Piaget, "A Conversation with Jean Piaget," *Psychology Today*, vol. 3, no. 12 (1970), p. 30.

16. Piaget, "Piaget's Theory," p. 716.

17. Jean Piaget, "Need and Significance of Cross-Cultural Studies in Genetic Psychology," in D. Inhelder and H.H. Chipman (eds.), *Piaget and His School* (New York: Springer Verlag, 1976), p. 260.

18. See, for example, P.R. Ammon, "Cognitive Development and Early Childhood Education," in H.L. Homs and P.A. Robinson (eds.), *Psychological Processes in Early Education* (New York: Academic Press, 1977); C.J. Brainerd, "Learning Research and Piagetian Theory," in L.S. Siegel and C.J. Brainerd (eds.), *Alternatives to Piaget: Critical Essays on the Theory* (New York: Academic Press, 1978); G. Brown and C. Desforges, *Piaget's Theory: A Psychological Critique* (London: Routledge and Kegan Paul, 1979); D.W. Hamlyn, *Experience and the Growth of Understanding* (London: Routledge and Kegan Paul, 1978); D.C. Phillips and M.E. Kelly, "Hierarchical Theories of Development in Education and Psychology," *Harvard Educational Review*, vol. 45, no. 3 (1975), pp. 351–75; and Jean Piaget, *Psychology and Epistemology*, trans. Arnold Rosin (New York: Grossman, 1971).

19. P.R. Dasen, "Cross-cultural Piagetian Research: A Summary," *Journal of Cross Cultural Psychology*, vol. 3 (1972), pp. 23–39.

20. M. Cole, "An Ethnographic Psychology of Cognition," in R.W. Brislin et al. (eds.), *Cross Cultural Perspectives in Learning* (New York: Sage, 1975).

21. See, for example, S. Boonsong, "The Development of Conservation of Mass, Weight, and Volume in Thai Children," master's thesis, College of Education, Bangkok, Thailand, 1968 (cited in P.T. Ashton, "Cross-cultural Piagetian Research: An Experimental Perspective," *Harvard Educational Review*, vol. 45 [1975], pp. 475–506); M. Bovet, "Cross-

cultural Study of Conservation Concepts: Continuous Quantity and Length," in B. Inhelder, H. Sinclair, and M. Bovet (eds.), *Learning and the Development of Cognition*, trans. Susan Wedgwood (Cambridge, Mass.: Harvard University Press, 1974); M.M. de Lemos, "The Development of Conservation in Aboriginal Children," *International Journal of Psychology*, vol. 4 (1969), pp. 255–69; P.R. Dasen, "Cognitive Development of Aborigines in Central Australia: Concrete Operations and Perceptual Activities," doctoral dissertation, Australian National University, Canberra, 1970 (cited in Brown and Desforges, *Piaget's Theory*); D.M. Hyde, "An Investigation of Piaget's Theory of the Development of Number," doctoral dissertation, University of London, 1959 (cited in Ashton, "Cross-cultural Piagetian Research").

22. Ashton, "Cross-cultural Piagetian Research," p. 478. *See also* J.J. Goodnow, "Cultural Variations in Cognitive Skills," in D.R. Price-Williams (ed.), *Cross-Cultural Studies* (Harmonsworth: Penguin, 1969); S. Modgil, *Piagetian Research: A Handbook of Recent Studies* (Slough, England: National Foundation of Educational Research, 1974); S. Modgil and C. Modgil, *Piagetian Research: Compilation and Commentary* (Slough, England: National Foundation of Educational Research, 1976).

23. E.g., Jean Piaget and B. Inhelder, *Le Développement des Quantités chez l'enfant* (Neuchâtel and Paris: Delachaux et Niestlé, 1941).

24. Inhelder, Sinclair, and Bovet (eds.), *Learning and the Development of Cognition*, p. 246.

25. For example, David Elkind, "Children's Discovery of Conservation of Mass, Weight, and Volume: Piaget Replication Study II," *Journal of Genetic Psychology*, vol. 98 (1961), pp. 219–27.

26. Jean Piaget and B. Inhelder, *The Child's Conception of Space* (London: Routledge and Kegan Paul, 1956), p. 220.

27. Donaldson, *Children's Minds*.

28. Inhelder, Sinclair, and Bovet, *Learning and the Development of Cognition*.

29. Jean Piaget, "Intellectual Evolution from Adolescence to Adulthood," *Human Development*, vol. 15 (1972), pp. 1–12.

30. P.C. Wason and P.N. Johnson-Laird, *Psychology of Reasoning: Structure and Content* (London: Batsford, 1972).

31. Goodnow, "Cultural Variations in Cognitive Skills," p. 250.

32. J.G. Wallace, "The Course of Cognitive Growth," in V.P. Varna and P. Williams (eds.), *Piaget, Psychology and Education* (London: Hodder and Staughton, 1976), p. 16.

33. Brown and Desforges, *Piaget's Theory*, p. 106.

34. Jan Smedslund, "Piaget's Psychology in Practice," *British Journal of Educational Psychology*, vol. 47 (1977), pp. 1–6.

35. See, for example, Brown and Desforges, *Piaget's Theory*; J.H. Flavell, *The Developmental Psychology of Jean Piaget* (Princeton, N.J.: Van Nostrand, 1963); Isaacs, *Intellectual Growth in Young Children*; and

L. Vygotsky, *Thought and Language* (Cambridge, Mass.: MIT Press, 1962).

36. Smedslund, "Piaget's Psychology in Practice," pp. 3–4.
37. Jean Piaget, "Problems of Equilibration," in C. Nodine, J. Gallagher, and R. Humphrey (eds.), *Piaget and Inhelder on Equilibration* (Philadelphia: Jean Piaget Society, 1972), p. 14.
38. B. Inhelder and J. Piaget, *The Growth of Logical Thinking from Childhood to Adolescence* (New York: Basic Books, 1958).
39. Jean Piaget, *Biology and Knowledge*, p. 181.
40. B. Inhelder and H. Sinclair, "Learning Cognitive Structures," in P.H. Mussen, J. Langer, and M. Covington (eds.), *Trends and Issues in Developmental Psychology* (New York: Holt, Rinehart and Winston, 1969), p. 5.
41. T.E. Moore and A.E. Harris, "Language and Thought in Piagetian Theory," in Siegal and Brainerd (eds.), *Alternatives to Piaget*, pp. 149–50.
42. M. Donaldson, *Children's Minds*, p. 69.
43. For example, A.R. Luria, "The Directive Function of Speech in Development and Dissolution," *Word*, vol. 15 (1959), pp. 341–52; and A.R. Luria, *Cognitive Development: Its Cultural and Social Foundations* (Cambridge, Mass.: Harvard University Press, 1976).
44. S.A. Rose and M. Blank, "The Potency of Context in Children's Cognition: An Illustration Through Conservation," *Child Development*, vol. 45 (1974), p. 502.
45. L. Vygotsky, *Thought and Language*.
46. Piaget, "Piaget's Theory," p. 714.
47. Piaget, *Biology and Knowledge*, p. 316.
48. Inhelder, Sinclair, and Bovet, *Learning and the Development of Cognition*, p. 28.
49. See, for example, D.W. Brison, "Acceleration of Conservation of Substance," *Journal of Genetic Psychology*, vol. 109 (1966), pp. 311–22; G.E. Gruen, "Note on Conservation: Methodological and Definitional Considerations," *Child Development*, vol. 37 (1966), pp. 977–83; R. Kingsley and V.C. Hall, "Training Conservation of Weight and Length Through Learning Sets," *Child Development*, vol. 38 (1967), pp. 1111–26; L. Wallach and R.L. Sprott, "Inducing Number Conservation in Children," *Child Development*, vol. 35 (1964), pp. 1057–71; and L. Wallach, A.J. Wall, and L. Anderson, "Number Conservation: The Roles of Reversibility, Addition/Subtraction, and Misleading Perceptual Cues," *Child Development*, vol. 38 (1967), pp. 425–42.
50. Inhelder, Sinclair, and Bovet, *Learning and the Development of Cognition*, p. 19.
51. *Ibid.*, p. 24.
52. Piaget, "Piaget's Theory," p. 716.
53. Inhelder, Sinclair, and Bovet, *Learning and the Development of Cognition*, p. 25.

54. *Ibid.*, p. 25.
55. *Ibid.*, p. 25.
56. For more extensive reviews of this literature, see H. Beilin, "The Training and Acquisition of Logical Operations," in M.F. Rosskopf, L.P. Steffe, and S. Taback (eds.), *Piagetian Cognitive Developmental Research and Mathematical Education* (Washington: National Council of Teachers of Mathematics, 1971); C.J. Brainerd, "Neo-Piagetian Training Experiments Revisited: Is There any Support for the Cognitive-Developmental Stage Hypothesis?" *Cognition*, vol. 2 (1973), pp. 349–70; C.J. Brainerd, "Cognitive Development and Concept Learning: An Interpretive Review," *Psychological Bulletin*, vol. 84 (1977), pp. 919–39; C.J. Brainerd, "Learning Research and Piagetian Theory," in Siegal and Brainerd, (eds.) *Alternatives to Piaget*; R. Glaser and L.B. Resnick, "Instructional Psychology," *Annual Review of Psychology*, vol. 23 (1972), pp. 207–76; and B.J. Zimmerman and T.L. Rosenthal, "Observational Learning of Rule-Governed Behavior of Children," *Psychological Bulletin*, vol. 81 (1974), pp. 29–42.
57. Inhelder, Sinclair, and Bovet, *Learning and the Development of Cognition*, p. 49.
58. J.L. Sheppard, "Compensation and Combinatorial Systems in the Acquisition and Generalization of Conservation," *Child Development*, vol. 45 (1974), pp. 717–30.
59. R. Gelman, "Conservation Acquisition: A Problem of Learning to Attend to Relevant Attributes," *Journal of Experimental Child Psychology*, vol. 7 (1969), pp. 167–87.
60. F.B. Murray, "Acquisition of Conservation Through Social Interaction," *Developmental Psychology*, vol. 6 (1972), pp. 1–6.
61. J.A. Emrick, "The Acquisition and Transfer of Conservation Skills by Four-year-old Children," doctoral dissertation, University of California at Los Angeles, 1968 (cited in Brainerd, "Learning Research and Piagetian Theory.")
62. J. Smedslund, "The Acquisition of Conservation of Substance and Weight in Children. II. External Reinforcement of Conservation of Weight and Operations of Addition and Subtraction," *Scandinavian Journal of Psychology*, vol. 2 (1961), pp. 71–84; "The Acquisition of Conservation of Substance and Weight in Children. III. Extinction of Conservation of Weight Acquired 'normally' and by Means of Empirical Controls on a Balance Scale," *Scandinavian Journal of Psychology*, vol. 2 (1961), pp. 85–87; "The Acquisition of Conservation of Substance and Weight in Children. IV. An Attempt at Extinction of the Visual Components of the Weight Concept," *Scandinavian Journal of Psychology*, vol. 2 (1961).
63. G. Hatano, "A Developmental Approach to Concept Formation: A Review of Neo-Piagetian Learning Experiments," *Kokkyo University Bulletin of Liberal Arts and Education*, vol. 5 (1971), pp. 59–76.

64. G. Hatano and Y. Suga, "Equilibration and External Reinforcement in the Acquisition of Number Conservation," *Japanese Psychological Research*, vol. 11 (1969), pp. 17–31.

65. J.F. Wohlwill, "Un essai d'apprentissage dans le domaine de la conservation du nombre," *Etudes d'Épistémologie Génétique*, vol. 9 (1959), pp. 125–35; J.F. Wohlwill and R.C. Lowe, "An Experimental Analysis of the Conservation of Number," *Child Development*, vol. 33 (1962), pp. 153–67.

66. A. Karmiloff-Smith, "On Stage: The Importance of Being a Non-conserver," p. 159. Commentary on C.J. Brainerd's "The Stage Question in Cognitive-Developmental Theory," *The Behavioral and Brain Sciences*, vol. 2 (1978), pp. 188–90.

67. *Ibid.*, p. 189.

68. *Ibid.*, p. 190.

69. T. Trabasso, "Representation, Memory, and Reasoning: How Do We Make Transitive Inferences?" in A.D. Pick (ed.), *Minnesota Symposium on Child Psychology*, vol. 9 (Minneapolis: University of Minnesota Press, 1975).

70. P. Tulviste, "On the Origins of Theoretic Syllogistic Reasoning in Culture and the Child." *The Quarterly Newsletter of the Laboratory of Comparative Human Cognition*, vol. 1, no. 4 (1979), pp. 73–80.

71. E. H. Gombrich, *Art and Illusion* (Princeton, N.J.: Princeton University Press, 1960).

72. Piaget, *The Child and Reality*, p. 30.

73. Jean Piaget, *Science of Education and the Psychology of the Child*, trans. Derek Coltman (New York: Orion Press, 1970), p. 51. *See also* Jean Piaget, *To Understand Is to Invent: The Future of Education*, trans. George-Anne Roberts (New York: Grossman, 1973).

74. Jean Piaget, Foreword to *Piaget in the Classroom*, Milton Schwebel and Jane Raph (eds.) (New York: Basic Books, 1973), p. x. Some might see it as ironic that this absolute assertion follows Piaget's endorsement of the principles that "the field of experimental pedagogy must remain autonomous" and that "all hypotheses derived from psychology must be verified, through actual classroom practices and educational results, rather than merely based on simple deduction" (p. ix).

75. Piaget, "A Conversation with Jean Piaget," p. 30.

76. John Dewey, *Experience and Education* (1938; New York: Collier Books, reprint, 1963), pp. 62, 63.

77. Schwebel and Raph (eds.), *Piaget in the Classroom*, p. 14.

78. *Ibid.*

79. Jean Piaget, *The Mechanisms of Perception* (London: Routledge and Kegan Paul, 1969), p. 364.

80. See Brainerd's review of these experiments in "Learning Research and Piagetian Theory."

81. See B.J. Zimmerman and T.L. Rosenthal, "Conserving and Retaining

Equalities and Inequalities Through Observation and Correction," *Developmental Psychology*, vol. 10 (1974), pp. 369–78.

82. G.T. Botvin and F.B. Murray, "The Efficacy of Peer Modeling and Social Conflict in the Acquisition of Conservation," *Child Development*, vol. 46 (1975), pp. 796–99.

83. P. Gal'perin, in Brian Simon (ed.), *Psychology in the Soviet Union* (London: Lawrence and Wishart, 1957), p. 217.

84. A.A. Williams, "Number Readiness," *Educational Review*, vol. 11, no. 1 (1958).

85. Marilynne Adler, "Jean Piaget, School Organization, and Instruction," in Irene J. Athey and Duane O. Rubadeau (eds.), *Educational Implications of Piaget's Theory* (Waltham, Mass.: Xerox, 1970), p. 12. But see Scott A. Miller, "Candy Is Dandy and Also Quicker: A Further Nonverbal Study of Conservation of Number," *The Journal of Genetic Psychology*, vol. 134 (1979), pp. 15–21.

86. See Brainerd, "Neo-Piagetian Training Experiments Revisited."

87. *Ibid.*

88. Inhelder, Sinclair, and Bovet (eds.), *Learning and the Development of Cognition.*

89. *Ibid.*, p. 25.

90. *Ibid.*, p. 26.

91. Athey and Rubadeau (eds.), *Educational Implications of Piaget's Theory*, p. xviii.

92. Schwebel and Raph (eds.), in *Piaget in the Classroom*, p. 290.

93. Deanna Kuhn, "The Application of Piaget's Theory of Cognitive Development to Education," *Harvard Educational Review*, vol. 49, no. 3 (1979).

94. Constance Kamii, in Schwebel and Raph (eds.), *Piaget in the Classroom*, p. 204.

95. Schwebel and Raph (eds.), *Piaget in the Classroom*, p. 22.

96. *Ibid.*, p. 280.

97. Hermina Sinclair, in Schwebel and Raph (eds.), *Piaget in the Classroom*, p. 42.

98. John W. Renner, "What This Research Says to Schools," in John W. Renner, *et al.* (eds.), *Research, Teaching, and Learning with the Piaget Model* (Norman, Oklahoma: University of Oklahoma Press, 1976), p. 176.

99. Hans Aebli, *Didactique psychologique: application à la didactique de la psychologie de Jean Piaget* (Neuchâtel: Delachaux et Niestlé, 1951), p. 60. Quoted in John H. Flavell, *The Developmental Psychology of Jean Piaget*, p. 369.

100. Eleanor Duckworth, "Piaget Rediscovered," in Ripple and Rockcastle (eds.), *Piaget Rediscovered*, p. 2.

101. Hans G. Furth, quoted in Schwebel and Raph (eds.), *Piaget in the Classroom*, p. 281.

102. Constance Kamii, in Schwebel and Raph (eds.), *Piaget in the Class-room*, p. 203.

103. A rather tautological way of stating the first half of this advice: "No learning occurs when the subjects are too young for there to be a possibility of extending the zone of assimilations to the new factors introduced" (Jean Piaget, Foreword to Inhelder, Sinclair, and Bovet, *Learning and the Development of Cognition*). Or, as Marilynne Adler summed up the results of E. Turiel's doctoral dissertation, "An Experimental Analysis of Developmental Stages in the Child's Moral Judgment" (Yale University, 1964): "This study strongly implies that educative efforts are likeliest to lead the child to accommodate his mental structure when they are just far enough ahead of him to induce a moderate degree of mental discrepancy, but not so far ahead as to be beyond his range of understanding." Marilynne Adler, in Athey and Rubadeau (eds.), *Educational Implications of Piaget's Theory*, p. 9.

104. Marilynne Adler, in Athey and Rubadeau, *Educational Implications of Piaget's Theory*, p. 10.

105. D.H. Crawford, "The Work of Piaget as It Relates to School Mathematics," *Alberta Journal of Educational Research*, vol. 6 (1960), pp. 133–34.

106. I should perhaps give greater stress to how far Piaget's theory is primarily influential on curriculum design and teaching in a restrictive way. Exemplary is the following quotation from John W. Renner, "What This Research Says to Schools" in Renner et al. (eds.), *Research, Teaching, and Learning with the Piaget Model*, p. 184: "The acceptance of the Piagetian levels concepts by the teacher can have a profound effect on the learner. To accept the Piagetian concept, we must accept his learning model, as well as his intellectual–development model. . . . The acceptance of the latter gives the teacher an entirely new set of *expectations* with respect to what a learner can do. As one teacher told us about a second–grade child, 'I always thought that child was lazy and that that was why he did not learn to subtract. Now that I know he cannot reverse his thinking, I no longer feel he doesn't want to learn to subtract, I know he can't.'" The new set of expectations, it should be pointed out, are not about what children can do, on the whole, rather they are about what children supposedly cannot do. It perhaps does not need pointing out that laziness and lack of reversibility in thinking do not exhaust the range of possibilities why a particular second–grade child does not learn to subtract.

107. Marilynne Adler, in Athey and Rubadeau, *Educational Implications of Piaget's Theory*, p. 10.

108. To refer to only one of many studies, if Ragan J. Callaway, Jr., is right in his claims about, for example, the critical or sensitive period for

learning to read (see his *Modes of Biological Adaptation and Their Role in Intellectual Development*, Perceptual Cognitive Development Monographs, vol. 1, no. 1, The Galton Institute, 1970), then Marilynne Adler's suggestion, if implemented, could lead to an educational disaster.

109. See, for example, John W. Renner, in Renner et al. (eds.), *Research, Teaching, and Learning with the Piaget Model*, ch. 1. He asks what is the purpose of the kind of "educational institution" he is advocating, and answers, "to lead children toward intellectual development" (p. 4). And how will one know that this goal of education has been achieved? "A way of determining the progress that has been made is represented by the intellectual–development model of Piaget" (p. 6). See also Hans G. Furth, *Piaget for Teachers* (Englewood Cliffs, New Jersey: Prentice-Hall, 1970), p. ix: "I suggest that the *spontaneously* growing intelligence of the child should be the focus of grade-school activities and that all else should be subordinated to this priority."

110. John W. Renner, in Renner et al. (eds.), *Research, Teaching, and Learning with the Piaget Model*, ch. 10, advocates "acceptance by schools of the responsibility for the intellectual development of students, rather than assuming it exists and teaching accordingly" (p. 188). The former seems to be what Piaget has characterized as "completely useless," and the latter he seems to claim is precisely what must be done.

111. I have perhaps not brought out well enough the analogous confusion and ambiguity that Piaget's claims contribute to teaching methods. On the same page, for example, Furth and Wachs tell us that the teacher's task is to design activities that "are developmentally appropriate so as to challenge the child's thinking but not too difficult so as to invite failure," and also that "Each child must be left alone to work within the structure at his own level, at his own rate, and in his personal style." H.G. Furth and H. Wachs, *Thinking Goes to School: Piagetian Theory in Practice* (New York: Oxford University Press, 1974), p. 45.

112. H. Aebli, quoted in Edmund V. Sullivan, *Piaget and the School Curriculum* (Ontario: The Ontario Institute for Studies in Education, Bulletin No. 2, 1967), p. 23.

113. Piaget and Inhelder, *The Child's Conception of Space*.

114. "Piaget's evidence that the child of nine or ten can handle many of the basic concepts of Euclidean spatial representation and measurement is mirrored in SMSG's [School Mathematics Study Group] placement of such topics in the elementary curriculum." Jeremy Kilpatrick, "Cognitive Theory and the SMSG Program," in Ripple and Rockcastle (eds.), *Piaget Rediscovered*, p. 130.

115. Sullivan, *Piaget and the School Curriculum*, p. 20. Sullivan's analysis

of particular Piagetians' claims shows the "considerable amount of vagueness in interpretation" (p. 21) that follows a close look at attempts to move from Piaget's theory to recommendations for a mathematics curriculum.

116. L.S. Vygotsky, "Interaction Between Learning and Development" (1935), in L.S. Vygotsky, *Mind in Society: The Development of Higher Psychological Processes* (Cambridge, Mass.: Harvard University Press, 1978), p. 85.

117. *Ibid.*, pp. 86, 88.

118. *Ibid.*, p. 89.

119. One occasionally sees in Piagetian literature the claim that it is best to keep a little way ahead of the child's achieved level of development so that some motivating accommodation is activated. This brings us to a fundamental problem with the Piagetian assimilation/accommodation model, a problem raised in D.W. Hamlyn, "The Logical and Psychological Aspects of Learning," in R.S. Peters (ed.), *The Concept of Education* (London: Routledge and Kegan Paul, 1967), pp. 24–43. It seems to me that Piaget's theory has great difficulty accommodating to this common-sense observation that one should aim teaching somewhat ahead of a child's achieved level of development.

120. Vygotsky, *Mind in Society*, p. 90.

121. Hanne Sonquist, Constance Kamii, Louise Derman, in Athey and Rubadeau (eds.), *Educational Implications of Piaget's Theory*, p. 101.

122. J. McV. Hunt, "The Psychological Basis for Using Preschool Enrichment as an Antidote for Cultural Deprivation," *Merrill-Palmer Quarterly*, vol. 10 (1964), p. 239. *See also* N.D. Kephart, *The Slow Learner in the Classroom* (Columbus, Ohio: Merrill, 1960).

123. Vygotsky, *Mind in Society*, p. 89. This, we might note, was a criticism aimed in the 1930s at a former system undermined by experience.

124. Charles J. Brainerd, *Piaget's Theory of Intelligence* (Englewood Cliffs, N.J.: Prentice-Hall, 1978), p. 298.

125. *Ibid.*, p. 293.

126. Eleanor Duckworth, "Piaget Rediscovered," in Ripple and Rockcastle, *Piaget Rediscovered*, p. 3.

127. Piaget, *Science of Education and the Psychology of the Child*, p. 151.

Chapter 4: Educationally Useful Theories

1. See, for example, D.J. O'Connor, *An Introduction to the Philosophy of Education* (London: Routledge and Kegan Paul, 1957), and "The Nature of Educational Theory" *Proceedings of the Philosophy of Education Society of Great Britain* (Oxford: Blackwell, 1972), vol. 6, no. 1, pp. 97–117. See also the responses to these two statements by Paul H. Hirst, "Philosophy and Educational Theory," in Israel Scheffler (ed.),

Philosophy and Education (Boston: Allyn and Bacon, 1966), pp. 78–95; and pp. 110–17 of the same volume of the *Proceedings of the Philosophy of Education Society of Great Britain* as O'Connor's article. See also Ernest Nagel, "Philosophy of Science and Educational Theory," *Studies in Philosophy and Education*, vol. 7, no. 1 (Fall, 1969).

2. Lawrence Kohlberg and Rochelle Mayer, "Development as the Aim of Education," *Harvard Educational Review*, vol. 42, no. 4 (November, 1972), pp. 449–96.

3. See, for example, R.S. Peters, "Education and Human Development," in *Education and the Development of Reason* (London: Routledge and Kegan Paul, 1972), esp. pp. 517–18.

4. Deanna Kuhn, "The Application of Piaget's Theory of Cognitive Development to Education," *Harvard Educational Review*, vol. 49, no. 3 (1979).

Chapter 5: Psychology and Education

1. Hugh G. Petrie, *The Dilemma of Inquiry and Learning* (Chicago: University of Chicago Press, 1982). Even casual discussion of the kind of learning that properly interests educators leads Oakeshott to conclude that "only human beings are capable of learning" in this sense. See Michael Oakeshott, "Learning and Teaching" in R.S. Peters (ed.), *The Concept of Education* (London: Routledge and Kegan Paul, 1967), pp. 156–57.

2. This point is made in D.C. Phillips and M.E. Kelly, "Hierarchical Theories of Development in Education and Psychology," *Harvard Educational Review*, vol. 45, no. 3 (August, 1975). For a discussion of epistemology and psychology, see Jean Piaget, *Psychology and Epistemology*, trans. Arnold Rosin (New York: Grossman, 1971); and Jean Piaget, "What Is Psychology?" *American Psychologist*, vol. 3, no. 7 (1978), pp. 648–49.

3. Or, as Richard C. Atkinson puts it: "The learning models that now exist are totally inadequate to explain the subtle ways by which the human organism stores, processes, and retrieves information." In "Ingredients for a Theory of Instruction," *American Psychologist*, vol. 27 (1972), p. 929.

4. It often seems to be taken as bad manners, or poor taste, for someone outside a field to point out what the best practitioners within the field all acknowledge—in this case the fundamental insecurity of psychological theories. This is taken as some kind of accusation or attack only if practitioners are unaware of the epistemological status of the theories they use, and fail to see that we are all in this together, trying to make sense of, and establish secure knowledge about, the bewildering complexities of human behavior and thinking.

5. Critics of this program have followed two lines of attack: one theoretical, the other empirical. The theoretical one argues that the reconceptualization of human behavior made necessary by the ambition to fit such behavior to the appropriated methods has succeeded at the cost of eliminating its distinctively human features. The empirical one points out that while it is perfectly proper to base a program of research on a questionable presupposition, it needs to be remembered that the program is an empirical test of claims embedded in that presupposition. Critics' evaluations of the evidence accumulated over a half century of research tend to conclude that the presupposition is not supported: while this program has secured some laws about some behaviors near the physiology end of a continuum of human behavior, where conditions common to physical phenomena still hold with more or less reliability, it has failed to produce any laws about significant aspects of human behavior or any theories with the explanatory power of those common in the physical sciences. When workers in this program pay any attention to such critics, they either claim that they have securely established laws about significant human behaviors, or argue that, even if they have not yet, there is no *a priori* reason to suggest that their program will not lead to such laws in the future.

6. B.F. Skinner, *Science and Human Behavior* (1953; New York: Free Press, reprint, 1965), p. 20 and *passim*.

7. One might note here Hugh G. Petrie's observation: "It is somewhat ironic that in one of the few cases in the history of human thought when science listened seriously to philosophy about scientific method, behaviorism was the result. For a case can be made that the main methodological features of behaviorism were drawn directly from a positivistic philosophy which, it was thought, represented 'real' science. And yet positivism in philosophy is all but dead, killed partly by the very fact that it did *not* accurately represent science, but rather tried to reconstruct it." *The Dilemma of Inquiry and Learning*, pp. 307–08.

8. For an account of this earlier method for finding out the truth, see E.E. Alison Peers, *Ramón Lull* (London: SPCK, 1932), and Martin Gardner, *Logic, Machines, and Diagrams* (New York: Schocken, 1958). *See also* J.N. Hillgarth, *Ramón Lull and Lullism in Fourteenth-Century France* (New York: Oxford University Press, 1971). Lull's method seems to have been the model for a part of Swift's "Laputa" section of *Gulliver's Travels*.

9. Lee J. Cronbach, "Beyond the Two Disciplines of Scientific Psychology," *American Psychologist*, vol. 30, no. 2 (1975), p. 123.

10. Lee J. Cronbach, "The Two Disciplines of Scientific Psychology," *American Psychologist*, vol. 12, no. 11 (1957), p. 671.

11. A somewhat related issue is discussed by Vygotsky: "The concept of a historically based psychology is misunderstood by most research-

ers. . . . For them, to study something historically means, by definition, to study some past event. Hence, they naïvely imagine an insurmountable barrier between historic study and study of present–day behavioral forms. *To study something historically means to study it in the process of change* . . . 'it is only in movement that a body shows what it is.' Thus, the historical study of behavior is not an auxiliary aspect of theoretical study, but rather forms its very base. As P.P. Blonsky has stated, 'Behavior can be understood only as the history of behavior.' " L.S. Vygotsky, *Mind in Society: The Development of Higher Psychological Processes* (Cambridge, Mass.: Harvard University Press, 1978), pp. 64–65.

12. Cronbach, "Beyond the Two Disciplines of Scientific Psychology," p. 116. The methodological problems that scientific psychology is wrestling with overlap considerably with those faced in all the human sciences. It is odd that the methodological discussions, experiments, and innovations in historiography, in the hermeneutic tradition, in structuralism, in critical theory seem to have had so little influence in even the discussions of methodology among North American psychologists. The determined association with physical-science methods perhaps makes such innovations seem too exotic.

13. Piaget, "What Is Psychology?" pp. 648–49.

14. "There is in fact a growing feeling in the field that Piaget's stage model of cognitive development is in serious trouble." John H. Flavell, "Commentary" on Charles J. Brainerd's "The Stage Question in Cognitive-Developmental Theory," *The Behavioral and Brain Sciences*, vol. 2 (1978), p. 187.

15. Jean Piaget, *Psychology and Epistemology*, p. 148.

16. *Ibid.*, p. 21.

17. Cronbach, "Beyond the Two Disciplines of Scientific Psychology," p. 125.

18. The third condition, excessive sensitivity to questions at the expense of concern for methodology and phenomena, leads to the bottomless pit of epistemology.

19. See, for example, Roger Gehlbach, "Individual Differences: Implications for Instructional Theory, Research, and Innovation," *Educational Researcher*, vol. 8, no. 4 (April, 1979), pp. 8–14.

20. See, for example, Michael Duncan and Bruce Biddle, *The Study of Teaching* (New York: Holt, Rinehart and Winston, 1974).

21. N.L. Gage, *The Scientific Basis of the Art of Teaching* (New York: Teachers College Press, 1978), p. 18.

22. *Ibid.*, p. 91.

23. Jerome S. Bruner, *Towards a Theory of Instruction* (Cambridge, Mass.: The Belknap Press, 1966). Some elaboration of his model has appeared but in general this scheme is widely accepted.

24. *Ibid.*, p. 40.

25. I raise this particular question as an example because this is precisely, and explicitly, what is happening in a number of Piagetian programs. See Deanna Kuhn, "The Application of Piaget's Theory of Cognitive Development to Education," *Harvard Educational Review*, vol. 49, no. 3 (1979), pp. 697–706.

26. Cronbach, "The Two Disciplines of Scientific Psychology," p. 681.

27. Cronbach, "Beyond the Two Disciplines of Scientific Psychology." *See also* Lee J. Cronbach and Richard E. Snow, *Aptitudes and Instructional Methods: A Handbook for Research on Interactions* (New York: Irvington, 1977).

28. Cronbach, "Beyond the Two Disciplines of Scientific Psychology," p. 119.

29. *Ibid.*, p. 119.

30. *Ibid.*, p. 125.

31. *Ibid.*, p. 125.

32. Richard Snow, "Individual Differences and Instructional Theory," *Educational Researcher*, vol. 6, no. 10 (1977), p. 12.

33. *Ibid.*, p. 12.

34. Roger Gehlbach, "Individual Differences," p. 10.

35. *Ibid.*, p. 12.

36. G. Pask and B.C.E. Scott, "Learning Strategies and Individual Competence," *International Journal of Man-Machine Studies*, vol. 4 (1972), pp. 217–53.

37. Richard C. Atkinson, "Ingredients for a Theory of Instruction," p. 923.

38. See W.J. Popham et al., *Instructional Objectives* (Chicago: Rand McNally, 1969).

39. For a discussion of some of these problems see Hugh Sockett, "Curriculum Aims and Objectives: Taking a Means to an End," *Proceedings of the Philosophy of Education Society of Great Britain* (Oxford: Basil Blackwell, 1972), pp. 30–61.

40. W.J. Popham, *Criterion-Referenced Instruction* (Belmont, California: Fearon, 1973), p. 13.

41. Robert Mager, *Behavioral Objectives* (Belmont, California: Fearon, 1962), p. 13.

42. W.J. Popham and Eva L. Baker, *Systematic Instruction* (New Jersey: Prentice-Hall, 1979), p. 20.

43. See for example, Phillippe C. Duchastel and Paul F. Merrill, "The Effects of Behavioral Objectives on Learning: A Review of Empirical Studies," *Review of Educational Research*, vol. 43 (1973), pp. 53–69; and O.K. Duell, "Effect of Type of Objective, Level of Test Questions, and the Judged Importance of Tested Materials upon Post-test Performance," *Journal of Educational Psychology*, vol. 66 (1974), pp. 225–32.

44. This notion that education accumulates merely from the accumulation of sets of facts, concepts, and whatever is hardly new or restricted to any particular subject area. As William Hazlitt noted about the same

abuse: "Anyone who has passed through the regular gradations of a classical education, and is not made a fool by it, may consider himself as having had a very narrow escape." "On the Ignorance of the Learned," in W.E. Williams (ed.), *A Book of English Essays* (Harmondsworth, Middlesex: Penguin Books, 1951), p. 147.

45. In my *Educational Development* (New York: Oxford University Press, 1979), I try to show that facts, concepts, whatever, become educational aliments by being organized according to what, in chapter 1, I have called "paradigmatic forms of understanding," and which, in the earlier book, I identify as a sequence of stages called mythic, romantic, philosophic, and ironic. These form contexts of meaning in which students make sense of things at different stages of their educational development; an educational unit is anything that is organized according to the principles which determine what is meaningful at each stage.

46. It seems fair to note that if one does not look beyond the typical practice of many schools, one may be encouraged to remain insensitive to this distinction, and may be encouraged to view education as a fact- or "concept"-accumulating activity. Particularly in North America, where the influence of psychology has been so pervasive on educational practice—which the proponents of more of such influence might doubt—there has been a massive technologizing that has, in my view, greatly perverted education into a largely mindless process of conveying disjointed bits of information, measuring retention of some of these bits, and allotting "credits"—grades or whatever—on the results of these crude and educationally irrelevant measures. Education seems to have become in many people's minds indistinguishable from what is reflected from these procedures. They seem unable to distinguish between the procedures of schooling and the process of education. There is nothing at all wrong with technologizing certain aspects of schooling; the problems arise when no distinction is made between the central educational function of schools and their various socializing functions.

47. Fred N. Kerlinger, "The Influence of Research on Educational Practice," *Educational Researcher*, vol. 6, no. 8 (September, 1977), and Robert E. Slavin, "Basic vs. Applied Research: A Response," *Educational Researcher*, vol. 7, no. 2 (February, 1978).

48. Slavin, "Basic vs. Applied Research," p. 16. Philosophy seems, in Slavin's account, indistinguishable from the mindless acceptance of any passing fad.

49. *Ibid.*

50. For an extended argument of this point, see R.S. Peters, "Education and the Educated Man," *Proceedings of the Philosophy of Education Society of Great Britain*, vol. 4 (January 1970), pp. 5–20.

51. For a fuller argument of this point, and the section immediately following, see A.R. Louch, *Exploration and Human Action* (Berkeley and Los Angeles: University of California Press, 1966).

52. E.R. Hilgard, *Theories of Learning* (New York: Appleton-Century-Crofts, 1956), p. 486.

53. I owe this analogy, and much more of what follows, to Jan Smedslund. See his *Becoming a Psychologist* (New York: Halstead Press, 1972); "Bandura's Theory of Self-Efficacy: A Set of Common-sense Theorems," *Scandinavian Journal of Psychology*, vol. 19 (1978), pp. 1–14; "Some Psychological Theories Are Not Empirical: Reply to Bandura," *Scandinavian Journal of Psychology*, vol. 19 (1978), pp. 101–02; "Between the Analytic and the Arbitrary: A Case Study of Psychological Research," *Scandinavian Journal of Psychology*, vol. 20, (1979). Smedslund acknowledges debts to F. Heider, *The Psychology of Interpersonal Relations* (New York: John Wiley, 1958); K.J. Gergen, "Social Psychology as History," *Journal of Personality and Social Psychology*, vol. 36 (1973), pp. 309–20; K.J. Gergen, "Social Psychology, Science, and History," *Personality and Social Psychological Bulletin*, vol. 2 (1976), pp. 373–83; and U. Laucken, *Naïve Verhaltenstheorie* (Stuttgart: Klett, 1974).

54. B.F. Skinner, *Reflections on Behaviorism and Society* (Englewood Cliffs, N.J.: Prentice-Hall, 1978), p. 10.

55. J.A. Poteet, *Behavior Modification: A Practical Guide for Teachers* (London: University of London Press, 1974), p. 23.

56. *Ibid.*, p. 45.

57. *Ibid.*, p. 49.

58. Perhaps it needs to be noted here that much learning in education does not require memorization of the facts used to support or establish certain generalizations or, even, ways of seeing things. The development of a sophisticated historical consciousness, for example, does not depend on memorizing all the facts which it has been necessary to note—to "learn" in some short-term way—in the process.

59. Jan Smedslund, "A Re-examination of the Role of Theory in Psychology," paper presented to 21st International Congress of Psychology, Paris, 1976.

60. Poteet, *Behavior Modification*, p. 85.

61. Jack Martin, "External versus Self-Reinforcement: A Review of Methodological and Theoretical Issues," forthcoming. *See also* his "Laboratory Studies of Self-Reinforcement (SR) Phenomena," *Journal of General Psychology*, vol. 101 (1979), pp. 103–49.

62. Albert Bandura, "Self-efficacy: Towards a Unifying Theory of Behavioral Change," *Psychology Review*, vol. 84 (1977), pp. 191–215.

63. Smedslund, "Bandura's Theory of Self-efficacy."

64. Smedslund, "Some Psychological Theories Are Not Empirical."

65. See also Smedslund's devastating reduction of an article, chosen at random, to a set of common-sense theorems: "Between the Analytic and the Arbitrary."

66. Petrie, *The Dilemma of Inquiry and Learning*, p. 313.

67. R.O. Sleep, "Epistemology and Aims in Education," doctoral dissertation, Ontario Institute for Studies in Education, 1970, p. 165.

68. H.S.H. McFarland, *Psychological Theory and Educational Practice* (London: Routledge and Kegan Paul, 1971), p. 300.

69. *Ibid.*, p. 301.

70. L. Wittgenstein, *Philosophical Investigations*, trans. G.E.M. Anscombe (Oxford: Blackwell, 1963), p. 232.

Conclusion

1. Eric Hobsbawm, "Is Science Evil?" *New York Review of Books*, vol. 15, no. 9 (November 19, 1970), p. 14.

2. Cesare Pavese, *The Devil in the Hills*, trans. D.D. Paige (Harmondsworth, Middlesex: Penguin, 1967), p. 149.

Index

Education and Psychology

Education and Psychology

PLATO, PIAGET AND SCIENTIFIC PSYCHOLOGY

Kieran Egan

Methuen & Co. Ltd
London

First published in 1983 by
Teachers College Press

First published in Great Britain in 1984 by
Methuen & Co. Ltd
11 New Fetter Lane
London EC4P 4EE

Printed in Great Britain by
Richard Clay (The Chaucer Press), Bungay, Suffolk

British Library Cataloguing in Publication Data

Egan, Kieran
    Education and psychology : Plato, Piaget
    and scientific psychology.
    1. Educational psychology
    I. Title
    370.15   LB1051

    ISBN 0-416-38100-6
    ISBN 0-416-38110-3 Pbk